AESTHETICS AND COUNTER-AESTHETICS
OF INTERNATIONAL JUSTICE

Aesthetics and Counter-Aesthetics Of International Justice

Editors

Christine Schwöbel-Patel
Robert Knox

Assistant Editor

Rosie Woodhouse

COUNTERPRESS
COVENTRY

First published 2024
Counterpress, Coventry
http://counterpress.org.uk

© 2024 Christine Schwöbel-Patel and Robert Knox

Rights to publish and sell this book in print, electronic, and all other forms and media are exclusively licensed to Counterpress Limited. An electronic version of this book is available under a Creative Commons Attribution-NonCommercial (CC-BY-NC 4.0) International license via the Counterpress website:

https://counterpress.org.uk

ISBN: 978-1-910761-17-5 (Paperback)
ISBN: 978-1-910761-18-2 (Ebook)

Typeset in 10.5 on 12pt Sabon

The cover art is an OSPAAAL poster by Cuban graphic designer and artist Alfredo Rostgaard, created in 1968.
The cover design is by Peter Quach.

Global print and distribution by Ingram

In recent years, growing attention has been paid to the relationship between international law and aesthetics. This collection situates this relationship within its wider political context, demonstrating that the question of aesthetics in not neutral but rather connected to the social, economic, and political relationships in which international justice is deeply embedded. The first part of the collection is an invitation to reflect on what we see and register in international justice, in particular in representations of those who suffer violence, including the violence of law. The second part of the collection uses different forms to reflect on how aesthetics can be turned against the dominant aesthetics and politics of international law, in the form of 'counter-aesthetics' through cartoons, interviews, parables, and a screenplay. This collection is the first of its kind to make visible the dominant and normalized aesthetics of violence and justice through a political economy lens; and to take seriously the limitations of the aesthetic forms that give violence and justice their expression.

Christine Schwöbel-Patel is Professor of Law at the University of Warwick, Alexander von Humboldt Fellow, and co-Director of the Centre for Critical Legal Studies.

Robert Knox is a Senior Lecturer in Law at the University of Liverpool, and an Editor of *Historical Materialism: Research in Critical Marxist Theory* and the *London Review of International Law*.

Acknowledgments

This project goes back so far that the list of people to acknowledge could encompass almost a decade of colleagues, comrades, family, healthcare professionals, childcare professionals, friends, and acquaintances. To spare you, the reader, this long list, and to spare the strain on our memories, we would like to thank those who have helped in pulling this together in the last months. First, we thank the contributors for their patience and for taking a leap of faith when we promised that this time, it really was going to get wrapped up. Second, enormous thanks go to the assistant editor Rosie Woodhouse, without whose fantastic editing this would still be a promise of a book rather than a real one. Third, we would like to thank the Counterpress editors Illan Wall and Gilbert Leung, who were not only enthusiastic about the proposal for this book, but also embraced the suggestions for various unorthodox contributions. Fourth, we thank the interlocutors from the two conferences/workshops who have not contributed to this collection, but whose valuable contributions to the discussions remain an important part of the collection: This includes Sean Columb, Thierry Cruvellier, Alma Itzhaky, Tor Krever, Vinh Nguyen, Jerusha Owino, Klaartje Quirijns, Sophie Rigney, Diana Sankey, Ben Stolk, and Immi Tallgren. Finally, our heartfelt thanks to our families and partners.

A book that centres political economy should mention some of the resources drawn on: The project was initiated through a project grant from the University of Liverpool's Research and Development Fund when we were colleagues there; it was completed with funding from Warwick Law School's Legal Research Institute and an Alexander von Humboldt Fellowship for Experienced Researchers awarded to Christine.

Contents

PART I: AESTHETICS OF INTERNATIONAL JUSTICE

1. Aesthetics of International Justice 1
   CHRISTINE SCHWÖBEL-PATEL AND ROBERT KNOX
   Form: Academic chapter

2. The International Criminal Court in Focus:
   The Representation of Victimhood on YouTube 14
   SOFIA STOLK
   Form: Screenplay

3. Displaying the Victim: Essentialized Aesthetics of
   Victimhood in Transitional Justice Debates 40
   PADRAIG MCAULIFFE
   Form: Academic chapter

4. The Image of the Asylum Seeker and Spectacular Deterrence
   in UK Asylum Law 63
   ANNE NEYLON
   Form: Academic chapter

5. Aesthetics and the Construction of the 'Grateful Refugee':
   Critical Perspectives from Law and Design 89
   CHRISTINE SCHWÖBEL-PATEL AND DEGER OZKARAMANLI
   Form: Academic chapter

6. International Trials and Justice for Victims:
   A View from Practice 115
   RUBY MAE AXELSON AND WAYNE JORDASH
   Form: Academic chapter

7. The International Justice Robe 136
   TERRY DUFFY
   Form: Artwork

PART II: COUNTER-AESTHETICS OF INTERNATIONAL JUSTICE

8. Counter-Aesthetics of International Justice 143
   CHRISTINE SCHWÖBEL-PATEL AND ROBERT KNOX
   Form: Academic chapter

9. Provocation and Possibility in Counter-Aesthetics 155
   ANASTASIA TATARYN
   Form: Academic chapter

10. Recasting Atrocities as Public Health Catastrophes 168
    RANDLE DEFALCO
    Form: Academic chapter

11. Violence 200
    JO FRANK
    Form: Poem

12. Why Eichmann Couldn't Laugh:
    Fifteen One-Minute Parables 205
    GERRY SIMPSON
    Form: Parables

13. 'Poetic Justice Products': International Justice, Victim
    Counter-Aesthetics, and the Spectre of the Show Trial ... 216
    ALEX BATESMITH
    Form: Academic chapter

14. Pinan: Comics and International Justice 243
    CAROLINA ALONSO BEJARANO AND PETER QUACH
    Form: Comic and Interview

15. Alternative Superheroes 270
    KATE EVANS
    Form: Interview

Biographies

Carolina Alonso Bejarano is a DJ and scholar-activist teaching Law at the University of Warwick in the UK. Her work has appeared in Feminist Formations, The Believer, WritersMosaic, Revista BLAST and Jadaliyya, among others. Along with her fellow immigrants' rights activists, Carolina produced the play Undocumented/Unafraid (2015) about the rights of undocumented workers in the US. Her book, Decolonizing Ethnography: Undocumented Immigrants and New Directions in Social Science (2019, Duke UP), was written with her field collaborators about the liberatory possibilities of ethnographic research.

Ruby Mae Axelson is a Senior Legal Consultant at Global Rights Compliance with expertise in international criminal law, international humanitarian law and gender justice. Ruby is appointed to the defence team of Jovica Stanišić before the UN International Residual Mechanism for Criminal Tribunals ('IRMCT'). Prior to this she was on the defence team of Ratko Mladić at the International Criminal Tribunal for the former Yugoslavia ('ICTY').

Alex Batesmith is a Lecturer in Legal Profession at the School of Law, University of Leeds. His research on legal professions, cause lawyering, professional identity, and law and emotion focuses on lawyers in international criminal justice and in post-conflict and authoritarian regimes. This is informed by his previous 20-year career as a domestic and international criminal lawyer, including five years as a United Nations war crimes prosecutor in Kosovo and Cambodia and six years as a post-conflict justice consultant.

Randle DeFalco is an Assistant Professor of Law at the University of Hawai'i at Mānoa William S. Richardson School of Law. His research focuses on atrocity, genocide, international criminal law, and transitional justice, especially in relation to less visible forms of mass violence such as the enforcement of famine conditions and socio-economic oppression. He is the author of Invisible Atrocities: The Aesthetic Biases of International Criminal Justice (CUP, 2022).

Terry Duffy is a renowned international artist with a reputation for unique, challenging work. His artworks encompass sublime minimal abstracts to culturally figurative paintings to large-scale installations. He is an independent artist willing to confront issues of cultural importance such as 'Victim, no Resurrection'. He has received several commissions to create unique religious vestments, including for Coventry and Dresden reconciliation, the WW1 Centenary Commemorations, Archbishop Desmond Tutu, and Windrush commemorations. "Art attempts to open minds and heal wounds".

Kate Evans is a cartoonist, graphic novelist, artist, author, mother and activist. She was living in a tree on the route of the Newbury Bypass road protest, when she was commissioned by *The Guardian* newspaper to draw cartoons from the tree tops. The subject of her pen is wide-ranging – from feminist fairy stories, through birth and breastfeeding to refugee relief and revolutionary socialism. She does the regular strip "Thoughts from a Broad" for *New Internationalist* magazine.

Jo Frank is a writer and translator based in Berlin. Jo is publisher and editor for the award-winning publishing house Verlagshaus Berlin. His latest books include GEWALT (Violence, 2023) and TRAUER (GRIEF, 2023).

Wayne Jordash is the Director of Global Rights Compliance and a leading lawyer specialising in international human rights and humanitarian law, particularly in high risk and conflict-affected areas. Wayne is also an internationally recognised expert in the global network of international tribunals, having had cases before the International Court of Justice, International Criminal Court, the International Criminal Tribunals and the Special Court for Sierra Leone.

Robert Knox is a Senior Lecturer in Law at the University of Liverpool, and an Editor of Historical Materialism: Research in Critical Marxist Theory and the London Review of International Law.

Prof. **Pádraig McAuliffe** is a graduate of University College Cork and teaches at the School of Law and Social Justice at the University of Liverpool. His main research interest lies in how global normative regimes like human rights, transitional justice and international criminal law are applied in states of limited administrative reach.

Anne Neylon is a Lecturer in Asylum and Immigration Law at the University of Liverpool. She has previously written on precariousness under law for refugees and asylum seekers in Europe and Canada, the museum and the border, and the border spectacle in asylum law and policy. She has published in the International Journal of Refugee Law, the European Journal of Migration and Law, and the London Review of International Law.

Deger Ozkaramanli is assistant professor at the Faculty of Industrial Design Engineering, at Delft University of Technology in the Netherlands. Her research critically examines ethical questions and moral dilemmas that arise when implementing design methods in inter- and trans-disciplinary projects to address socio-technical challenges. She studies dilemmas using multiple disciplinary lenses, mainly drawing from the ethics of technology and critical studies. Deger leads the Design Research Society Special Interest Group on Design Ethics in collaboration with an international team of conveners.

Peter Quach is a comic book artist, illustrator, graphic designer and karateka who lives in Brooklyn, New York. Peter's comic, I Am a Racist (And so Can You), an investigation into the historical roots of his internalized racism, was a notable comic in the Best American Comics 2013. Other works include But by Laughter, Gumdrops (with Carolina Alonso Bejarano), Temporary, Freedman, Transit, and You Don't Know Much About Jesus. Peter was a teacher at the Beverly Arts Center in Chicago and serves as an assistant karate instructor at Karatedo Honma Dojo in New York.

Christine Schwöbel-Patel is Professor of Law at the University of Warwick and co-Director of the Centre for Critical Legal Studies. Her work is at the intersection between international law and its structural harms and is informed by a political economy and aesthetics analytic. Her latest monograph is *Marketing Global Justice: The Political Economy of International Criminal Law* (Cambridge University Press 2021).

Gerry Simpson's latest work, *The Sentimental Life of International Law: Literature, Language and Longing in World Politics* – from which some of these parables are drawn - was published by Oxford University Press in late 2021. Gerry is currently writing a study of the Cold War (with Sundhya Pahuja and Matt Craven) as well as *The Atomics*, a philosophical memoir.

Sofia Stolk's research focuses on the visualization of international law. She is co-founder of the Legal Sightseeing research platform. Annually, she coordinates the 'Camera Justitia' programme on law and justice at the Movies that Matter Festival in The Hague.

Anastasia Tataryn is an Associate Professor at St Jerome's University at the University of Waterloo, Canada. She has previously worked, and completed a PhD in Law, in the UK. Her research and publications are primarily in migration and labour law, critical legal theory, and explore transformative epistemological thinking. Anastasia is also a professionally trained dancer, and a movement instructor. For more, see anastaziyatataryn.net

PART 1

AESTHETICS OF INTERNATIONAL JUSTICE

1

Aesthetics of International Justice

Christine Schwöbel-Patel and Robert Knox

Some projects require time to ripen, especially if they have yet to enter into conversation with others. When we began this project in early 2016, we found few critical interlocutors outside of the contributors to this collection. A rather large number of our colleagues thought that an international law project converging around the term 'aesthetics' was confusing, not of its time, or sesquipedalian. More than seven years later, there is an established and growing catalogue of projects on aesthetics and international law. Among these are a recent conference hosted on the theme of *The Aesthetics of International Law*;[1] the newly minted ICJ Judge Hilary Charlesworth delivered the 2022 ASIL Grotius Lecture on *The Art of International Law*;[2] Ruth Buchanan edited the special issue of *Visualizing Law and Development* in 2022;[3] Also in 2022, Randle DeFalco's book *Invisible Atrocities: The Aesthetic Biases of International Criminal Justice* was published;[4] Marina Aksenova and Karmia Bennoune edited the symposium *Art, Aesthetics, and International Justice* in 2020;[5] Sofia Stolk and Renske Vos initiated

---

1. 'The Aesthetics of International Law,' Department of Legal Studies, Central European University and ESIL Interest Group on Social Sciences and International Law, accessed 24 April 2023, https://legal.ceu.edu/sites/legal.ceu.hu/files/attachment/article/1387/ceu-esil-theaestheticsofinternationallaw-callforpapers.pdf.
2. 'The Art of International Law,' American University Washington College of Law, accessed 24 April 2023, https://www.wcl.american.edu/impact/initiatives-programs/international/24th-grotius-lecture/.
3. Ruth Buchanan ed., 'Special Issue: Visualizing Law and Development,' *Osgoode Hall Law Journal* 59/1 (2022), accessed 3 May 2023, https://digitalcommons.osgoode.yorku.ca/ohlj/vol59/iss1/.
4. Randle C. DeFalco, *Invisible Atrocities: The Aesthetic Biases of International Criminal Justice* (Cambridge: Cambridge University Press, 2022).
5. Marina Aksenova ed., 'Art, Aesthetics and International Justice,' *AJIL Unbound*

the project *Legal Sightseeing* in 2018.[6] These projects highlight a greater appetite for thinking about the discipline of international law outside of its usual text-based analysis, mostly by attending to visuality.

To complement attention to the visual life of international law, a lively discussion on materiality/materialism and (international) law has emerged.[7] This ranges from the consideration of objects of international law as with Jessie Hohmann and Dan Joyce's eponymous collection,[8] to international law's architecture, exemplified through Miriam Bak McKenna's work,[9] to the emerging discussions on posthumanism and new materialism in international law, as with Emily Jones and Matilda Arvidsson's edited volume.[10] An attention to the material life of international justice can also be noted in the literature on cultural rights and cultural property and heritage.[11] In a different key of materiality, historical materialism, which focuses on the material conditions under which international justice is made real particularly in relation to capital accumulation and its class relationships, has also received greater attention in international law. Recent notable contributions include Ntina Tzouvala's *Capitalism as Civilisation*,[12] and Rose Parfitt's *The Process of International Legal Reproduction*,[13] or indeed our own scholarship.[14]

---

114 (2020), accessed 24 April 2023, https://www.cambridge.org/core/journals/american-journal-of-international-law/ajil-unbound-by-symposium/art-aesthetics-and-international-justice.

6. 'Legal Sightseeing,' accessed 24 April 2023, https://legalsightseeing.org/.

7. See Hyo Yoon Kang and Sara Kendall, 'Legal Materiality,' in *The Oxford Handbook for Law and Humanities*, eds. Maksymilian Del Mar, Bernadette Meyler, and Simon Stern (Oxford: Oxford University Press, 2020).

8. Jessie Hohmann and Daniel Joyce eds., *International Law's Objects* (Oxford: Oxford University Press, 2018).

9. Miriam Bak McKenna, 'Designing for International Law: The Architecture of International Organisations 1922-1952,' *Leiden Journal of International Law* 34/1 (2020).

10. See Emily Jones, *Feminist Theory and International Law: Posthuman Perspectives* (London: Routledge, 2023).

11. See critically on expert rule and cultural heritage law, Lucas Lixinski, *International Heritage Law for Communities: Exclusion and Re-Imagination* (Oxford: Oxford University Press, 2019).

12. Ntina Tzouvala, *Capitalism as Civilisation: A History of International Law* (Cambridge: Cambridge University Press, 2020).

13. Rose Parfitt, *The Process of International Legal Reproduction: Inequality, Historiography, Resistance* (Cambridge: Cambridge University Press, 2019).

14. Robert Knox, 'Valuing race? Stretched Marxism and the logic of imperialism,' *London Review of International Law* 4/1 (2016); Christine Schwöbel-Patel, *Marketing Global Justice: The Political Economy of International Criminal Law*

A third area of significance has emerged through research and policy groups that use images and design for evidence-gathering, including for investigations that lead to strategic litigation. The perhaps most prominent of these is Forensic Architecture. Forensic Architecture is a research group that uses techniques in spatial and architectural analysis, digital modelling, and other forms of design to create causal connections and storytelling of human rights violations, including violence committed by states, police forces, militaries, and corporations.[15]

Finally, the growing field of law and emotion draws on questions of affect, and its role in shaping forms of justice. Kamari Maxine Clarke's *Affective Justice* and Gerry Simpson's *A Sentimental Life of International Law*, for example, set out the experiences and emotions of international justice and international lawyers.[16] Imagery and language are studied here in relation to their ordering and world-making properties in the scholarship and practice of international justice.

Given the increased attention to aesthetics and international justice, and this project's stalling and interruption, one could ask whether we have anything novel to contribute with this book? We believe that we (still) do; and we hope that you as the reader will agree. Above all, our project has always been concerned with situating the aesthetics of international law within its wider *political* context. Drawing on radical conceptions of the aesthetic, the project seeks to explain the interconnection between international law's 'aesthetic' and the construction of hegemony on the global stage. Such hegemony, of course, cannot simply be reduced to the jostling of various 'interest' groups, but rather is rooted in the political-economic (and aesthetic!) structures of global capitalism.

This particular frame has important consequences for how we approached the concept of the 'aesthetic' in this project. First, we maintain that there remains an important place in the discussion for understanding the dominance of certain types of aesthetic

---

(Cambridge: Cambridge University Press, 2021); Serena Natile and Christine Schwöbel-Patel, 'Rosa Luxemburg and International Law: About the project,' University of Warwick, accessed 3 May 2023, https://warwick.ac.uk/fac/soc/law/research/projects/rosa-luxemburg-and-international-law/about-the-project/.

15. 'Agency,' Forensic Architecture, accessed 24 April 2023, https://forensic-architecture.org/about/agency.

16. Kamari Maxine Clarke, *Affective Justice: The International Criminal Court and the Pan-Africanist Pushback* (Durham: Duke University Press, 2019); Gerry Simpson, *The Sentimental Life of International Law: Literature, Language, and Longing in World Politics* (Oxford: Oxford University Press, 2021).

(re)presentations of international justice, and by extension the invisibilization of other forms of (re)presentation. This frame also aims to act in contrast to what can appear like an elitist engagement with (predominantly Western) 'high art' forms, in the appreciation of particular paintings, sculptures, or literature forms. In explaining the dominance of certain representations of justice, we set out that international justice and its representations cannot be divided from the neoliberal capitalist circumstances in which they are made real. Second, on a practical level, and building on the theorization of the dominance of a certain type of aesthetics, this volume brings together a large variety of different *forms* of engaging with themes of international justice. Indeed, it is remarkable that despite the growing engagement with aesthetics, the formal academic journal article, book chapter, or monograph remain the dominant forms of expression in international legal scholarship, perhaps scattered with some images for good measure. Aside from the more familiar academic contributions, this volume offers, among others, parables, comics, and a screenplay as (alternative or disruptive) forms of thinking about international justice – attempts at what we bundle together under the term counter-aesthetics.

In understanding international law's aesthetic in this political context, this project, then, has from its beginning been structured by a (not always very neat) division between the 'aesthetics' of international justice on the one hand, and the 'counter-aesthetics' of international justice on the other hand. Whilst the former, we argue, is associated with those hegemonic forces which operate across the international field, the latter represents those attempts to contest—and ultimately overturn—both international law and its dominant aesthetic.

This book is divided into two parts to give expression to this division. The first part on Aesthetics of International Justice aims to make sense of the dominant representation and constitution of international justice through a political-economic lens. This Introduction is intended as a frame for the first part. The second part considers various forms of counter-aesthetics, by which we mean visions of international justice that do not conform with hegemonic ideas, representations, and materiality. To give a theoretical form to counter-aesthetics, we propose three potential techniques, namely (a) rupture, (b) détournement, and (c) solidarity aesthetics, as rooted in radical theoretical and practice approaches to aesthetics. We explain these techniques in more depth in the framing chapter on Counter-Aesthetics of International Justice (Chapter 8).

What is Aesthetics?

Aesthetics is often explained as the theory of art and beauty. In a wider interpretation, and the most common association in international justice, it is about visualization. Indeed, a common entry point into aesthetic enquiries is to begin with the observation that we live in a visual world.[17] We too are interested in visual representations of international justice. For understanding international justice projects, it is important to highlight the visual storytelling of films and documentaries and to question photographic depictions of perpetrators, victims, or lawyers.[18] We consider it instructive to consider how the view is directed and how representations are made natural.[19] In joining this debate about common visual representations, we also want to problematize that visual representations are the first port of call for aesthetic enquiries. In other words, we also question why the visual is the sense that is given the greatest importance.

In our exploration of thinking about aesthetics as not only about seeing but also about a broader sense experience, we have been guided by Jacques Rancière's notion of aesthetics as an enquiry relating to distribution and participation in the sense experience.[20] Rancière argues that every community is based on a particular 'distribution of the sensible.' Aesthetics is a means of understanding the *formalization* of experience and meaning; it is an enquiry into what is experienced as the common sense, what this enables, and what this obscures.[21]

---

17. See for example, Rloand Bleiker ed., *Visual Global Politics* (Oxford: Routledge, 2018); Nikolas M. Rajkovic, 'The Visual Conquest of International Law: Brute Boundaries, the Map, and the Legacy of Cartogenesis,' *Leiden Journal of International Law* 31/2 (2018); Kirsten Ainley, Stephan Humphries and Immi Tallgren eds., 'International Criminal Justice on/and Film,' *London Review of International Law* 6/1 (2018); Christiane Wilke, 'The Optics of War: Seeing Civilians, Enacting Distinctions, and Visual Crises in International Law,' in *Sensing Law*, ed. Sheryl Hamilton (Oxford: Routledge, 2017); 'Legal Sightseeing'; Immi Tallgren, 'Come and See? The Power of Images and International Criminal Justice,' *International Criminal Law Review* 17/2 (2017).
18. See Kate Miles, *Visual International Law: Image, Symbol, Art and Architecture* (Cambridge: Cambridge University Press, forthcoming); Ainley, Humphreys and Tallgren, 'International Criminal Justice on/and Film.'
19. The questions of perspectives of viewing art as a form of critique were famously introduced to a British audience through John Berger's 1972 television series *Ways of Seeing*, adapted in John Berger, *Ways of Seeing* (London: Penguin, 1972).
20. Jacques Rancière, *The Politics of Aesthetics*, trans. Gabriel Rockhill (London: Bloomsbury, 2004), 8.
21. Rancière, *The Politics of Aesthetics*.

This 'distribution of the sensible' is defined by Rancière as the 'system of self-evident facts of sense perception that simultaneously discloses the existence of something in common and the delimitations that define the respective parts and positions within it.'[22] In other words, every social collective will rely upon a series of common experiences that are able to mediate their relationship to the wider world. Crucially for Rancière, these experiences are not benign or neutral. Particular societies are not simply inclusive of all senses and sensibilities but also exclusive. By setting out what the 'common' sensible experience is and who is entitled to participate in the creation and reception of this experience, any given aesthetic will also—implicitly or explicitly—*exclude* certain sensible experiences, perspectives, etc. In this way, the aesthetic is inherently political.

An enquiry into aesthetics and international justice according to Rancière, then, is to question what is deemed to be included in the sense experience of justice—what kinds of language, images, symbols, sounds, smells, texts, designs, objects—and what is deemed to be outside of it.[23] This includes an appreciation for international justice's knowledge production more generally.[24] It follows that we are not simply concerned with a selection of *unusual* ways of thinking about experiencing international justice; we are interested in discerning certain patterns in the sense experience of law to identify forms of legitimation. The aesthetic enquiry is therefore a project of drawing attention to the usual presentations and representations and appreciating that this common-sense creation is a political act. In this way, Rancière draws our attention to the ideological dimension of the aesthetic. As Althusser (Rancière's former mentor) noted, ideology 'represents the imaginary relationship of individuals to their real conditions of existence.'[25] The aesthetic plays a crucial role in this process, insofar as it constitutes its sensuous dimension.

---

22. Ranciere, *The Politics of Aesthetics*, 12.
23. On sounds, see 'TWAILR Mixtape: A Playlist for Rethinking the Spirit and Purpose of International Law,' 4 March 2020, accessed 24 April 2023, https://twailr.com/twailr-mixtape-a-playlist-for-rethinking-the-spirit-and-purpose-of-international-law/; James Parker, *Acoustic Jurisprudence: Listening to the Trial of Simon Bikindi* (Oxford: Oxford University Press, 2015); Gilbert Leung, 'Law is a Fugue,' *Critical Legal Thinking*, 15 March 2018, accessed 24 April 2023, http://criticallegalthinking.com/2018/03/15/law-is-a-fugue/.
24. Andrea Bianchi and Moshe Hirsch eds., *International Law's Invisible Frames* (Oxford: Oxford University Press, 2021).
25. Louis Althusser, *Lenin and Philosophy and Other Essays*, trans. Ben Brewster (New York: Monthly Review Press, 2001), 108.

However, whilst Rancière establishes the general notion that aesthetics is political and politics is inherently aesthetic, he tells us very little about the *specific* relationship between political projects, actors, forms, and periods. Accordingly, it becomes difficult to track the varying levels of importance that aesthetics takes on in particular contexts and who certain aesthetic projects will favour. In order to explore these issues, it is useful to turn to the work of Guy Debord and the artistic-political movement of the Situationist International, of which Debord was a key figure. Debord and the Situationist International usefully demarcate the type of politics with which we are confronted when it comes to aesthetics, and are able to delimit the relationship between aesthetics and different modes of socio-economic organisation. They shared, then, a similar insight to Rancière, but attempted to situate this insight historically, thinking through how the dominance of the aesthetic represents a distinct and particular form of ideology.

For Debord, whilst aesthetics has always had a political function, it is only under late capitalism that it assumes its key role. In his book *The Society of the Spectacle*, Debord argued that 'in societies where modern conditions of production prevail, all life presents itself as an immense accumulation of spectacles' accordingly 'everything that was directly lived has moved away into a representation.'[26] In late capitalism, therefore, everything is mediated by 'the image'. Crucially, for Debord, the spectacle is not simply 'a collection of images' but rather 'a social relation among people, mediated by images.'[27] In this way, the spectacle plays a central role in *ordering* and *producing* the social. In particular, the spectacle is key for integrating populations—particularly 'the masses'—into late capitalism.

Writing (mostly in France) in the 1950s and 1960s, the Situationist International were able to anticipate the increasing dominance of media over social life. Although they were only dealing with rudimentary forms of mass media, technological and communications developments over the course of the twentieth and twenty-first centuries seem to have buttressed their insights. Vitally, however, the theorists of the SI were not simply concerned with observing 'empirically' the growth and predominance of aesthetic representations. Rather, they sought to root this process in the deeper logic and expansion of capitalist social relations. Debord argued that the predominance of 'mediation' that marked

---

26. Guy Debord, *The Society of the Spectacle*, trans. Kenn Knabb (Berkeley: Bureau of Public Secrets, 2014), 2.
27. Debord, *The Society of the Spectacle*, 2.

the spectacle was connected to the central role that the commodity plays in mature capitalist societies. Following Marx, Debord understood that capitalist societies were deeply marked by *commodity fetishism*, whereby the products of human social relations appear as though they are entirely disconnected from said social relations.[28] In this act of disconnection these products of human action—commodities, capital, labour, etc.—come to dominate human life, dictating and structuring its reproduction.[29] For Debord, the dominance of images that characterises the spectacle is the perfection of commodity fetishism:

> this is the principle of commodity fetishism, the domination of society by "intangible as well as tangible things," which reaches its absolute fulfilment in the spectacle, where the tangible world is replaced by a selection of images which exist above it, and which simultaneously impose themselves as the tangible par excellence.[30]

Crucially for Debord, the spectacle is not simply a generic domination of images, and nor is its aesthetic capable of being filled by any political content. Rather, the spectacle represents a particular politics linked to the dominance of capitalist social relations, limiting its ability to simply be 'hijacked' by all political forces.

In this way, Debord and the SI identified the *totalising* effect of the contemporary aesthetic. Whilst this is well taken, the spectacle is nonetheless simultaneously composed of specific forms of representation, matching particular political-economic and—accordingly—aesthetic configurations. In order to advance this form of inquiry, especially in the contemporary neoliberal context, one might add the work of Stuart Hall to that of Rancière and Debord. Hall noted, echoing what we already know, that to analyse representations we must study the material forms in which symbolic meaning is circulated, being 'the actual signs, symbols, figures, images, narratives, words and sounds.'[31] Where Hall becomes particularly instructive is in his work on the spectacle of 'the Other.' Here, Hall studies representations of difference, introducing the importance of race in this respect: 'people who are in any way significantly different from the majority—'them' rather than 'us'—are frequently

---

28. Karl Marx, *Capital: A Critique of Political Economy: Volume 1*, trans. Ben Fowkes (London: Penguin, 1976), ch. 1.
29. Marx, *Capital*, ch. 1.
30. Debord, *The Society of the Spectacle*, 14.
31. Stuart Hall, 'Introduction' in Stuart Hall ed., *Representation: Cultural Representations and Signifying Practices* (Milton Keynes: The Open University, 1997), 9.

exposed to [a] binary form of representation.'[32] These sharply opposed forms of representation might be in the register of good/bad, civilized/primitive, ugly/excessively attractive, or repelling-because-different/compelling-because-strange-and-exotic. The 'Other' according to Hall is often required to be '*both things at the same time.*'[33] This is especially the case when the 'Other' is to be included into processes of capital accumulation (for the benefit of the capitalist metropole). For Hall, a catalogue of racialization was established through historical moments of encounter of Western exploration, such as sixteenth century trading of Europeans with African kingdoms, the formal colonization of Africa in the nineteenth century, and the post-Second World War migrations from the Third World into Europe and North America.[34] These were key historical moments in which 'commodity racism' emerged from representational practises. A hierarchisation through race *and* through global capital flows emerged, yoking the otherwise 'excluded' to capital and commodity flows. With this, Hall showed the deep connections between mass advertising, imperialism, and commodity flows to and from Africa.[35]

Drawing on Rancière, Debord, and Hall, at the centre of our enquiry into aesthetics and international justice is the link between the dominance of certain representations of international justice and the (racialized) capitalist structures in which they exist. In this way, we can speak of a 'dominant' aesthetic – dominant both in terms of particular *forms* and *modes* of representation, and in the content expressed through these forms. Indeed, the crucial lesson we can take from these thinkers is that form and content are in fact inseparable from the production of such dominant aesthetics.

This approach thus prompts us to ask specific questions in relation to the aesthetics of international justice: who benefits from a certain type of common-sense approach to international justice? Who benefits from a view of international justice that is inflected with punitive notions of individual perpetrators of great crimes? Who benefits from the dominant racialized narratives and images of 'deserving' victims and refugees? Whose interests are served through the exhibiting of a particular photograph or artefact of 'justice'?

---

32. Stuart Hall, 'The Spectacle of the "Other"' in Hall, *Representation*, 229.
33. Hall, 'The Spectacle of the "Other",' 229.
34. Hall, 'The Spectacle of the "Other",' 239.
35. Hall, 'The Spectacle of the "Other",' 239-242.

What is Made Visible in International (Criminal) Justice?

What is the aesthetic experience of films, as an example of the above dynamics, that broach international criminal law (ICL)? We are, in a way, always presented with the same narrative, namely one which begins with the Second World War and its reframing of the idea of justice. ICL films, whether fictional or documentary, are a direct affirmation of a redemptive story of the Western world. The Nuremberg trials after the Second World War mark the starting point of ICL films, with a reminder of the 'never again' warning and promise. Victims in ICL films are typically aesthetically compared with Jewish victims of the Holocaust and perpetrators are typically likened with Hitler. Roles of helpless victims, the monstrous savage and their saviours are assigned.[36] They are of a morality which is constantly conscious of the 'absolute crime' as one of genocide; where other wrongs pale in comparison. Poverty, inequalities in economic power, environmental problems are placed on the side-lines of this narrative. To exemplify international (criminal) justice's dominant subculture, one might pick out the opening scenes of one of the anti-impunity documentaries that became popular in the 2000s.

'Across the world, in the silent wake of horror, a yearning, a reckoning with crimes against humanity.'[37] These words appear slowly on the screen at the beginning of the documentary *The Reckoning. The Battle of the International Criminal Court*. The words are accompanied by the following images. We see:

> Sun-parched land with a setting sun and the silhouette of two African men walking towards the camera.
>
> Black children, arm in arm, walking slowly towards a mud hut.
>
> An African village with heavy black clouds.
>
> Black hands turning a scull.
>
> A bird of prey taking flight.

---

36. See Makau Mutua, 'Savages Victims and Saviors: The Metaphor of Human Rights,' *The Harvard International Law Journal* 42 (2001).
37. 'The Reckoning: The Battle of the International Criminal Court' by Pamela Yates (Skylight Pictures, 2009).

Bloodied Black bodies in a field.

Footage of a pick-up truck with a gunman.

The images of violence and poverty continue, the scenes change rapidly, they are underlined by dramatic and sad music; short victim testimonies spoken to the camera follow. Then, the music finds a resolution, the words 'The Promise of Justice' appear. We see:

The white modern building of the ICC against a blue and white sky.

A modern courtroom filled with gowned lawyers.

The First Prosecutor of the court at a press conference.

Then again, the music becomes more dramatic. The words on the screen read: 'But the Hand of Justice is not always Welcome.' We see:

The UN Security Council and the representatives of China and the US.

A community meeting where Black people raise their hands to note their desire for dropping arrest warrants.

It is not difficult to identify the recurring themes: the repetition of images of good versus bad; conflict and resolution; images and symbols of death and hope; violence as located largely in Africa; poverty as the backdrop. The combination of images, narrative, and music are all components of a particular aesthetic. It is not only the use of film as an evidentiary medium that is significant here. Rather, as Lawrence Douglas observes, the filmic landscape we inhabit is very much part of a 'visual legacy of films.'[38] This visual legacy is constituted by films like *Nazi Concentration Camps*, the selection of shorts and images shown at the Nuremberg trials at the end of the Second World War.[39] The repetition of these images renders some victims hyper-visible, creating a hierarchy between those deemed deserving and those deemed undeserving, which is closely mapped onto the register of those who are productive and reproductive of capitalist structures (including the closely linked story of Western redemption), and those who are not.

---

38. Lawrence Douglas, 'Film as Witness: Screening *Nazi Concentration Camps* Before the Nuremberg Trial,' *The Yale Law Journal* 104/2 (1995), 464.
39. Douglas, 'Film as Witness'; Cornelia Vismann, *Medien der Rechtsprechung* (Frankfurt: S. Fischer Verlag, 2019).

Paying attention to a dominant aesthetic also means to pay attention to that which has been invisibilized, silenced, or hidden. Whilst our attention is directed towards the blindingly hyper-visible, our view is distracted from other forms of knowing and world-making. Counter-aesthetics is an attempt at drawing attention to such hierarchies that structure who benefits and is exploited within international justice, and challenging these with alternative, disruptive, and oppositional forms of aesthetics that draw on radical anti-racist, anti-capitalist, and anti-imperial movements and struggles.

The Aesthetics of International Justice, as Exemplified in This Collection

This collection begins with a chapter by Sofia Stolk that engages with aesthetics and international criminal justice through a screenplay of an institutional video produced by the International Criminal Court. By presenting the video as a screenplay, including specifying angles, close-ups, and the type of music used, this chapter brings alive that this institutional video is the product of multiple aesthetic and narrative choices that communicate a very specific story about the work of the ICC. Stolk draws attention to the framing of victimhood by the ICC, a theme that is picked up in the next chapter by Padraig McAuliffe, who turns attention to the field of Transitional Justice. McAuliffe traces how over time different aesthetics of the victim emerged through legal definition (by others) and self-definition (by survivors) in the struggles over the field's orientation. As different aspirations, emphases, or teleologies are advocated with reference to the interests of victims, six different aesthetics of victimhood emerged. These are a) the victim as active liberal citizen, b) the victim as witness, c) the victim as patient and saint, d) the victim as normal, e) the victim as indigent, f) the victims as indigene. Anne Neylon continues with the theme of aesthetic archetypes, drawing attention to the image of asylum seekers arriving at the shores of the United Kingdom in small boats. Neylon argues that such images are also law-creating moments where migrants and asylum seekers are depicted and narrated as illegitimate and 'illegal,' indeed criminal, arrivals to the state. In their co-authored contribution, Christine Schwöbel-Patel and Deger Ozkaramanli are also concerned with stereotypes. They analyse, with the visual aid of commissioned cartoons and familiar images, the construction of the 'grateful refugee' through their disciplines of law and design. Placing this construction in the context of the global neoliberal capitalist order that enables the flow of capital over people, they identify a dilemma presented for migrants and refugees, namely that they are expected to be at once deferential *and* entrepreneurial. Wayne Jordash and Ruby Axelson complement and ground the discussions on justice for victims with an overview from practice. The chapter, which is based on a keynote speech held by Wayne Jordash KC at the first conference on The Aesthetics and Counter-Aesthetics of International Law at the University of Liverpool, provides an important overview of the case law that has narrowed the scope of victim participation and reparation in international criminal courts and tribunals. The view from practice brings into focus the gap between the claims made and the rights afforded to victims.

The first part of this collection closes with an artwork that was commissioned for this project. Terry Duffy, a socially and culturally engaged international artist based in Liverpool, attended the project workshops we organised and visited The Hague with the aim of artistically capturing a counter-aesthetics of international justice. The result of his work is a striking judge's gown, following the pattern of a religious cope. The artwork, we believe, is fitting for a transition between the first part of this book on aesthetics to the second part on counter-aesthetics. Whilst we had imagined—in a naively abstract fashion—a radical departure from the kinds of dominant aesthetics we encountered in our research of international justice, the result appeared to us to be largely a reproduction of familiar themes. There is the religious symbolism of the cope/gown, the visceral imagery of mass graves, skulls and bones, emaciated victims, and the imperative to 'End Genocide Now!' Nevertheless, the depictions of Jacques Vergès and Justice Radhabinod Pal introduces different and unexpected characters to the storytelling. Vergès was a famous (and controversial) radical anti-imperial defence lawyer, known for his use of the method of trial of rupture; Justice Pal was the author of a remarkable dissenting opinion at the post Second World War Tokyo tribunal, which, despite many limitations, has become particularly meaningful for the story told about the relationship between imperialism and the development of international law. And yet, their depiction on the gown is somehow in dissonance with the other familiar tropes, reaffirming some of the aesthetics of international justice rather than going beyond them. Perhaps, though, this makes visible the limitations of conceptualising a 'counter'-aesthetic that is separated from a specific political movement. To identify whether a radical vision of counter-aesthetics is possible or feasible, we turn to Part Two.

2

The International Criminal Court in Focus

The Representation of Victimhood

Sofia Stolk

The larger part of this chapter takes the form of a screenplay. It dissects the texts, images, and editorial choices in the 17:32 minutes long video 'Victim's participation before the International Criminal Court' (2013).[1] The video is produced for educational purposes by the International Criminal Court's (ICC) Public Information and Documentation section and distributed through its website and YouTube channel, where it is one of the most popular ICC videos.[2] By presenting the video as a screenplay, this chapter aims to emphasize that this institutional video is not a neutral information device; it is the product of many aesthetic and narrative decisions, both small and large, that communicate a very specific story about victimhood and the work of the ICC.[3]

For this chapter, I selected three sequences of scenes in the video that engage with the depiction of victimhood. The first sequence contains the introductory scenes and illuminates how a certain tone is set. Moreover, it introduces a particular type of editing that frequently recurs throughout the video: a split screen.[4] In these split screens, two scenes appear next to each other in one frame. The same formula applies for all such scenes. In one half, we see meetings between victims/affected communities and ICC representatives 'in the field.' In the other half,

---

1. 'Victims' participation before the International Criminal Court (ICC),' IntlCriminalCourt, accessed 4 April 2023 https://youtu.be/chymGL8teX4.
2. At the time of writing: 26,000 views (23 February 2021).
3. Gillian Rose, *Visual Methodologies: An Introduction to Researching with Visual Materials*, 4th ed. (London: Sage Publications, 2016).
4. Split scenes can be found at min.: 2:00; 2:44; 5:35; 5:10; 9:00; 6:17; 11:36; 12:50; 15:00; 16:06.

we see an ICC staff member from his or her office who explains a part of the victim participation procedures. The second sequence further highlights the textual and expert-focus character of the video. Most shots show how ICC staff members talk to or about victims. Victims are passive rather than active subjects. A remarkable shot is the 'Over the Shoulder Shot' (OSS), where we look over the shoulder of the victim at the talking ICC staff; we take the perspective of the victim, but one can wonder if the victim is the actual protagonist. The third sequence further emphasizes the paradoxical silence of the victims in a video that emphasizes that their voices must be heard. In the rare moments that we hear the actual voice of the victim, what is said is often dismissed or reinterpreted by an expert commentator.

The screenplay reaffirms that the voice of the victim in international criminal law (ICL) is mediated through representation.[5] This happens in the courtroom and the audio-visual materials alike. In 'Victim's participation before the International Criminal Court,' the title of the video and images of victims and affected communities suggest that they are the main subjects. However, the ICC staff members are the central figures who actively explain, organize, travel, etc. Their voices speak. The listening victims in the video primarily facilitate the rather textual explanation of the victim participation procedures. This emphasizes the bureaucratic reality that is behind the promises of 'ending impunity' and 'helping victims make their voice heard,'[6] and the procedural constraints inherent to the legal response to 'unimaginable atrocities that deeply shock the conscience of humanity.'[7] In this, the video shows a tension similar to the dissonance in ICC courtrooms that has been observed

---

5. Sara Kendall and Sarah Nouwen, 'Representational Practices at the International Criminal Court: The Gap between Juridified and Abstract Victimhood,' *University of Cambridge Faculty of Law Legal Studies Research Paper Series* 24 (2013); Christine Schwöbel-Patel, 'Spectacle in International Criminal Law: The Fundraising Image of Victimhood,' *London Review of International Law* 4/2 (2016); Kieran McEvoy and Kirsten McConnachie, 'Victimology in transitional justice: Victimhood, innocence and hierarchy,' *European Journal of Criminology* 9/5 (2012); Rachel Killean and Luke Moffett, 'Victim Legal Representation before the ICC and ECCC,' *Journal of International Criminal Justice* 15/4 (2017); Sofia Stolk and Wouter Werner, 'Moving Images: Modes of Representation and Images of Victimhood in Audio-Visual Productions,' in *The Oxford Handbook of International Criminal Law*, ed. Kevin Jon Heller et al. (Oxford: Oxford University Press, 2020).
6. 'Helping Victims Make Their Voice Heard. The Office of Public Counsel for Victims, 5 Years of Activities,' International Criminal Court, accessed 28 August 2015, https://www.icc-cpi.int/NR/rdonlyres/01A26724-F32B-4BE4-8B02-A65D6151E4AD/282846/LRBookletEng.pdf.
7. Rome Statute, Preamble.

by critical ICL research between the urge to listen to victims and the failure to let them speak directly and individually.[8] The screenplay below is a textual translation of audio-visual material, but it nevertheless strongly 'visualizes' the division between who speaks and who is silent.

The screenplay follows the usual screenplay conventions, including some abbreviation. Characters that appear for the first time are written in capital letters. Other words in capital letters are important props (objects, clothes, etc.) and specific camera shots. The most important terms and abbreviations are in this short glossary:

ANGLE ON = Change of focus within the same scene.

CLOSE UP = A certain feature or part of the subject takes up the whole frame.

INT. = Indoors.

ESTABLISHING SHOT = Extreme wide shot providing an overview of the setting.

EXT. = Outdoors.

MID/MEDIUM SHOT = Part of the subject is visible in more detail, still giving an impression of the whole subject

OSS = Over the Shoulder shot.

PAN SHOT = Horizontal camera movement.

SPLIT SCREEN = two or more different scenes taking place in different sections within one frame.

SUPERIMPOSE = Letters placed over the film.

WIDE SHOT = Subject takes up full frame, environment visible.

---

8. Kendall and Nouwen, 'Representational Practices'; Sofia Stolk, 'The Victim, the International Criminal Court and the Search for Truth: On the Interdependence and Incompatibility of Truths about Mass Atrocity,' *Journal of International Criminal Justice* 13/5 (2015).

The International Criminal Court in Focus

1 LEADER - MONTAGE SHOT 1 FADE IN

Dramatic ORCHESTRA playing.

MONTAGE SHOT:

- WIDE PAN ESTABLISHING SHOT of a desert village landscape.

- A GROUP OF WOMEN in TRADITIONAL AFRICAN CLOTHING sit around a TABLE. A RADIO stands on the table. Women are listening to radio. We see a STONE HOUSE VILLAGE in the background.

- Man in African shirt speaks in RADIO MICROPHONE. A GIRL sits in the back.

SUPERIMPOSE: SPLIT SCREEN MONTAGE SHOT - 9 INSERTS

- EXT. WOMAN in GREEN SCARF holds up a PAPER SIGN. She is surrounded by other women in COLOURED HEADSCARVES. PAN TO man in white shirt with a PAPER in his hand, speaking to the women. CUT TO: meeting group of men in white clothes sitting on the ground or a carpet. Desert surrounding. CUT TO: meeting of group of women in coloured veils sitting on the ground.

- EXT. WIDE PAN SHOT. MARCHING SOLDIERS in desert.

- EXT. TWO SHOT. Black MAN and white WOMAN facing a group of people (not visible). Woman is explaining something with use of hands. VILLAGE and WOODEN BENCH visible in background. CUT TO: OSS we see the back of the man and the woman. We see a GROUP OF MEN on BENCHES listening. Woman is still moving hands and explaining. White building and other villagers in the back.

- INT. COURTROOM SHOT. MARIA KAMARA standing in courtroom. Formal posture. Talking to camera (inaudible).

- EXT. PICK-UP TRUCK with SOLDIERS. Moving. SUPERIMPOSED right lower corner: 23.1.2003.

- INT. COURTROOM. MONTAGE SHOT. CLOSE UPS JUDGES and other courtroom participants listening, wearing HEADPHONES.

- INT. MAN talks to group of people in PLASTIC CHAIRS.

- INT. OSS. We see the back of the head of a man who talks to a WOMAN and a MAN.

- INT. COURTROOM. JUDGES enter and have a seat.

IRIS IN TO:

EXT. WHITE ICC BUIDLING MAANWEG - DAYLIGHT

TITLE OVER (centre):

VICTIMS' PARTICIPATION BEFORE THE INTERNATIONAL CRIMINAL COURT

CUT TO:

2 EXT. ENTRANCE ICC BUILDING - DAYLIGHT

Outreach coordinator MARIA KAMARA stands outside the ICC BUILDING to introduce 'victim participation'. She wears WINTER COAT and a SCARF. Formal pose, clutched hands, one leg slightly in front of the other. We see the entrance of the court in the back, the ICC NAME SIGN visible. No other background action.

SUPERIMPOSE: Maria Kamara, Outreach Coordinator, Uganda and Kenya

MARIA KAMARA

(speaking clearly and slowly)

For the first time in the history of international criminal justice systems, the Rome Statute, the founding document of the international criminal court, which has been signed and ratified by over 120 states is putting victims at the centre of its proceedings.

(making circle with hands)

Victims have the right to participate and request for reparations. But what does it mean and how does it work in practice?

WIPE TO:

3 INT. COURTROOM - CONTINIOUS ACTION

STATIC CAMERA. Empty COURTROOM. Maria walks from back to front, while talking. Arms loosely bend. Important words are emphasized by hand gestures.

MARIA KAMARA

In the courtroom, victims are represented by lawyers who ensure that their views and concerns are are heard by the judges

(pointing at bench, stops walking)

> But the process of victims
> participation starts on the ground
>> (finger points to the ground)
> in the situation related countries,
> in affected communities, in the
> towns and villages where the
> victims reside.

CUT TO:

4 INT. FRONTSEAT OF CAR - DAYLIGHT - DRIVING

We see a road and green borders viewed from a front window of a DRIVING CAR. We see the dashboard and the forehead of the DRIVER in the mirror. We hear ENGINE SOUND. We see a WHITE VAN driving in front of us.

SUPERIMPOSE: Central African Republic

ANGLE ON: Side view on front-seat passenger. LEATITIA BONNET, woman in her thirties, sunglasses on her head, looking outside.

CUT TO:

5 EXT. AFRICAN VILLAGE - CAR STOP - DAYLIGHT

We see the parked car from the outside, ENGINE SOUND. Driver gets out. Nature surrounding.

ANGLE ON: back of the car. WOMAN carrying a plate on her head walks by. CHILDREN playing in tree. HOUSES of village vaguely visible in the back.

CUT TO:

6 EXT. COMMUNITY GATHERING - DAYLIGHT

We see a GROUP of around 15 COMMUNITY MEMBERS gathered. In front MAN IN WHEELCHAIR. We see parked MOTORCYCLES and BIKES. Village in the background. Surrounded by trees. Sandy terrain. Four WOMEN in TRADITIONAL CLOTHING walk over to the group.

PAN SHOT following the woman, who sit down on the benches on which the others are already sitting. FRENCH female voice speaking and INDISTINCT CHATTER in background.

REVERSE ANGLE on LEATITIA BONNET and translator. OSS of two women in the audience. Wooden TABLE.

Behind Bonnet and TRANSLATOR where a white woman with LAPTOP and PAPER is seated. Bonnet speaks, translator stands next to her with his arms crossed.

SUPERIMPOSED: Leatitia Bonnet. Field Officer, VPRS

>   LEATITIA BONNET
> (supports talking with gestures)
> (translated)
> So, I work for the Victims Participation and Reparation Section. Our job is to help victims request participation and ask for reparations. I am going to explain it further.[9]

---

[9]. Wherever the original spoken language is other than English, I included the translated text. This is due to the lack of proficiency of the author in most other languages. For the sake of consistency, the parts in French are also displayed in their English translation.

INSERT SHOT:

SPLIT SCREEN

left: group of about 20 COMMUNITY MEMBERS sitting in rows wearing AFRICAN TRADITIONAL CLOTHES. Listen silently. ANGLE ON: MAN IN WHEELCHAIR, listening. Village background. CUT TO: close-up, other listening villagers in background.

right: MEDIUM SHOT. MIKEL DELANGRANGE sits in ICC OFFICE, PINBOARD with PAPERS pinned on it in background.

SUPERIMPOSED: Mikel Delangrange, Associate Legal Officer, VPRS

> MIKEL DELAGRANGE
> The proceedings that we have before us, we're looking at war crimes, crimes against humanity and genocide. So, to be a victim, to qualify as a victim before the court...you need to be someone who has suffered harm from one of the crimes that has been charged by the prosecutor.

Voice LEATITIA BONNET starts speaking.

BACK TO SCENE:

We see LEATITIA BONNET from behind, next to translator. Same setting, community members listening. We see the village and another group of people in the back.

                    LEATITIA BONNET

               (translated)

          In order to be recognized
          as a victim in the Jean-Pierre Bemba
          trial, specifically in that trial,
          you have to be a victim of the crimes
          that Mr Bemba is charged with, which
          in this case are murder, pillaging
          and rape. So the people who would be
          recognized as victims by the Judges
          will be those who have suffered from
          these three crimes.

                                        INSERT SHOT:

SPLIT SCREEN

Left: Leatitia Bonnet continues (mute). ANGLE ON: close-up first row of listening community members.

Right: Mikel Delagrange in office.

                    MIKEL DELAGRANGE

          Now, the traditional way for a
          victim to participate in the
          proceedings is by submitting an
          application form to my office, the
          VPRS.

BACK TO VILLAGE SCENE

LEATITIA BONNET

If someone wants to be recognized by
the Judges as a victim, he or she has

to make a request and fill in this
form, as we have discussed earlier.

ANGLE ON: man, WHITE SHIRT, stands up between other community members.

VILLAGER

(points at forms)

(translated)

We did fill in the form but we
haven't had any response yet.

(indistinct chattering in the back)

CUT TO:

7 INT. COURTROOM ICC

MEDIUM SHOT Maria Kamara stands in front of desks in courtroom.

MARIA KAMARA

As you could see, the participation
process starts with the direct
contact with the victims. Once the
victims decide to apply to
participate in the proceedings, the
application forms are sent from the
field offices to the court in The Hague.

Notes on Scene 1-7

This first sequence highlights how a certain tone is set through the central characters, locations, and props. In this section, we listen to three ICC staff members. Maria Kamara, the outreach coordinator, represents the voice from the ICC headquarters. She introduces and summarizes what we see in the video. She frames victim participation as an historical milestone and invites us to look at the practical side of the victim participation process. The two Victims Participation and Reparations Section officers represent the nuts and bolts of the victim participation process. Leatitia Bonnett represents the direct contact with the victims, and Mikel Delagrange explains what her work with victims involves. The images of the visits to affected communities do not speak for themselves, they are embedded by the two layers of textual explanation from more formal office environments, offered by Kamara and Delagrange. What happens in the villages is an illustration of the textual commentary, and no independent footage with explanatory power of its own. The footage gives an idea of what the work 'in the field' looks like, but the core message resides in the text rather than the images.

The community members are anonymous characters that mainly feature in a role as 'the affected community' or 'the victims.' The only individual that is singled out is the man in the wheelchair, as a visual depiction of those 'affected.' The main props are papers, both in the field and the offices, emphasizing the bureaucratic character of the proceedings. At the end of scene six, one of the victims critically addresses the procedure by saying that 'we did fill in the form but we haven't had any response yet.' The comment is included, but not responded to in any way. The VPRS officer in the field might have responded, but this did not make the final cut. The following scene, featuring Maria Kamara again, does not react to the comment, but summarizes what has been explained before.

The next sequence further emphasizes the centrality of the ICC staff, contrasted with the anonymity of victims—and the related security issues.

```
                15 INT. ICC HALLWAY
```

We see Maria Kamara walking towards us through a hallway in the ICC.

SUPERIMPOSE: Maria Kamara, Outreach Coordinator, Uganda, and Kenya

                    MARIA KAMARA
              (moving left hand)
        One of the main challenges facing the court is locating the victims of the crimes to inform them of their rights to participate in the processes. This is true especially so given the fact that the court has limited resources. The court relies on its own outreach capabilities in cooperation with civil society groups, intermediaries and the media.

16 EXT. BUILDING KENYA.

We see a GREY THREE STORY APARTMENT BUILDING from the outside. WIDE SHOT. CARS are driving by. ZOOM IN on red door.

SUPERIMPOSE: Kenya

                                            CUT TO:

INT. OFFICE IN KENYA

                                            CUT TO:

17 EXT. VILLAGE CHURCH INT. ICC OFFICE

SPLIT SCREEN

Left: EXT. VILLAGE (mute).

Two INTERMEDIARIES (a man and a woman) arrive with WHITE VAN, they unload CARDBOARD BOXES and carry them inside a BRICK CHURCH BUILDING.

CUT TO: INT. church building, where COMMUNITY MEMBERS (women, men, children) are sitting in pews, some dressed in TRADITIONAL AFRICAN CLOTHING.

PAN TO: left, view on the audience.

REVERSE ANGLE: intermediaries on the stage, talk in MICROPHONES (OSS of audience).

CUT TO: audience reading BOOKLETS with images.

CLOSE UP: SMALL CHILD looking into the camera, sitting on an adult's lap who is reading a booklet.

CUT TO: shot from the back of the church. OSS of the audience at the intermediaries on stage.

INSERT Right: INT. ICC OFFICE

MID SHOT Mikel Delagrange, sitting in office.

> MIKEL DELAGRANGE
>
> (talks into camera)
>
> Locating victims, wherever they may reside within the given country, the situation country, our central challenge is really to ensure the security of those that are engaging with

the court. Ehm, we don't have a standing
army or police force that we can rely
upon to ensure their security. So what
we do rely on is our best practices
that we've developed over the years
to ensure the confidentiality and the
security of those seeking to participate.
We do this mainly by training
intermediaries on these best practices.
So that when victims choose to come
forward and engage in this participation
process, they do so knowing that they've
undertaken a certain amount of risk but
also how to mitigate that risk.

CUT TO:

18 INT. OFFICE NGO KENYA

ANGLE ON: AIMEE ONGESO (MEDIUM CLOSE UP) with a bookshelf in the back, viewed OSS, behind the back of a bald head of the VICTIM. Aimee is attentively listening to the victim, nodding, and humming.

 VICTIM

 (translation)

 So—I came to ask for advice.
 As a victim –how can I ensure
 my security?

MEDIUM CLOSE UP: Aimee Ongeso and EDIGAH KAVULAVU. Both nodding.

MEDIUM CLOSE UP: Aimee Ongeso. Back of the head of the victim visible. ZOOM OUT: include Edigah KAVULAVU in frame. OSS of victim.

> EDIGAH KAVULAVU
> (translated)
> Mr Simon - concerning your security, you have to know that your security starts with you. Even when the police and the ICC are involved, your security depends on you.

INTER CUT: hands of Edigah Kavulavu holding pen, paper in front.

CLOSE UP: Edigah Kavulavu.

SUPERIMPOSE: Edigah Kavulavu - Kituo Cha Sheria, NGO

> EDIGAH KAVULAVU
> If you go through your village and tell everyone that you are on the ICC's list, you have already put your life in danger.
> (humming AIMEE ONGESO on the background)

WIDE SHOT: Aimee and Edigah sitting at TABLE in office, PAPER on the table, BOOKSHELVES, MAP and CLOSET in the back. We see the BACK OF THE VICTIM, wearing a WHITE SHIRT with BLACK VEST.

                    EDIGAH KAVULAVU

          (translation) Police have the

          obligation to ensure your protection.

          If someone is threatening you

          -the first thing you need to do is

          go and report it to the police.

CUT TO: BOOKS on the shelves 'Laws of Kenya'. PAN SHOT bookshelf.

                    EDIGAH KAVULAVU

          (voice only)

          (translation)

          Then -inform us—because our organization

          can meet with the police or your

          village chief to make sure that you

          are safe.

ClOSE UP: back of the head of the nodding victim.

                                             CUT TO:

Notes on Scene 15-18

The main theme in this sequence is confidentiality and security. These concerns affect participation procedures and video production alike; restraining what and who we can show, and what not. In the first part of the sequence, we encounter a by now familiar setting of ICC intermediaries that visit a community in order to explain the victim participation procedure.[10] Emphasis is placed on 'best practices,' which are

---

10. On intermediaries, see Mariana Pena, 'The Role of Intermediaries and Third Par-

visualized by the booklets that are handed to the community members. The role of the victims is again that of the listening audience, while the ICC intermediaries speak before the group. The main storyline is again presented by Mikel Delagrange from his office.

Scene eighteen introduces an 'actual' victim participant—insofar as the community members in previous scenes where not 'victims.'[11] The nature of the conversation is mainly procedural; the participation procedure is central, not the victim's story. The bureaucratic tone is illustrated again by the imagery; the scene is set in an office and ends with a long shot of the legal books on the shelves. An attempt has been made to reduce the recognizability of the victim, by filming him from behind. Full anonymity however is not realized; the victim's voice is not manipulated, and his body is still visible. The absence of speaking victims certainly has a connection to the protection of victims. As evidenced by this scene, security is one of the major concerns of the victims who participate. Interestingly, the response of the intermediaries to the concerns of security emphasize that this is a matter mainly of the victim's own responsibility. Another striking contrast is the depiction of effort of the ICC officials to speak to entire communities in public meetings, to locate and recruit victim participants, and simultaneously the remark that spreading the word in your village about your participation in the procedure equals putting your life in danger. The former—making ICC participation known, sits uncomfortably with the latter—the demand for victims to keep their participation secret.

The tension between expectations of victims on the one hand and what the ICC can offer on the other hand is one of the prominent themes in this and the following scenes. This tension is not presented as a fault in the procedural design. Rather, it is presented as a problem that can be solved by educating victims, by explaining why their expectations are not appropriate. This again places the victims in a passive role. The requests or demands of victims that the ICC cannot meet are rendered unrealistic. The video is part of an attempt to temper these 'unrealistic' expectations, without reflection on the roots and validity of these expectations. The ICC has emphasized the importance of an 'effective system of two-way communication,' but this video

---

ties in Victim Participation,' in *Victim Participation in International Criminal Justice*, ed. Kinga Tibori-Szabó and Megan Hirst (The Hague: TMC Asser Press, 2017), 81.
11. On the inclusion and exclusion of particular types of victims into the procedures, and the 'pyramid of victimhood,' see Kendall and Nouwen, 'Representational Practices.'

primarily shows one-way communication from the ICC to the victims.[12] The following sequence further illustrates this tension.

```
26 EXT. VILLAGE GATHERING - DAYLIGHT
```

We see COMMUNITY MEMBERS gathering outside in a DESERT-like environment. Some are sitting on the ground, some are standing. Most of the women are wearing COLOURFUL HEADSCARVES. One WOMAN in a BLACK ROBE, blurred face, is standing in front of the group, she addresses herself to A WOMAN IN A COLOURFUL SHIRT (black hair, faced towards the talking woman). Three MEN stand close aside, one holding PAPERS.

>   WOMAN
>
>   (moving hands)
>
>   (translated) All I am asking is that
>   the procedure should be accelerated
>   that we receive a response within two
>   or three months, since Omar Al-Bashir's
>   involvement in these crimes is common
>   knowledge. I would also like to know
>   how we will return to our country.
>   Here, as you know, we have old people,
>   children and the destitute who have
>   suffered a lot. What will you do to
>   take us back home?

---

12. 'Strategic Plan for Outreach of the International Criminal Court,' *International Criminal Court*, 29 September 2006, accessed 6 April 2023, http://www.icc-cpi.int/NR/rdonlyres/FB4C75CF-FD15-4B06-B1E3- E22618FB404C/185051/ICCASP512_English1.pdf. See also Stolk, 'The Victim, the International Criminal Court and the Search for Truth.'

SPLIT SCREEN

Left: CONTINUOUS ACTION in the sandy village (mute). Group of CHILDREN walking around, looking into the camera, we see the village gathering in the back, women in COLOURFUL ROBES. ANGLE ON: middle circle of village gathering. Four men discussing. ANGLE ON: woman in yellow robe and headscarf.

INSERT right: MID SHOT Aimee Ongeso in OFFICE, BOOKSHELF in the back.

> AIMEE ONGESO
> Then we have the expectations
> of that justice will be served
> quickly. So when are they going
> to get arrested? When is the
> judgement going to come? When
> are we going to see this happening?
> And, now, we all realize of
> course justice is a slow process,
> so the expectation that there
> is going to be quick or expeditious
> delivery of justice is another
> expectation.

CUT TO:

27 INT ICC COURTROOM

Victim hearing. We see lawyer MARIE-EDITH DOUZIMA LAWSON, in GOWN and BAND. She wears HEADPHONES. In the back, we see the COMPUTER SCREENS of other courtroom participants.

SUPERIMPOSED: Marie-Edith Douzima Lawson, Legal representative of victims

> DOUZIMA LAWSON
> (translated)
> Madam witness, after everything that happened to you, after everything that happened to your community, how do you feel?

SUPERIMPOSED: Pulchérie Makiandakama, Victim

> PULCHÉRIE MAKIANDAKAMA
> (translated)
> In my community, I am no longer considered a human being—and I think that all across the Central African Republic, I am no longer considered a human being. You see, I was a human being but I was treated like an animal.

SPLIT SCREEN

Left: CONTINUOUS ACTION courtroom (mute). CLOSE-UP witness. Listening JUDGES. Courtroom images.

INSERT right: MID SHOT Aimee Ongeso in OFFICE, BOOKSHELF in the back.

AIMEE ONGESO

Victim participation is very important because, first of all, the victims need to be heard. They need to tell their story. And they need to know that someone is listening to their story and that something is going to be done about their story. So the first important thing that you give them audience, that they're being heard is very important. You know, the worst thing would be, yes we have victims and no one is even bothered about what is happening, that would be horrible. So in terms of victim participation, I would like to see yeah, the ICC has done a good job. We are very happy that victims can be heard, they can talk, and yes the court is listening.

CUT TO:

29 EXT. ENTRANCE ICC BUILDING - DAYLIGHT

BACK TO SETTING SCENE 2. Outreach coordinator Maria Kamara stands outside the ICC BUILDING.

MARIA KAMARA
Victims are entitled to truth and justice. The processes at the ICC might help them to deal with the past and to move forward. Participation is voluntary. Some victims might prefer not to participate. From those participating, only some of them will personally address the court, and others will have their voices heard through their lawyers. Not all victims of the crimes will participate in the proceedings. But the court acknowledges their sufferings and is mindful of their situations and their needs.

CUT TO:

30 CREDITS

BLUE SCREEN

SUPERIMPOSE: Produced by the ICC Public Information and Documentation Section with support from the European Commission. ICC-CPI © 2012.

SUPERIMPOSE: TWO LOGOS

10 Years Fighting Impunity ICC (left)

European Commission (right)

Notes on Scene 26-30

In the first scene, a similar interaction described earlier is taking place. An anonymized victim is requesting the ICC to expedite the proceedings. An ICC intermediary is explaining from her office that this is one of the 'unrealistic' expectations that victims have. In an earlier sequence, she noted that 'it has been quite a challenge to be honest with you in trying to manage these expectations.'[13] This vocabulary of 'managing' expectations fits with the overall bureaucratic tone of the video. That a managerial logic has captivated international law, and international criminal law particularly, has been noted elsewhere.[14] Instead of emphasizing the importance of the independent voice of the victim, this scene emphasizes the importance of victims as part of a proceeding.

In this light, it is worth noting the remark in the next scene. The ICC intermediary repeats a phrase often repeated in the victim participation context by victim representatives, VPRS officers and prosecutors alike: that victims need to be able to tell their stories, that they must be heard.[15] To give victims an audience is important to the ICC.

---

13. 'Victims' participation before the International Criminal Court (ICC),' min. 11:36.
14. Richard Clements, 'Governing international criminal justice: Managerial practices and the International Criminal Court' (PhD Thesis, University of Cambridge, 2021); Frédéric Mégret, 'International Criminal Justice as a Juridical Field,' *Champ Pénal/Penal Field* 13 (2016); Christine Schwöbel-Patel, 'The Rule of Law as Marketing Tool: The International Criminal Court and the Brand of Global Justice,' in *Research Handbook on the Rule of Law*, eds. Christopher May and Adam Winchester (Cheltenham: Edward Elgar Publishing, 2018); Christopher Hutton, 'Linguistic Landscape, Law and Reflexive Modernity,' in *Law, Culture and Visual Studies*, eds. Anne Wagner and Richard K. Sherwin (New York: Springer, 2014); Martti Koskenniemi, 'The politics of international law—20 years later,' *European Journal of International Law* 20/1 (2009); Stolk and Werner, 'Moving Images.'
15. For example, in interviews, press releases, documentaries, and outreach documents. See Esther Addler, 'Fatou Bensouda, the woman who hunts tyrants,' *The Guardian*, 5 June 2016; Fatou Bensouda in 'The Reckoning: The Battle for the International Criminal Court' by Pamela Yates (Skylight Pictures, 2009), min. 39:30; ICC, 'Helping Victims Make Their Voice Heard'; 'The Office of Public Counsel for Victims, 5 Years of Activities,' International Criminal Court, accessed 11 April 2023, http://www.icc-cpi.int/NR/rdonlyres/01A26724- F32B-4BE4-8B02- A65D6151E4AD/282846/LRBookletEng.pdf. See also, *Prosecutor v Lubanga Dyilo* (Hearing) ICC-01/04-01/06 (26 January 2009) [34]-[35], [51]; 'Statement to the Press by the Prosecutor of the International Criminal Court (Abidjan, Côte d'Ivoire, 20 July 2013),' *International Criminal Court*, 20 July 2013, accessed 11 April 2023, https://www.icc-cpi.int/news/statement-press-prosecutor-internation-

One way of doing this, is calling victims to give testimony in court, as is illustrated by the excerpt from the evidence of Victim a/0866/10, or Pulchérie Makiandakama. However, only a few victims are allowed to speak in court. In the Bemba case, in which Ms Makiandakama participated, only two of 5229 participating victims were permitted to present evidence in court.[16] Another way to make these voices heard is through the other outreach channels of the ICC such as YouTube. The video presented in this chapter primarily aims to explain the victim participation procedures. Still, the lack of victims' voices is striking. As this is the video selected by ICC officials as their main video on their YouTube channel, it seems like a missed opportunity to leave the actual voice of the victims and their experiences largely out of the narrative. The final words of Maria Kamara recognize that not all victims will participate, and not all participants will be able to speak directly. She notes that 'the court acknowledges their sufferings and is mindful of their situations and their needs'. This affirmation can be contrasted with a report by the Human Rights Center at the University of California, Berkeley, based on 622 interviews with victims, which shows that victims feel frustrated by the proceedings, that they are not well informed, and that their expectations are not met.[17] These are serious concerns that can be contrasted with the seemingly ideal participation procedure put forward in the video.

---

al-criminal-court-abidjan-cote-divoire-20-july-2013; 'Statement of the Prosecutor of the International Criminal Court, Fatou Bensouda, in Relation to the Escalating Violence in the Central African Republic,' *International Criminal Court*, 9 December 2013, accessed 11 April 2023, https://www.icc-cpi.int/news/statement-prosecutor-international-criminal-court-fatou-bensouda-relation-escalating-1; Fatou Bensouda, 'The Incidence of the Female Child Soldier and the International Criminal Court', *International Criminal Court*, 4 June 2012, accessed 11 April 2023, https://www.icc-cpi.int/sites/default/files/NR/rdonlyres/316A88F6-86B4-488D-8FEB-526D0E515062/284579/04062012DPSpeechNYGirlChildSoldiers.pdf; 'Ruto and Sang Trial Opens at the International Criminal Court,' *International Criminal Court*, 10 September 2013, accessed 11 April 2023, https://www.icc-cpi.int/news/ruto-and-sang-trial-opens-international-criminal-court.

16. See *Prosecutor v Bemba Gombo* (Decision) ICC-01/05-01/08 (22 February 2012); Wairagala Wakabi, 'Victims to Testify in Bemba Trial This Week,' *International Justice Monitor*, 30 April 2012, accessed 6 April 2023, https://www.ijmonitor.org/2012/04/victims-to-testify-in-bemba-trial-this-week/.

17. Human Rights Center, 'The Victims' Court? A Study of 622 Victim Participants at the International Criminal Court' (UC Berkeley School of Law, 2015).

Final Remarks

In sum, the ICC clearly chose to present its work in this video in a procedural way, with a central role for ICC staff members. Presented in this way, the video does not differ in content from a leaflet on the participation procedures. The scenes in the field present an illustration of how the ICC interacts with victims but the victims never actively contribute to the story in the video in a substantive way. Rather, they are depicted as silent audience members that facilitate the story of ICC staff about the victims' need for explanation of the proceedings and its limits.

The video emphasizes a problem of the ICC that has been identified elsewhere: It reduces victims of mass atrocity to a stereotype that can only speak indirectly through ICC representation; the stereotype of a passive, silent, suffering victim in need of support. This chapter aims to show how, in this video, the silent victim stereotype is constructed through an accumulation of choices regarding the texts, props, locations, editing, and characters, resulting in a film about victims in which the voice of the victim is absent. Based on this, one can start thinking about the alternative paths that could have been taken. The content of a video is not predetermined, and neither is a legal procedure. If we can identify the choices, we can identify the room for change.

3

Displaying the Victim

Essentialized Aesthetics of Victimhood in Transitional Justice Debates

Padraig McAuliffe

This chapter explores how the aesthetics and counter-aesthetics of victimhood are manifested in the field of transitional justice (TJ) as it emerged from a set of isolated practices in Latin America in the 1980s to something 'normalized' (some might say 'banalized') in the sense of now forming a part of the presumptive toolkit for peacebuilding and memory politics. Popularized by the mid-1990s, within a decade TJ was firmly ensconced in the popular imagination, official peacebuilding discourse and foreign policy. In the past ten years, the nature of the claims made for TJ have become ever-more expansive as its practice moved from its historically exceptionalist origins (initially conceived in a relatively limited manner as the study of tools for establishing stability in transition from authoritarian rule to liberal democracy around the time of the Cold War's dénouement) to the current mainstream, globalized, 'steady-state' phase. This contemporary phase departs from an exclusive concern for past violence to treat conditions of persistent conflict, laying the foundation for a normalized law of violence where transitional justice became commonplace as opposed to exceptional.[1] Once transitional justice moved from the question of whether something should be done to how it should be done, it was discovered that standardized approaches from prior practice needed significant amendment or compromise in novel transitional political contexts. Difficulties in applying past models or idealized archetypes

---

1. Ruti Teitel, 'Transitional Justice Genealogy,' *Harvard Human Rights Journal* 69 (2003), 89–93.

to given transitional contexts have required constant innovation and adaptation. The field has, at various points, alternated between the transnational and the local, the holistic and the specific, the liberal and the communitarian, accentuating different imaginaries of justice (retributive, restorative, grassroots, feminist, indigenous, etc.). These innovations have at times yielded beneficial outcomes in terms of justice, truth, and restoration, but persistently generate additional dilemmas and make manifest underlying issues the various mechanisms have not and perhaps cannot address.

The primary reason both the practise and the discourse surrounding TJ has expanded has not been because of its success—as Pablo de Greiff argues, no transitional state that can legitimately claim to have generated a morally adequate number of trials or revealed all complex truths or generated sufficient reparations,[2] while others note a 'hollowness' inherent in the field produced by the overcharging of existing mechanisms and unrealistic public expectations.[3] Instead, TJ has metastasized as theory and practice are reflexively reinvented in the attempt to fully capture real world complexities. In attempting to remedy the shortcomings every new intervention makes apparent, it consistently adopts new mechanisms, perspectives, and goals in a range of diverse, context-specific sites of intervention as theorists and practitioners grapple with new forms of ambivalence, animus, and the unknown. Most of the controversies in its advocacy-cum-policy-oriented literature therefore revolve not only around the conceptual terrain for intervention, but also the field's self-identity. This identity has become highly contested, a site for moral and political struggle over the meanings attached to justice, the teleology implied by transition, and the most relevant audiences. Over time, TJ's constantly expanding symbolic capital led to increased claims for inclusion and insistence by scholars and activists of the need to 'reframe' the field to include ever broader agendas that incorporate structural, gender, ethnocultural and post-colonial agendas.[4]

---

2. Pablo de Greiff, 'Theorizing Transitional Justice,' in *Transitional Justice*, ed. Melissa Williams, Rosemary Nagy and Jon Elster (New York: New York University Press, 2012), 35.
3. Rama Mani, 'Editorial: Dilemmas of Expanding Transitional Justice, or Forging the Nexus Between Transitional Justice and Development,' *International Journal of Transitional Justice* 2/3 (2008), 255.
4. Christine Bell, 'Transitional Justice, Interdisciplinarity and the State of the "Field" or "Non-Field,"' *International Journal of Transitional Justice* 3 (2009), 13.

Though some argue that the victim as political actor has been absent in TJ and that a 'victims turn' only emerged in the middle of the last decade, in reality victims have been at the core of TJ policy-making since the very start.[5] We can see over time the gradually different aesthetics of the victim that emerges through legal definition (by others) and self-definition (by survivors) in the struggles over the field's orientation, as different aspirations, emphases or teleologies are advocated with reference to the interests of victims. These interests are always considered paramount but permit competing visions as to what they actually consist of in the different critical cycles the field has manifested over time. This chapter suggests a number of different aesthetics of victimhood that have emerged at various stages in the evolution of TJ as a field of study and practice:

a) The victim as active liberal citizen
b) The victim as witness
c) The victim as patient and saint
d) The victim as normal
e) The victim as indigent
f) The victim as indigene

This list is not exhaustive. The victim as female has an entire literature to itself that might dwarf the others combined.[6] The collective aspects of victimhood are also increasingly coming to the fore as TJ grapples with abuses committed against aggregated groups like LGBT communities[7] and ethnic minorities.[8] The six aspects considered here arguably suffice to demonstrate that victimhood is socially constructed as TJ praxis fosters, shapes, and defines subjectivities that influence how victims

---

5. Jemima García-Godos, 'Victims in Focus,' *International Journal of Transitional Justice* 10/2 (2016), 350.
6. See for example Katherine Franke, 'Gendered Subjects of Transitional Justice,' *Columbia Journal of Gender & Law* 15 (2006), 813; Olivera Simic, 'Feminist Research in Transitional Justice Studies: Navigating Silences and Disruptions in the Field,' *Human Rights Review* 17/1 (2016), 95; Julieta Lemaitre and Kristin Bergtora Sandvik, 'Beyond Sexual violence in Transitional Justice: Political Insecurity as a Gendered Harm,' *Feminist Legal Studies* 22 (2014), 243.
7. Pascha Bueno-Hansen, 'The Emerging LGBTI Rights Challenge to Transitional Justice in Latin America,' *International Journal of Transitional Justice* 12/1 (2018), 126.
8. Chris Chapman, 'Transitional Justice and the Rights of Minorities and Indigenous Peoples,' in *Identities in Transition: Challenges for Transitional Justice in Divided Societies*, ed. Paige Arthur (Cambridge: Cambridge University Press, 2011), 251.

represent (if not necessarily self-understand) themselves.[9] Though these imaginaries of the victim are very different, the perennial theme is the asserted centrality of victims vis-à-vis perpetrators and society as a whole. The mainstreaming of TJ intervention has been attended by the constant reiteration of immeasurable trauma and physical/psychological/emotional damage suffered by victims before, during, and after conflict. This became visible with the growth of satellite television and the internet in the years after the Cold War, as greater exposure to global news ensured images of victimization were widespread, making it extremely difficult for governments to ignore suffering or the need for some form of accountability.[10] As Louis Bickford notes,

> the human rights movement has strongly influenced the development of the field, making it self-consciously victim-centric. Transitional justice practitioners tend to pursue strategies that they believe are consistent with the rights and concerns of victims, survivors, and victim's families.[11]

In post-conflict and post-authoritarian states, victims are seen to be used as political tools by policy-makers to gain moral authority.[12] External TJ experts 'legitimize their existence on the basis of speaking about and for victims.'[13] For example, the first claim in the 'About Us' section of the International Center for Transitional Justice's website states that it works with victims and other groups and organizations 'to ensure redress for victims and to help prevent atrocities from happening again.'[14] Indeed, the TJ industry 'produces' victims in the process of making claims or seeking

---

9. Vincent Druliolle and Roddy Brett, 'Introduction: Understanding the Construction of Victimhood and the Evolving Role of Victims in Transitional Justice and Peacebuilding,' in *The Politics of Victimhood in Post-conflict Societies: Comparative and Analytical Perspectives*, eds. Vincent Druliolle and Roddy Brett, (Berlin: Springer, 2018), 5.
10. M. Cherif Bassiouni, 'Justice and Peace: The Importance of Choosing Accountability over Realpolitik,' *Case Western Reserve Journal of International Law* 35/2 (2003), 203.
11. Louis Bickford, 'Transitional Justice,' in *The Encyclopaedia of Genocide and Crimes Against Humanity, Vol. III*, ed. Dinah Shelton (London: MacMillan, 2004), 1045.
12. Marie Smyth, 'Putting the Past in its Place: Issues of Victimhood and Reconciliation in Northern Ireland's Peace Process,' in *Burying the Past: Making Peace and Doing Justice after Civil Conflict*, ed. Nigel Biggar (Georgetown: Georgetown University Press, 2003), 126–127.
13. Tshepo Madlingozi, 'On Transitional Justice Entrepreneurs and the Production of Victims,' *Journal of Human Rights Practice* 2/2 (2010), 208.
14. 'About Us,' International Center for Transitional Justice, accessed 12 April 2023, https://www.ictj.org/about.

support for projects.[15] They are able to do this because a large body of norms and soft law promote the active engagement by and with victims. Their participation is seen as the *sin qua non* of any TJ initiative. The success of TJ initiatives is increasingly judged by (a) the quantity and quality of public and victim consultation carried out (facilitating a better understanding of the dynamics of repression/conflict, patterns of discrimination and types of victims)[16] and (b) the degree of victims' agency in establishing their interests and preferences when designing TJ policies of transitional justice.[17] However, this consultation and participation can be used to justify almost any form of justice intervention on the spectrum from inactivity to thoroughgoing justice, grassroots processes to distant internationalized tribunals given the inescapable reality that victims 'differ remarkably in their desires for revenge, for granting forgiveness, for remembering, and for moving on.'[18] All TJ measures are justified on the basis that they seek to provide recognition to victims, but historically victims have been used by policy-makers and theorists to justify different forms of recognition. The aesthetic of the victim has hence been subjected to some wild oscillations, which form the subject of this chapter. There is no dominant aesthetic of victimhood. However, neither is it the case that victim constructions are as varied as the lived experiences of victimhood; idiosyncratic experiences of conflict and repression are shoehorned into generic, prefabricated but slowly evolving imaginaries.

The Victim as Active Liberal Citizen

By the late 1980s the universal language of human rights had begun to permeate political discourse in states where Cold War authoritarianisms were losing their grip on power. Initially tentative debates over the possibility of accountability in the waves of transition in Latin America and Eastern Europe would employ this language to secure some measure of punishment and redress. At the time, both advocates and politicians were preoccupied with the existential dilemma of how

---

15. Madlingozi, 'Production of Victims,' 208 (abstract).
16. Report of the Secretary-General, The Rule of Law and Transitional Justice in Conflict and Post-Conflict Societies (23 August 2004) UN Doc S/2004/616, para 16.
17. Independent study on best practices, including recommendations, to assist States in strengthening their domestic capacity to combat all aspects of impunity, by Professor Diane Orentlicher, (27 February 2004) UN Doc E/CN.4/2004/88.
18. Martha Minow, *Between Vengeance and Forgiveness* (Boston: Beacon Press, 1998), 135.

to balance moral and legal demands for criminal accountability for past political violence with the constraints imposed by transitional power-balances as authoritarian state apparatuses relinquished power slowly. In what could be characterized as the stability/democracy versus justice debate (and later, peace versus justice debate), policymakers and scholars measured risks of future military coups or revanchist seizure of power against opportunities for democratic development.[19] Without the guarantee of amnesty, powerholders like the National Party in South Africa, Pinochet in Chile or Uruguay's dictatorship would have walked out of democratization negotiations altogether. In Argentina, criminal prosecutions were circumscribed by Full Stop and Due Obedience laws, while those military offenders prosecuted were eventually excused from sentences rendered against them. The fear of victims and civil society was that the dominant paradigm might be transitional politics instead of transitional justice in which the rights of victims to trial were sidelined in the interests of stability that impunity was assumed to foster. It was in these contexts that a realist versus idealist contest of TJ ideas would see its first iteration. Realists argued that new rulers should follow a Weberian ethical 'maxim of responsibility' by considering the predictable (negative) consequences of accountability instead of an ethic of conviction in which a trial was imperative.[20] Idealists, by contrast, contended that impunity would inevitably call into question the rights-based legitimacy and credibility of the new dispensation. What is significant was how the notion of victimhood was employed in these idealist arguments. Idealists drew on the verdicts of treaty-based human rights tribunals and provisions in international human rights law to propose prosecutions as an essential part of the remedy states must guarantee victims of right to life or humane treatment violations. Retributive theories of punishment were augmented by an emphasis on respect for the victim and his or her rights.[21] Scholars like Nigel Biggar argued that 'thinking of criminal justice primarily in terms not of retribution but of the vindication of victims significantly relaxes the tension between justice and the politics of making peace.'[22]

---

19. For a review of the debate in these terms see Aurelien Colson, 'The Logic of Peace and the Logic of Justice,' *International Relations* 15/1 (2000).
20. José Zalaquett, 'Balancing Ethical Imperatives and Political Constraints: The Dilemma of New Democracies Confronting Past Human Rights Violations,' *Hastings Law Journal* 43/6 (1991), 1429.
21. Aryeh Neier, *War Crimes: Brutality, Genocide, Terror, and the Struggle for Justice* (New York: Times Book, 1998), 83, 222.
22. Biggar, *Burying the Past*, 16–17.

On this understanding, impunity meant the bartering of justice for a political settlement, as victims' rights 'become the objects of political trade-offs, and justice becomes, depending upon one's perspective, the victim of the means of Realpolitik.'[23] It was instead argued that it was essential to introduce the experiences of individuals in a field otherwise dominated by politics. Scholars and activists propounded and explored a trilateral relationship between the state, the *ancien* regime, and victims as rights-holders, one where government's choice of accountability or impunity policy depended to a determinative extent on the relative strength of the public's demand for truth and/or accountability and the outgoing rulers' insistence on amnesty and impunity.[24]

This public demand was most visible in organized survivors' groups pressing the new governments to act.[25] The vision of victims as active, organized campaigners for state-based retribution was most apparent in groups like Madres de la Plaza de Mayo who marched and campaigned in Buenos Aires to demand the Argentine government reveal the fate of 'disappeared' family members. The Madres resisted a proposed truth commission 'because they perceived it as an attempt to avoid full disclosure and accountability for what had been done to their loved ones' and rejected all proposals for reparations, dismissing them 'as blood money.'[26] In the face of junta denials and post-authoritarian foot-dragging, the Madres focused global attention on the government's human rights violations. On similar lines, the Guatemalan Alliance Against Impunity and Assembly of Civil Society were central in securing the exclusion of amnesty for gross human rights abuses in the peace deal there.[27] Likewise, in East Germany, citizens who had been 'victimized by petty affronts, personal acts of betrayal and outright crimes actively campaigned to prevent the worst offenders from being restored to positions of authority' in reunified Germany.[28] They did so most notably by breaking into local Stasi headquarters and demanding

---

23. M. Cherif Bassiouni, 'Searching for Peace and Achieving Justice: The Need for Accountability,' *Law and Contemporary Problems* 59/4 (1996), 11–12.
24. Elin Skaar, 'Truth Commissions, Trials - or Nothing? Policy Options in Democratic Transitions,' *Third World Quarterly* 20/6 (1996), 1109.
25. David Backer, 'Civil Society and Transitional Justice: Possibilities, Patterns and Prospects,' *Journal of Human Rights* 2/3 (2003), 297.
26. Eric Brahm, 'Transitional Justice, Civil Society, and the Development of the Rule of Law in Post-conflict Societies,' *International Journal of Not-For-Profit Law* 9 (2006), 66.
27. Brahm, 'Transitional Justice,' 63–64.
28. A. James McAdams, 'Transitional Justice: The Issue that Won't Go Away,' *International Journal of Transitional Justice* 5/2 (2011), 307.

use of secret files therein to review the 'suitability' of politicians and public officials for continued employment in unified Germany.[29] These and similar groups were presented in heroic fashion, valorized for the rockiness of their relationship with the government and portrayed as active citizens speaking truth to power.[30]

As democratic norms became consolidated in post-authoritarian states, retributive appeals for justice were augmented by more generalized rule of law-based appeals. The presentation of the criminal justice interests of victims changed from the 'emotively retributive' demands of groups like the Madres to more abstract, long-term term desires to end cultures of impunity.[31] Even in this Argentinian example the Madres laid down a template for public demonstration in Buenos Aires that became the model for other protests decades later. These groups insist 'that they were exercising their rights and performing their duties as citizens, asserting what the state's role should be, and demanding that it meet its obligations.'[32] This evolution may reflect a form of maturation into liberal democratic citizenship as narratives of trauma and pain gave way to imaginaries of *a* civil society, instantiating the nascent democracy and serving as a bulwark against revanchism.[33] Criminal justice was not to be interpreted merely as an attempt to provide recognition to victims by denying the implicit claim of superiority made by the criminal's behaviour, but instead as reaffirming the enduring salience of norms that grant equal rights to all citizens in the reforming polity.[34] As such, those who demanded justice did so to see recognition 'not only as victims, but as rights bearers.'[35] Over time, the demand for punishment owed less to a desire to transform victims' attitudes

---

29. McAdams, 'Transitional Justice,' 306.
30. Brahm, 'Transitional Justice,' 63.
31. Robert Sloan, 'The Expressive Capacity of International Punishment: The Limits of the National Law Analogy and the Potential of International Criminal Law,' *Stanford Journal of International Law* 43/39 (2007), 50–51.
32. Karen Ann Faulk, 'Solidarity and Accountability: Rethinking Citizenship and Human Rights,' in *Human Rights at the Crossroads*, ed. Mark Goodale (Oxford: Oxford University Press, 2012), 98.
33. Report of the Special Rapporteur on the promotion of truth, justice, reparation and guarantees of non-recurrence, Pablo de Greiff (7 September 2015) UN Doc A/HRC/30/42, para 85–88.
34. De Greiff, 'Theorizing,' 43.
35. Pablo de Greiff, 'Articulating the Links Between Transitional Justice and Development: Justice and Social Integration,' in *Transitional Justice and Development: Making Connections*, eds. Pablo de Greiff and Roger Duthie (New York: Social Science Research Council, 2009), 58.

towards former abuses from the past, but to transform victim attitudes towards the state in the present and future.[36]

What's notable about this line of broader citizenship-based reasoning is that it was a short step to embracing an entirely different sort of logic (one that also underpinned realist-based arguments), namely that 'survivors' attitudes about prosecutions were relevant but could never be determinative here because the society as a whole has been wronged as well, meaning that collective perspectives on justice beyond those of direct victims would gradually emerge to prominence.[37] Gradually, the image of the victim as active citizen was overshadowed by notions of the victim as patient and saint (truth commissions) and the victim as indigent (reparations).

The Victim as Witness

With a settled consensus on the need for accountability, debate in the field shifted from whether or not to permit impunity to what type of justice should be pursued. As truth commissions emerged to challenge trials as the best route for justice, a simplified binary choice of truth versus justice was widespread in the TJ literature.[38] This dynamic of truth versus justice encapsulated a broader conflict between the demands of justice, history, and memory.[39] Truth commissions, for example, were viewed as an explicit trade of justice for rejection of a 'criminal justice first' approach. In pursuance of argument that a criminal trial was the only appropriate or effective approach to past injustice, advocates initially argued that the opportunity a trial offered to victims to publicly outline their suffering would 'provide victims with a sense of justice and catharsis,'[40] that giving them 'their day in court' was inherently restorative of dignity,[41] and/or that 'psychologically

---

36. Pádraig McAuliffe, *The Rule of Law and Transitional Justice: A Contentious Relationship* (London: Routledge, 2013), 42-82.
37. Minow, *Between Vengeance and Forgiveness*, 135–136.
38. See Robert I. Rotberg and Dennis F. Thompson, eds., *Truth v. Justice: The Morality of Truth Commissions* (Princeton: Princeton University Press, 2010); Donald W Shriver, 'Truth Commissions and Judicial Trials: Complementary or Antagonistic Servants of Public Justice?,' *Journal of Law and Religion* 16/1 (2001), 1.
39. Teitel, 'Genealogy', 81.
40. Michael Scharf and Paul R. Williams, 'The Functions of Justice and Anti-justice in the Peace-building Process,' *Case Western Reserve Journal of International Law* 35/2 (2003), 175.
41. Jorge S. Correa, 'Dealing with Past Human Rights Violence: The Chilean Case after Dictatorship,' *Notre Dame Law Review* 67/5 (1991), 1459–1460.

healthy expression of grief and anger may be obtained through judicial proceedings.'[42] However, having observed some trials in action, critics of the primacy of criminal punishment began to respond that reliving their experiences through testimony could in reality be traumatic,[43] a problem exacerbated by the lack of resources or capabilities to deal with psychological trauma in states outside the Global North, to say nothing of the lack of security.[44] In addition, the adversarial nature of cross-examination was argued to undermine the dignity of the victim. The inherently adversarial nature of the trial process risked exacerbating the suffering of the victim by forcing him/her to undergo intrusive cross-examination in the divisive atmosphere of a courtroom, imperilling any latent potential for closure.[45] A prime example is Mark Osiel's observation of trial processes in Argentina:

> at the Argentina junta trial, witness-survivors found themselves facing questions concerning, for instance, their membership in guerrilla groups, questions identical to those their abductors asked them under torture. The witnesses, of course, found such questions deeply offensive; the experience of public testimony was thus personally degrading, rather than empowering.[46]

This was built into a broader critique of trials as something contrary to the interests of peace and reconciliation. Even if not actively traumatising, 'the adversarial and confrontational' nature of trials was believed to exacerbate hostility between victim and offender.[47] The adversarial nature of retributive justice also came under attack for its focus on perpetrators, which was deemed by many critics to have the consequence of relegating the needs of victims to second place and making truth less easily disclosed. Adversarial trials were therefore seen as inimical to reconciliation or reintegration.[48]

---

42. Robert L. Birmingham, 'The War Crimes Trial: A Second Look,' *University of Pittsburg Law Review* 24/1 (1962), 132.
43. Rachel Kerr and Eirin Mobekk, *Peace & Justice: Seeking Accountability After War* (Cambridge: Polity Press, 2007), 9.
44. Kerr and Mobekk, *Peace & Justice*, 119.
45. Lorna McGregor, 'Individual Accountability in South Africa: Cultural Optimum or Political Façade?,' *American Journal of International Law* 95/1 (2001), 36.
46. Mark Osiel, *Mass Atrocity, Collective Memory and the Law* (New Brunswick: Transaction Publishers, 1997), 104.
47. Rama Mani, 'Rebuilding an Inclusive Political Community After War,' *Security Dialogue* 36/4 (2005), 515.
48. Jonathan Doak, 'The Therapeutic Dimension of Transitional Justice: Emotional Repair and Victim Satisfaction in International Trials and Truth Commissions,' *Inter-

At the core of retributive justice theory was the notion that crime is an offence against the state. In establishing offender accountability, the experiences and interests of the victim took second place to the over-riding purpose of isolating the offender from society and to inflicting a punishment in proportion to the crime. Furthermore, because non-retributive consequentialist justifications like social pedagogy, deterrence, containment, and reconciliation were associated with criminal punishment, it became apparent that victims themselves might become secondary actors in transitional trials to the state. As David Crocker noted at the time, there was always a risk that the impersonality or neutrality of the law that lay at the core of the argument for prosecutions as a means of restoring liberal citizenship could be confused for, or conflated with, an indifference to the personal or unique aspects of a case, suggesting judicial processes and penalties gave little regard to victims.[49] Critics noted that victims could be reduced to a status of 'mere witnesses' in processes where the state and accused became the main parties.[50] As the Office of the High Commissioner for Human Rights noted, both domestic and international trial processes have often failed to appreciate the central importance of protecting the dignity of victims. The reality is that lack of appropriate training and work pressures frequently relegate victims to instruments of proof, rather than human beings and citizens with rights and needs.[51]

By contrast, truth commissions were justified as a superior policy choice on the grounds that victims could benefit from special rules of procedure that were designed to address the particular needs of those giving testimony instead of being treated as mere witnesses to be 'harvested by judicial actors in the service of larger goals of justice.'[52] Testimony could go beyond material facts to express the trauma and social disturbance felt by victims. As one South African TRC witness put it, its deliberations

---

national Criminal Law Review 11/2 (2011), 272–3.
49. David Crocker, 'Punishment, Reconciliation, and Democratic Deliberation,' *Buffalo Criminal Law Review* 5/2 (2002), 519.
50. Christine Bell, 'The "New Law" of Transitional Justice,' in *Building a Future on Peace and Justice: Studies on Transitional Justice, Peace and Development*, ed. Kai Ambos, Judith Large and Marieke Wierda (Springer: Berlin, 2009) 112.
51. OHCHR, 'Rule of Law Tools for Post-Conflict States: Prosecution Initiatives' (2008) UN Doc HR/PUB/06/4, 18.
52. Katherine M. Franke, 'Gendered Subject of Transitional Justice,' *Columbia Journal of Gender & Law* 15/3 (2006) 827, 821.

created a safe environment where we can actually feel that we are human beings and we have dignity, we have a name, we have a face ... The Truth Commission exposes ... all the bad things and the good things, and it exposes what perpetrators have done and it also explains how victims were victimized ... the way they conduct their hearing, their tactics, their methods that they use to get information actually sets you free.[53]

Similar findings were noted in studies of TRC participants in other countries.[54] Indeed, without victim participation, truth commissions risked becoming a dry, technocratic inquiry. Martha Minow, notably, argued that truth commissions could 'mov[e] beyond statistics to real people of blood, flesh and tears' gathering individual testimony to present human consequences of atrocities that would otherwise seem 'unfathomable and overwhelming.'[55]

The Victim as Patient and Saint

As noted above, at the core of the truth versus justice debate was the notion that ideals of retribution and reconciliation pull in different directions.[56] This is important because one of the main impetuses behind advocacy for truth commissions as something essential and not merely as a second-best to trial was the gradual recognition by peacebuilders, TJ actors and development agencies that psychosocial healing is a necessary precursor to reconciliation within communities. As John Torpey noted, greater weight was given to psychic harms and 'trauma' in reparations politics after the Cold War than in the legalistic Nuremberg paradigm. This reflected the 'triumph of the therapeutic' in domains beyond individual psychology and a paradigm shift in the conception of trauma from an exclusively physical construction to a something predominantly mental.[57]

In this intellectual environment, Rama Mani argued 'those who suffered during conflict, whether they lost a life, a limb or a family

---

53. As interviewed and cited in Paul Gready, 'Analysis: Reconceptualising Transitional Justice: Embedded and Distanced Justice,' *Conflict, Security & Development* 5/1 (2005), 5.
54. See for example Lisa Laplante and Kimberly Theidon, 'Truth with Consequences: Justice and Reparations in Post-Truth Commission Peru,' *Human Rights Quarterly* 29/1 (2007), 239.
55. Minow, *Between Vengeance and Forgiveness*, 76.
56. David Little, 'A Different Kind of Justice: Dealing with Human Rights Violations in Transitional Societies,' *Ethics & International Affairs* 13/1 (1999), 79.
57. Torpey, 'Introduction', 4.

member' were referred to ubiquitously as victims. The usage of this term made 'them appear ill and in need of treatment, or impotent and in need of help. Many arguments for truth commissions are based on their imputed value in contributing to healing victims.'[58] Indeed, at the height of advocacy for truth commissions (and hence a time before a sufficient number of them could have their modalities and legacies assessed), these mechanisms were automatically assumed to be healing.[59] Because of their emphasis on victim testimony, their freedom from the cross-examinations and exclusions of evidence that underpinned fair trial, TRCs were therefore preferred to criminal proceedings because they could better balance the focus on offenders and their violations with a commensurate level of attention to victims and their suffering. Scholars contended that cathartic truth-telling had the benefits of 'compensating victims psychologically and materially, and telling a more coherent narrative than do trials focused narrowly on guilt of individuals.'[60] Most significantly for the purposes of this chapter, it was argued that TRCs could best serve the aspiration of 'healing for individuals and reconciliation across social divisions *the more they diverged from prosecutions*.'[61]

This emphasis on healing stemmed from a vision of the victim as a patient, but expanded to take in the perpetrator and society as a whole. As Richard Wilson notes, hearings in Cape Town were framed in a manner that made any expression of a desire for revenge by victims seem inappropriate. By contrast, 'virtues of forgiveness and reconciliation were so loudly and roundly applauded that emotions of vengeance, hatred and bitterness were rendered unacceptable, an ugly intrusion on a peaceful healing process.'[62] This clashed with commonplace retributive notions of victimhood among the populace at large.[63] Nevertheless, this ethos

---

58. Rama Mani, *Beyond Retribution: Seeking Justice in the Shadows of War* (Cambridge: Polity Press, 2002), 119–120.
59. A position noted, but not necessarily endorsed, in Frédéric Mégret, 'Of Shrines, Memorials and Museums: Using the International Criminal Court's Victim Reparation and Assistance Regime to Promote Transitional Justice,' *Buffalo Human Rights Law Review* 16 (2010), 5.
60. Leslie Vinjamuri and Jack Snyder 'Advocacy and Scholarship in the Study of International War Crime Tribunals and Transitional Justice,' *Annual Review of Political Science* 7/1 (2004), 357.
61. Minow, *Between Vengeance and Forgiveness*, 88. Emphasis added.
62. Richard Wilson, *The Politics of Truth and Reconciliation in South Africa: Legitimizing the Post-Apartheid State* (Cambridge: Cambridge University Press, 2001), 120.
63. Wilson, *Politics of Truth*, 129.

of absolution found echoes in the TRC's Report itself, where illustrative accounts of forgiveness by victims were prominently catalogued.[64] The process essentially generated pressure for forgiveness and reconciliation 'requiring exceptional virtue amounting to sainthood.'[65] As Siphiwe Ignatius Dube noted, those victims who expressed the willingness to forgive were the most commonly admired and appreciated participants, observing that in TJ scholarship at the time 'forgiveness and compassion are regarded as morally superior to anger and resentment' that earlier theories of retributive justice were thought to address.[66]

These arguments were valuable in establishing truth commissions as a morally legitimate and politically viable alternative to trials. However, as the truth versus reconciliation argument gave way to a less polarized acceptance that holistic blends of many mechanisms were the most appropriate response to the needs of society, a number of critiques emerged of the medicalized view of those who suffered and the routinized pressure to forgive the unforgivable. In the first place, it was clear that the imagery of healing did not fit the self-image of victims themselves. For example, in the paradigmatic example of South Africa, survivors argued that 'we have had these experiences, but we do not want to present ourselves as victims in need of healing.[67] Dissatisfaction with the TRC in South Africa flowed from the impossibility of identifying all victims of apartheid, the sense of unfairness of amnesty and the reality of ongoing impunity and ongoing impoverishment.[68] As Lisa Laplante notes, 'criticism that the South African truth commission equated truth with reconciliation, bypassing justice, and thus leaving many victims unsatisfied and angry, echoes a growing consensus that breaking with the past requires some form of justice.'[69]

The emergent therapeutic discourse of catharsis was criticized as disempowering of populations,[70] while the discourse of restorative

---

64. Claire Moon, *Narrating Political Reconciliation: South Africa's Truth and Reconciliation Commission* (Lanham, MD: Lexington Books, 2009).
65. Pablo De Greiff, 'The Role of Apologies in National Reconciliation Processes: On Making Trustworthy Institutions Trusted,' in *The Age of Apology: Facing up to the Past*, eds. Mark Gibney et al., (Philadelphia: University of Pennsylvania Press, 2008), 121.
66. Siphiwe Ignatius Dube, 'Transitional Justice Beyond the Normative: Towards a Literary Theory of Political Transitions,' *International Journal of Transitional Justice* 5/2 (2011), 183.
67. Mani, *Beyond Retribution*, 119–120.
68. Backer, 'Civil Society.'
69. Laplante and Theidon, 'Truth with Consequences,' 242.
70. Vanessa Pupavac, 'Therapeutic Governance: Psycho-social Intervention and

justice was argued to marginalize those who demand justice as citizens as opposed to health as metaphorical patients.[71] David Mendeloff famously argued that the theoretical assumption that truth-telling fosters healing was highly contentious and empirically unproven.[72] There also emerged a concern from those well-versed in restorative justice that TJ often seemed to co-opt the language (and imagery) of restorative justice in a cavalier fashion, distorting the familiar ethos of restorative justice which typically connotes giving ownership of justice to victims. In the TJ context, it became apparent that restorative justice was being employed as rhetorical cover for the continued appropriation by the state of the victim's role. A concern emerged that inasmuch as truth commissions were designed to use historical lessons to draw lines in the sand between regimes, governments could and did 'usurp the victim's exclusive right to forgive his oppressor.'[73]

The Victim as Normal

The instrumental use of victims in trial and truth commissions over time led to a gradual suspicion that the imagery and language of victimhood was becoming too complicit in macro-level projects that fetishized him or her as an object of reconciliation, truth, or forgiveness in the distant metropolis. Victimhood is (or at least should be) a matter of self-identity, and some individuals preferred to adopt the term 'survivor' over 'victim.'[74] A debate emerged concerning the use of both terms, with some contending that use of the 'victim' concept might implicitly or explicitly belittle the fact that they have come through and survived.[75] The term 'victim' also carries connotations of passivity, vulnerability, and definition by past events.[76] By contrast, as Mani argued, the concept of 'survivor' had more positive etymological connotations because the prefix *sur*

Trauma Risk Management,' *Disasters* 25/4 (2001), 358.
71. Rosemary Nagy, 'Transitional Justice as Global Project: Critical Reflections,' *Third World Quarterly* 29/2 (2008), 336.
72. David Mendeloff, 'Truth-seeking, Truth-telling, and Postconflict Peacebuilding: Curb the Enthusiasm?' *International Studies Review* 6/3 (2004), 355.
73. Aryeh Neier, cited in Minow, *Between Vengeance and Forgiveness*, 17.
74. Erica Bouris, *Complex Political Victims* (Sterling, VA: Kumarian 2007).
75. Mobekk and Kerr, *Peace & Justice*, 12.
76. Cheryl Lawther, 'Transitional Justice and Truth Commissions,' in *Research Handbook on Transitional Justice*, eds. Cheryl Lawther, Dov Jacobs and Luke Moffett (London: Edward Elgar Publishing, 2017), 346.

connoted 'moving beyond, overcoming, as in "surmount" or "surpass".'[77] More important, however, was the broadening of TJ to embrace holistic forms of justice that combined trial, truth commissions, reparations, indigenous/traditional mechanisms and memory projects which would interact with past harms in different ways. Some argued that the focus on individual victims might 'side-line' the wider community of survivors affected by injustice that were increasingly touched (or, more evidently, non-touched) by the flowering of different approaches.[78] It was posited that a discourse of survivors would acknowledge the complexities of conflicts and the interchangeable associations between and among victims and perpetrators. A moral imaginary of 'survivors of the conflict' could acknowledge the fluid changes between victims and perpetrators as a violent past gave way to a more democratic future and was more apt to be inclusive about their potential roles in the future.[79]

The change in emphasis from victim to survivor also corresponded with an increasing concentration on the day-to-day life of individuals as individuals, as opposed to avatars or objects of macro-level aspirations towards abstractions like peace, rights, democracy or reconciliation.[80] Critics argued the increasingly toolkit-based projects of TJ were abstracted from intra-community relations where survivors and perpetrators met on the street, in shops or the workplace, meaning that the field was open to the accusation it was disconnected from the everyday needs of the population. Jodi Halpern and Harvey Weinstein, for example, argued that

> while much attention has been paid to the reconstruction of infrastructure and the establishment of rule of law, little thought has been given to what is required at the day to day level in order to restore a sense of interpersonal security. To reverse the destruction of social and familial networks that normally sustain health and well-being, a process of rehumanization must occur.[81]

---

77. Mani, *Beyond Retribution*, 123.
78. Mani, *Beyond Retribution*, 88.
79. Chandra Lekha Sriram, Olga Martin-Ortega and Johanna Herman, 'Evaluating and Comparing Strategies of Peacebuilding and Transitional Justice,' Centre on Human Rights in Conflict Working Paper 2 (May 2009) accessed 12 April 2023, https://ciaotest.cc.columbia.edu/wps/chrc%20/0017258/f_0017258_14761.pdf, 23.
80. On the subordination of survivor needs to national meta-narrative projects, see Pádraig McAuliffe, 'Comprehending Ireland's Post-Catholic Redress Practice as a Form of Transitional Justice,' *Oxford Journal of Law and Religion* 6/3 (2017), 451.
81. Jodi Halpern and Harvey M. Weinstein, 'Rehumanizing the Other: Empathy and Reconciliation,' *Human Rights Quarterly* 26/3 (2004), 561.

In this sense, the discourse of survivorship and everyday existence drew on restorative justice's view of crime as harm to individuals and their surrounding community. On this view, peace and order for the community and vindication for the victim could only emerge from communication processes between victims, offenders, and community representatives.[82] A much more proactive image of survivors than the passive vision apparent in the therapeutic discourses of truth commissions emerged. It was also a more context appropriate view than that of the active citizen when advocating trials seen even earlier. The concepts of the local and the everyday draw on post-structural and postcolonial discourses to reveal structural forms of violence but also emphasized resistance and social solidarity against the influence of conservative or liberal power structures.

The Victim as Indigent

Since the mid-2000s, theorists and scholars have examined avenues for TJ to address the socio-economic roots of conflict. Indeed, it is increasingly argued that success in this regard is the metric by which practice should ultimately be judged. There are a number of reasons why liberal-legalist approaches to TJ emphasising direct physical abuses have given way to more structural, redistributive or transformative approaches that deal with less spectacularized but more widespread economic abuses, but three in particular are important. The first is the influence of consultations with victims as surveys of survivor populations became more systematic. Whereas until now, theorists presumed to know what populations wanted and needed (often on the basis of their own experiences or those familiar to their own liberal societies), now they would be told on the basis of structured polling and interviews.[83] The results of these polls showed victim interests to be distinctly different from those of the active liberal citizen, the instrumentalist witness or the passive patient-saint. Polls of survivor populations (incorporating victims of direct harms and their communities) repeatedly demonstrated that victimization occurred along lines of class and socio-economic position, while socio-economic concerns

---

82. Michael Gilbert and Tanya Settles, 'The Next Step: Indigenous Development of Neighborhood Restorative Community Justice,' *Criminal Justice Review* 32/1 (2007), 7.
83. See Eric Stover and Harvey M. Weinstein, eds., *My Neighbor, My Enemy: Justice and Community in the Aftermath of Mass Atrocity* (Cambridge: Cambridge University Press, 2004),

trump the desire for criminal justice or truth in transitions. Poverty, lack of welfare, and unemployment were the key concerns in societies like DR Congo, Uganda, and Kenya.[84] The second reason is the impact of feminist approaches to TJ. Above all, scholars argued that elevation of harms like torture and arbitrary detention over socio-economic harms like poverty and forced displacement privileged masculine conceptions of conflict, rendering invisible the variegated forms of loss and violence experienced predominantly by women.[85]

These revised approaches marked something of a tidal shift in TJ's justice imaginary. Before TJ expanded to encapsulate the economic, there was a sense abroad that claims by victims for redistribution or socio-economic justice exceeded what these individual or communities could demand, carrying mercenary or even scrounging connotations.[86] As Rolando Ames Cobián and Félix Reátegui put it, whereas heretofore TJ took as its starting point a particularized attention to serious human rights violations suffered by specific individuals, developmental or redistributive justice projects of necessity 'operate in the arena of massive and anonymous policies directed to whole categories of the population and is aimed at designing a general institutional framework.'[87] While this chapter has argued the imagery of victim has always been politicized, it did so within the context of a liberal politics that masked its interventions as neutral. The implicit notion that TJ should publicly take the side of victims, rather than that of any particular political agenda, would give way to this 'fourth phase' of economically transformational TJ that would politicize the economy and patterns

---

84. See Phuong Pham et al., 'Forgotten Voices: A Population-Based Survey of Attitudes About Peace and Justice in Northern Uganda' (Harvard Humanitarian Initiative, July 2005); Patrick Vinck and Phuong Pham, 'Ownership and Participation in Transitional Justice Mechanisms: A Sustainable Development Perspective from Eastern DRC,' *International Journal of Transitional Justice* 2/3 (2008), 398; Simon Robins, '"To Live as Other Kenyans Do": A Study of the Reparative Demands of Kenyan Victims of Human Rights Violations,' *International Center for Transitional Justice and Advocacy Forum*, 7 January 2011, accessed 12 April 2023, https://www.ictj.org/publication/live-other-kenyans-do-study-reparative-demands-kenyan-victims-human-rights-violations.
85. Fionnuala Ní Aoláin and Catherine Turner, 'Gender, Truth and Transition,' *UCLA Women's Law Review* 16 (2007), 229.
86. Tshepo Madlingozi, 'Good Victim, Bad Victim: Apartheid's Beneficiaries, Victims and the Struggle for Social Justice,' in *Law, Memory, and the Legacy of Apartheid: Ten Years after AZAPO v. President of South Africa*, eds. Wessel Le Roux, and Karin Van Marle (Pretoria: PULP, 2007), 112.
87. Rolando Ames Cobián and Félix Reátegui, 'Toward Systemic Social Transformation,' in de Greiff and Duthie, *Transitional Justice and Development*, 147.

of economic distribution.[88] The implicit notion that TJ should publicly take the side of victims, rather than that of any particular political agenda, would give way to approaches that would temper economic liberalization with redistribution. TJ could affect the transitional government's development plans[89] and/or 'expand ... not only the choices, but also the options and blueprint for society and individuals to improve their livelihoods and wellbeing.'[90]

The third trend compelling attention to the economic was the gradual embrace of reparations. This was something of a departure. As noted earlier, the Madres de la Plaza victim organizations could dismiss reparations proposals as blood money. Similarly, and around the same time, the 'comfort women' enslaved in the Japanese war effort argued legal compensation could only be accepted with an official apology.[91] While there was good reason to assume 'no market measures exist for the value of living an ordinary life, without nightmares or survivor guilt' and to fear that any reparations 'are likely to be grossly disproportionate to the damage caused, and many thus trivialize suffering,'[92] a more positive case could be made that reparations could actually serve as material evidence of a State's willingness to make amends after mass violence, and so could foster civic trust.[93] This argument was given greater force by the undoubted hollowness that attended the more metaphysical benefits of trials and truth commissions. Without reparations they 'provide no direct benefit to victims other than a sense of vindication that otherwise does not change the circumstances of their lives ... a policy based exclusively on prosecution is likely to be experienced by victims as an insufficient response to their own justice claims.'[94] The changing class basis of victims may also have contributed. The initial wave of TJ projects occurred on the basis of middle-class politicization of past atrocity in Latin America and Eastern Europe, but since then

---

88. Pádraig McAuliffe, *Transformative Transitional Justice and the Malleability of Post-Conflict Societies* (London: Edward Elgar, 2017).
89. Zinaida Miller, 'Effects of Invisibility: In Search of the 'Economic' in Transitional Justice,' *International Journal of Transitional Justice* 2/3 (2008), 267.
90. Yvette Selim and Tim Murithi, 'Transitional Justice and Development: Partners for Sustainable
Peace in Africa?,' *Journal of Peacebuilding and Development* 6/2 (2011), 64.
91. Norma Field, 'The Stakes of Apology,' *Japan Quarterly* 42/4 (1995), 405.
92. Minow, *Between Vengeance and Forgiveness*, 93, 104.
93. Naomi Roht-Arriaza and Katharine Orlovsky, 'A Complementary Relationship: Reparations and Development,' in de Greiff and Duthie, *Transitional Justice and Development*, 170.
94. De Greiff, 'Theorising,' 37.

most TJ has occurred in poverty-stricken areas of the developing world where hand-to-mouth survival in the aftermath of conflict arguably makes reparations more necessary and more justifiable. Consequently, the design of reparations programmes demanded processes to define who victims are, primarily with reference to categories of human rights violation suffered.[95]

The Victim as Indigene

As noted above in the treatment of the victim as everyday survivor, there emerged in scholarship a gradual realization that with the focus on elite bargains and national peace processes, too little attention had been given to the micro-level of village, town, and rural area where local cultures of violence could endure past state-level agreements. Bottom-up and ethnographic studies revealed that survivors at the local level 'focussed on historically specific grievances about who did what horrible thing to whom' which were radically at odds with the broader macro-level discourses of external academic consultants.[96] Indigenous populations in particular were less likely than others to be brought within spaces for dialogue in the aftermath of state crime.[97] As Elena Baylis argued, national process fail to properly account for or redress the crimes committed. New approaches were needed to render greater emphasis on local interest in justice.[98]

'Ownership,' 'the bottom-up, not the top-down,' and 'solidarity, not substitution' became core organizing principles (some might say mantras) of TJ on the ground. The most notable feature of this 'local turn' was the embrace of justice processes variously described as local, indigenous, customary, sub-national or traditional justice in states with underdeveloped legal systems and civil services. The initial concentration on legalist modalities of transitional justice appeared to exclude customary and traditional forms of justice that would depart from liberal procedural and institutional norms. However, indigenous

---

95. Jemima Garcias-Godos, 'Victims and Victimhood in Reparation Programs: Lessons from Latin America,' in Druliolle and Brett, *Politics of Victimhood*, 25.
96. Mark Osiel, 'The Banality of Good: Aligning Incentives Against Mass Atrocity,' *Columbia Law Review* 105/6 (2005), 1756.
97. Lawther, 'Transitional Justice and Truth Commissions,' 347.
98. Elena Baylis, 'Reassessing the Role of International Criminal Law: Rebuilding National Courts Through Transnational Networks,' *Boston College Law Review* 50/1 (2009), 14.

justice mechanisms like *gacaca* in Rwanda, *nahe biti* in East Timor and *mato oput* in Uganda were initially welcomed as an alternative to vigilantism in the community and as offering a useful means of treating lesser offences that national processes could not reach geographically or organizationally. However, the embrace of indigenous justice and reconciliation processes has been rationalized as a potentially more everyday form of justice for more intimate forms of violence suffered by victims.[99] This position has been articulated particularly with reference to the allegedly traumatizing and divisive nature of trials explored earlier. As Diane Orentlicher puts it, 'if victims' agency is a crucial value, does it not follow that victims should be able to opt out of these international norms if, say, in their culture and immediate circumstances they would prefer to reintegrate rebels who have committed atrocities into their community through a traditional ceremony of reconciliation than to prosecute them?.'[100] Imaginaries of the victim have also fed the counter-critique of indigenous justice too. To the extent that localized processes are valorized as a reflection of the importance of the community over the individual,[101] some now warn that these practices 'may privilege the communal over the individual to the degree that they obstruct goals of victim empowerment.'[102] Studies of victim attitudes to the *gacaca* process that was initially lauded as more responsive to the needs of localized victims revealed feelings of disillusionment (most notably over premature release of detainees) and the decline in participation over time.[103]

Conclusion

This chapter has made clear how 'sympathetic others' (i.e. policy-makers and scholars) often will be inclined 'to accord considerable

---

99. Gready, 'Embedded and Distanced Justice,' 14.
100. Diane Orentlicher, '"Settling Accounts" Revisited: Reconciling Global Norms with Local Agency,' *International Journal of Transitional Justice* 1/1 (2007), 19.
101. Eirin Mobekk, *Transitional Justice and Security Sector Reform: Enabling Sustainable Peace* (Geneva: Geneva Centre for the Democratic Control of Armed Forces, 2006), 49–50.
102. Ellen Lutz, 'Transitional Justice: Lessons Learned and the Road Ahead,' in *Transitional Justice in the Twenty-First Century: Beyond Truth Versus Justice*, eds. Naomi Roht-Arriaza and Javier Mariezcurrena (New York: Cambridge University Press, 2006), 335.
103. 'Integrated Report on Gacaca Research and Monitoring,' Penal Reform International, accessed 12 April 2023, https://www.penalreform.org/integrated-report-on-gacaca-research-and-monitoring-pilot-phase-january-2002-december.html.

authority' to victims as natural spokespeople in responding to past violations.¹⁰⁴ It further explored how the moral power of victimhood has been employed to undergird various aesthetics of victimhood that have been used to argue for and against different conceptualizations of justice (retributive, restorative, distributive) and different mechanisms of justice (trials, truth commissions, reparations, indigenous processes). These aesthetics of victimhood have changed, sometimes dramatically, over the last thirty years: citizens demanding accountability; patients in need of healing; saints as paragons of forgiveness; survivors knuckling down to the quotidian; indigenous communities tapping the folk wisdom of eons. There is a noticeable artificiality to all of these presentations, a simplified distilling of complex lives into imaginaries that tally with preferred mechanisms of justice. TJ scholars still tend to approach the concept of a victim more as a definitional category for analysis than an identity that need to be productively engaged with.¹⁰⁵ Privileging any particular aesthetic of 'victim' abrogates the reality that victimhood is complex, multidimensional, and often hidden. As Hugo van der Merwe notes, these debates are 'mainly being pursued at a normative level, with little consideration of the practical implications for victims or offenders or the measurement of social impact.'¹⁰⁶ The aesthetics of victimhood support political agendas of domestic and international actors and the ideological agendas of the scholar-activists who propose, support, run, and demand certain forms of response in relation to different mechanisms. Scholar-activists in particular brandish and popularize a certain distinct aesthetic of victimhood, consciously or unconsciously backgrounding other, equally valid forms of victimhood that are explicitly or impolitic rejected for being too liberal, too passive, too indigenous. Domestic justice constituencies borrow and abandon these to suit their own campaigns, but surely are conscious in a way scholar activists are not that these instrumentalist essentializations mask complex realities on the ground. This is so even as factions within epistemic TJ communities make their arguments on the basis that they better comprehend these complex realities than other factions.

However, it should be clear from the forgoing that foregrounding a certain victim aesthetic and invoking victim interests seldom serves

---

104. Osiel, *Mass Atrocity*, 143.
105. Druliolle and Brett, 'Introduction,' 4.
106. Hugo Van der Merwe, 'Delivering Justice During Transition: Research Challenges,' in *Assessing the Impact of Transitional Justice: Challenges for Empirical Research*, eds. Hugo Van der Merwe, Victoria Baxter and Audrey Chapman (Washington DC: USIP Press, 2009), 120.

as a rhetorical or political trump card. Adopting victim-centred approaches resolves none of the fundamental dilemmas transitional contexts throw up nor the normative disagreements they yield. Though presented chronologically, these presentations and self-presentations of victims are recurrent and contested—for example, the victim as active (middle-class) citizen is no less apparent in modern day Ukrainian campaigns for criminal justice than she was in late 80s Latin America,[107] even as it co-exists with an imagery of the collective victimhood of the socio-economically marginalized.[108] The assumption of the burden of criminal accountability by the state was initially considered empowering for victims as citizens, then was considered disempowering for subsuming the victim's experience by the state. Trials were considered cathartic and then were seen as traumatizing, truth commissions were variously presented as callously indifferent to victim experiences, then as healing victims and then as traumatizing. Reparations were rejected as insults to victims before being embraced as a form of respect for their material needs and/or citizenship. Essentialized images of disempowered and traumatized victimhood were used to argue for the ICC's creation as a 'victim-friendly' court,[109] essentialized claims about the racialized nature of these images are used to challenge the ICC's legitimacy.[110] Though often made in good faith and underpinned by genuine concern for victims, at all points both advocates and critics of certain TJ (and, it may be added, international criminal law) approaches used aesthetics of victimhood to gain moral authority for the claims they make and to legitimize their expertise without taking the necessary step of acknowledging that victim needs are various, inconsistent and, in most respects, impossible to satisfy.

---

107. Igor Lyubashenko, *Transitional Justice in Post-Euromaidan Ukraine: Swimming Upstream* (Bern: Peter Lang, 2017), 42–44.
108. Anna Klimina, 'The Role of Economic Class in Understanding Social Provisioning Processes in the Post-Soviet Transition: The Case of Ukraine,' *Journal of Economic Issues* 49/2 (2015), 415.
109. The ICC's self-presentation as a 'victim-friendly' court through the provisions of the Rome Statute is examined in Sam Garkawe, 'The Victim-Related Provisions of the Statute of the International Criminal Court: A Victimological Analysis,' *International Review of Victimology* 8/3 (2001), 269.
110. On the aesthetics of helpless victims faced with a 'savage' culture and former ICC Prosecutor Luis Moreno-Ocampo as 'white saviour', see Jeff Handmaker, 'Facing Up to the ICC's Crisis of Legitimacy,' *Recht der Werkelijkheid* 32 (2011), 100, 103.

4

The Image of the Asylum Seeker and Spectacular Deterrence in UK Asylum Law

Anne Neylon

Recent developments in law relating to asylum in the UK demonstrate that visual representations of the border have acted as catalysts for profound legal transformations. Images of refugees arriving to the shores of Britain have dominated much discourse about migrants, asylum seekers, and refugees. In this chapter, I demonstrate that such images are also law-creating moments where migrants and asylum seekers are depicted and narrated as illegitimate and 'illegal' arrivals to the state. The imagery and dramatization of migrants and asylum seekers in this way reinforces the role of the state as reasserting order amongst a chaotic and persistent arrival of unauthorized boats to the shores of the state. The *hypervisibility* of asylum seekers and migrants to the state and the public provides a focal point for anxiety about increased migration and asylum seekers that has been playing out in the media and in political talking points for decades. The use of imagery helps the state manufacture a call to action that has become increasingly draconian and dehumanizing, culminating in the development of measures including the UK-Rwanda Agreement, and proposals to keep asylum seekers arriving to the UK on boats or other irregular means, such as floating accommodation centres off the coast of Britain.[1]

---

1. 'Memorandum of Understanding between the Government of the United Kingdom of Great Britain and Northern Ireland and the Government of the Republic of Rwanda for the Provision of an Asylum Partnership Arrangement,' gov.uk, accessed 6 June 2023, https://www.gov.uk/government/publications/memorandum-of-understanding-mou-between-the-uk-and-rwanda/memorandum-of-understanding-between-the-government-of-the-united-kingdom-of-great-britain-and-northern-ireland-and-the-government-of-the-republic-of-r.

This chapter will consider the ongoing importance of the image and the spectacle of the migrant and asylum seeker as a driver of legal and policy change in the UK. First I will look at some of the key developments in terms of the spectacle of the migrant and the asylum seeker, examining this in the context of Guy Debord's 1967 account of spectacle as well as Nicholas De Genova's more recent work on the 'border spectacle.'[2] Then, examining the recent significant changes and proposals relating to refugee and asylum law in the UK, I will note how the use of this spectacular imagery has been relied upon to obfuscate the legal and practical realities that asylum seekers face, firstly under international law, and then specifically in relation to the UK's existing and emerging asylum policy.

I will then consider the concept of deterrence as a key factor in the UK's asylum policy, showing that the image and the spectacle has now become central to the UK's justification of its policies. Such spectacular images consistently present asylum seekers and migrants as sub-human and undeserving of decent treatment under the guise of breaking 'the business model of criminal smuggling gangs.'[3] The rhetoric about asylum seekers and the 'illegality' of their entrance to the state is now becoming more spectacularly spatialised. A variety of spatialising methods have been employed, including the spectacular use of ex-military barracks to house asylum seekers who may in turn be sent to Rwanda, and floating barges as asylum accommodation. Here, I show that these spaces are 'graduated zones of sovereignty' which allow different modes of governing segments of the population who in this instance do not relate to global markets.[4] Such spaces have the effect of 'shrinking' the legal space for asylum.[5] While states have previously established these spaces offshore, the UK has in this instance created this space within the frontiers of its mainland. As I will show, the use of spaces in this way marks a key moment in the shrinking of the space of UK asylum law. Access to the content of international refugee law

---

2. Guy Debord, *The Society of the Spectacle*, trans. Kenn Knabb (Berkeley: Bureau of Public Secrets, 2014); Nicholas De Genova, 'Spectacles of Migrant "Illegality": The Scene of Exclusion, the Obscene of Inclusion,' *Ethnic and Racial Studies* 36/7 (2013).
3. 'Channel Crossings, Migration and Asylum - Home Affairs Committee,' accessed 6 June 2023, https://publications.parliament.uk/pa/cm5803/cmselect/cmhaff/199/report.html.
4. Aihwa Ong, *Neoliberalism as Exception: Mutations in Citizenship and Sovereignty* (Durham, NC: Duke University Press, 2006).
5. Alison Mountz, 'The Enforcement Archipelago: Detention, Haunting, and Asylum on Islands,' *Political Geography* 30/3 (2011), 120.

is dependent on being present in the host state in order to avail the protection of the Refugee Convention. The UK is now beginning to use graduated zones of sovereignty to further avoid responsibility towards people seeking asylum.

Finally, I will demonstrate the connection between the current 'law-creating' moment in the UK in relation to asylum and the first iteration of the formal legal concept of asylum under UK law. I note that the spectacle or the imaginary of the asylum seeker has been crucial in both of these moments and directly informs legal responses where the concept of deterrence is at their core. Yet, as the legacy of deterrence efforts from the 1990s illustrates, there remain limits to the extent to which the logic of deterrence can be pushed to attack the human dignity of asylum seekers. As I will discuss, historical efforts to establish a policy of deterrence met with substantial pushback from local government, which in turn led to the establishment of minimum standards of treatment under law.

Spectacle

In 1967, Guy Debord stated that the spectacle is 'not a collection of images,' but rather 'a social relationship between people that is mediated by images.'[6] This 'new technique' of governance is grounded on the 'instantaneous propagation of mass-mediated public discourse and images, which is essentially one-way.'[7] In the same way that the commodity is attributed with a special character under capitalism, the spectacle influences the public's understanding and perception of public events by abstracting events from their 'concrete life' and transforming them into 'mere images.'[8]

Nicholas De Genova has recently taken the concept of the spectacle established by Debord and applied it to the site of the border. For De Genova, the border 'provides the exemplary theater [sic] for staging the spectacle of 'the illegal alien' that the law produces.'[9] At the same time, for De Genova, this 'border spectacle' influences the ways in which migrants are included and excluded within the state.[10]

---

6. Debord, quoted in Genova, 'Spectacles of Migrant "Illegality",' 1187.
7. Genova, 'Spectacles of Migrant "Illegality",' 1187.
8. Debord, *The Society of the Spectacle*, 11.
9. Nicholas De Genova, 'Migrant "Illegality" and Deportability in Everyday Life,' *Annual Review of Anthropology* 31/1 (2002), 436.
10. Nicholas De Genova, 'Migrant "Illegality" and Deportability in Everyday Life,' *Annual Review of Anthropology* 31/1 (2002), 436.

In the context of the UK, the presentation of the migrant is constantly abstracted from the legal realities that they encounter, as well as from the material circumstances that first forced them to leave their country of origin, and the material realities of their lives when they arrive in the UK to, for example, seek asylum. For decades, British nationals who ordinarily would have very little contact in their everyday lives with asylum seekers have been exposed to a keen corporate media image of a figure who is at once feckless and lazy yet taking British jobs. Asylum seekers are also regularly presented as recipients of an astonishing level of government largesse, with access to extravagant benefits and welfare.

As the image of the asylum seeker is filtered through the spectacle, their humanity is minimized. The asylum seeker emerges from this filter as a threat not just to the security of the state, but also to the everyday lives of the UK public. Their presence in the state is abstracted from the reasons that they fled their country of origin, which in many instances may be traced back to actions that the British state has historically engaged in. This can range from more recent historical moments such as interventions in Afghanistan, Iraq, and Libya in the early 2000s, to more distant historical events such as colonial exploitation which nonetheless still resonate to impact everyday lives, particularly in the form of the lack of economic opportunities as well as general regional instability.

The spectacle, and in particular the border spectacle, is therefore an important step in the abandonment of responsibility towards the asylum seeker and other forced migrants. As the figure of the migrant is reconstituted through the lens of the spectacle, their past, including the reasons for fleeing their country of origin, are overshadowed by the imagery and narrative of an asylum seeker as a figure divorced from the complex reasons that bring them to the country and is only understood as a threat to the UK.

The Spectacle of the Asylum Seeker in the UK

The idea of the asylum seeker or migrant has been a preoccupation of the British media for decades dating well back into the early twentieth century.[11] War, displacement, and the dissolution of the British Empire

---

11. See for example, Ron Kaye, 'Redefining the Refugee: The UK Media Portrayal of Asylum Seekers,' in *The New Migration in Europe: Social Constructions and Social Realities*, ed. Khalid Koser and Helma Lutz (London: Palgrave Macmillan, 1998), 163–82; Terence Wright, 'Moving Images: The Media Representation of Refugees,' *Visual Studies* 17/1 (2002), 53–66.

are all events that have factored in the movement of people to the British mainland. From the 1990s, the figure of the asylum seeker emerged in earnest. 'Asylum seeker' was a new term which is not referred to in the Refugee Convention but has emerged as a legal category to denote the period of time between when asylum in the host country has been applied for and when a decision is made on the application. 'Asylum-seeker' first appeared in the UNHCR ExCOM Conclusions is 1977.[12] This concept was embraced by European states that wished to emphasize a distinction between people who had full access to the rights set out in the Refugee Convention and those who still had not positively demonstrated that they fell within the refugee definition.[13] As 'asylum seeker' fell outside the ambit of the Convention, states began to carve out a particular legal space in which the person awaiting a determination would exist. The creation of the category allowed states to emphasise a legal and metaphorical border between those who were considered refugees and those who were not.

The emergence of this legal category also highlighted the possibility of an application being unfounded. Because asylum seekers have their application assessed based on their presence in the host state and the credibility of their fear of persecution as per the Refugee Convention, this category began to be cast in a negative light. In politics as well as in the media it is often portrayed as a means of accessing a host state without having to grapple with bureaucracy and restrictions of visas and the immigration system. This construction of asylum equates it with illegitimacy and illegality, ignoring the fact that the Refugee Convention explicitly refers to the fact that refugees may need to engage with clandestine methods in order to access asylum.[14]

The image of the asylum seeker and/or refugee in the media can be divided into three main categories. Firstly, there is the highly feminised image of the refugee, sometimes referred to as the 'Madonna and child.'[15] This image is often heavily relied upon in order to emphasise

---

12. Executive Committee of the High Commissioner's Programme, *Asylum No. 5 (XXVIII) - 1977*, 12 October 1977, accessed 6 June 2023, https://www.refworld.org/docid/3ae68c4388.html.
13. Jerzy Sztucki, 'Who Is a Refugee? The Convention Definition: Universal or Obsolete?,' in *Refugee Rights and Realities Evolving International Concepts and Regimes*, ed. Frances Nicholson and Patrick Twomey (Cambridge: Cambridge University Press, 1999), 70.
14. UN General Assembly, 'Convention and Protocol Relating to the Status of Refugees' (1951), art. 31, https://www.unhcr.org/media/28185.
15. Liisa Malkki, *Purity and Exile: Violence, Memory, and National Cosmology among Hutu Refugees in Tanzania* (Chicago: Chicago University Press, 1995), 11;

the vulnerability and abjectness of the refugee – one who is deserving of compassion and help. It is the type of image that is often used by aid agencies and Non-Governmental Organisations (NGOs) to solicit donations or political sympathy.

The second category is the figure of the male migrant/asylum seeker. Where the feminized image is often presented as immobile and fixed to a distant refugee camp, the masculine image is presented as mobile and on the move. A small number of asylum seekers are often presented in relief against the physical border wall or fence. Their attempt to cross the border is often communicated as the initial chipping away at the defences of the border, emphasizing the prospect of the continual and expanded attempts to cross.

The third category also highlights mobility, but in this instance the framing highlights the fact that a large group of migrants are moving across borders. Notable examples include the famous 'Breaking Point' image used by Nigel Farage in the run up to Brexit.[16] The image featured a large number of migrants in a snaking line along a road, supposedly at the borders of Europe. The focus of images like this is on the hyper-mobility and hypervisibility of large groups of migrants, symbolizing a loss of control over the borders of the state. More recently, this has manifested in images of groups of migrants crossing the Channel.

In the first category, it is heavily implied that the refugee in that image is 'genuine' and 'deserving.' This is not only because of the way in which the narrative associated with the image relies on stereotypes about women, mothers, and in particular women of colour in this role. On top of this, it feeds into narratives about who is a 'real' or 'genuine' refugee for the purpose of the host state's policy on asylum. In these narratives, the displaced person in the refugee camp is communicated as patiently waiting their turn to come to the host state, possibly through a refugee resettlement scheme. This image and the accompanying narrative in turn reinforce the state as sovereign, with absolute control over who can enter its borders.

The second and third categories however fundamentally upend this script and challenge the idea of absolute (state) control. Here the images are coded as asylum seekers who are dangerous because movement

---

Wright, 'Moving Images,' 58.
16. Heather Stewart and Rowena Mason, 'Nigel Farage's Anti-Migrant Poster Reported to Police,' *The Guardian*, 16 June 2016, accessed 13 July 2023 https://www.theguardian.com/politics/2016/jun/16/nigel-farage-defends-ukip-breaking-point-poster-queue-of-migrants.

across borders in an unanticipated way is presented as threatening. At times there is a clear overlap between the use of threatening and dehumanizing imagery in how the migrant is constructed. A notable example of this is David Cameron's reference to migrants arriving to the UK from Calais in 2015 as a 'swarm.'[17] In addition to the use of this language, the images often feature the asylum seekers attempting to overcome the securitization methods that have been employed to prevent migrants from entering the state. These images frequently depict asylum seekers attempting to climb over border fences or trying to evade border security through hiding in vehicles or other modes of clandestine entry.

In this way, the asylum seeker's mobility is portrayed as a key threat to the state's control over its borders and therein its identity as a sovereign state. Indeed, UK law on migration can be traced back to the royal prerogative, which eventually evolved into a near unfettered power to determine who can be admitted into the state.[18] The Refugee Convention challenges this power, limiting the absolute control of the state over its borders. Hypervisible and hypermobile asylum arrivals—who under the spirit of the Refugee Convention should at least be admitted to the state and given an opportunity to claim asylum—now embody a threat to this sovereignty.

Therefore, images of the 'boat arrival' to Britain via the Channel have been the source of particular anxiety in recent years, where the constructed hypermobility and hypervisibility of the asylum seekers and is played out through imagery. These images of migrants and asylum seekers crossing the Channel have seen a renewed focus since pandemic-era travel restrictions have been lifted.

Invisibilizing and Hypervisibilizing Asylum Seekers

For many years, there has been oscillation between obscuring migrants and particularly asylum seekers from view while at other moments, pushing a 'border spectacle' which helps justify some of the most punitive deterrence measures in the UK.[19] Since the 1990s, asylum seekers

---

17. 'Cameron: "Swarm" of Migrants Crossing Sea,' *BBC News*, accessed 6 June 2023, https://www.bbc.com/news/av/uk-politics-33714282.
18. Catherine Dauvergne, 'Sovereignty, Migration and the Rule of Law in Global Times,' *Modern Law Review* 67 (2004), 591.
19. Martina Tazzioli, 'Migrants' Displacements at the Internal Frontiers of Europe,' in *The Handbook of Displacement*, ed. Peter Adey and others (New York: Springer International Publishing, 2020).

in the UK have been subject to a parallel welfare system (Section 95 support) that excludes them from many aspects of mainstream society. Asylum seekers who are considered 'destitute' can apply for support from the Home Office in the form of accommodation and a small weekly stipend.[20] Asylum seeker accommodation is offered on a 'no choice' basis and asylum seekers are often sent to locations far from the capital, usually with little access to support and resources. Asylum seekers are also prohibited from working, apart from in very limited circumstances. Asylum seekers are therefore invisibilized within British society, where the restrictions on how they are allowed to live in the UK prevents interaction with the British public.

At the same time, despite this invisibilization, we have seen a sharp rise in the construction of the border spectacle, most acutely represented in the legal and policy responses to small boat arrivals to the UK. Namely, the UK-Rwanda Partnership, the proposed creation of large scale 'migrant camps' on ex-military bases, as well as new proposals on the creation of 'floating prisons' in locations offshore from the UK.[21]

The development of these practices demonstrates not only the articulation of a border spectacle, but also the provision of a kind of 'tutelage'—informed by the border spectacle—about the way in which asylum seekers should and deserve to be treated. This 'object lesson in the purpose of law' instructs the public that those who would seek asylum in the UK will be sent to spaces that emphasise their exclusion from British society and showcases their removability.[22] Further, it articulates a standard of treatment that would likely not be meted out to any other group within the British state. 'Tutelage' further articulates that the asylum seeker *deserves* this treatment. This position has been emphasized by the government on numerous occasions, including the Minister for Immigration who stated that asylum seekers must receive the most basic accommodation possible in order to save money as well as dissuade people from coming to Britain.[23] This has implications

---

20. Expert Participation, 'Immigration and Asylum Act 1999,' sec. 95, accessed 6 June 2023, https://www.legislation.gov.uk/ukpga/1999/33/contents.
21. '"Floating Prisons": Rishi Sunak's Plan for Migrant Barges Met with Fury by Local Leaders,' accessed 8 June 2023, https://inews.co.uk/news/floating-prisons-rishi-sunak-plan-migrant-barges-fury-local-leaders-2388997.
22. Joseph Pugliese, 'The Tutelary Architecture of Immigration Detention Prisons and the Spectacle of "Necessary Suffering",' *Architectural Theory Review* 13, no. 2 (1 August 2008): 216, https://doi.org/10.1080/13264820802216841.
23. Peter Walker and Peter Walker Political correspondent, 'Asylum Seekers Will Get the Most Basic Housing Possible, Says Robert Jenrick,' *The Guardian*, 29 March

not only for the development of current policies in relation to asylum seekers in the UK, but also the future trajectory of asylum policy that is informed by the goal of deterrence.

Joseph Pugliese has advanced the concept of 'necessary suffering' in the context of articulating the idea that detention is underpinned by the concept of retribution. This in turn is built into the architecture of prisons and detention sites and at times can result in people being 'spectacularly' exposed as undergoing punishment. That is, 'trauma-as-spectacle' is used as a means to push the rhetoric of deterrence. The migrant, detained behind razor-wire, has their experience presented as a telegenic spectacle – where the fence demarcating the citizen and the 'refugee prisoner' creates a social relation where 'spectacular images of riots and refugee self-harm' is 'telegenically mediated.'[24] Notorious examples of migrant (including asylum seeker) detention resulted in situations of riots and self-harm. In this way, their trauma becomes spectacularized due to the exposed nature of the detention in which they are held.

Using the example of former detention centres at Woomera and Baxter, Pugliese points out that enclosure of immigrants within the detention centre fencing has the effect of exposing the migrant to the citizen spectator. Conveying the image of the refugee's trauma establishes a 'carceral spectacle,' which 'enables a social relation between the prisoner and the citizen-subject.'[25]

As Debord has stated, 'the spectacle serves as a total justification of the condition and goals of the existing system.'[26] The presentation of the refugee/prisoner in Pugliese's example of a carceral subject is used as confirmation of the idea that the refugee is deserving of the treatment that they are subject to. As he points out, the state 'at once imprisons its target subjects, 'unauthorized' asylum seekers and refugees, whilst it dispenses object lessons on the power of the nation-state, its punitive rule of law and its life-negating power.'[27]

In the UK, the 'tutelary' spectacle has arguably emerged as the keystone of asylum policy. The use of military barracks as asylum accommodation during the pandemic in the Napier Barracks in Kent and Penally in Wales

---

2023, sec. UK news, https://www.theguardian.com/uk-news/2023/mar/29/asylum-seekers-housed-portakabins-maybe-ships-robert-jenrick.
24. Pugliese, 'The Tutelary Architecture of Immigration Detention Prisons and the Spectacle of "Necessary Suffering",' 210.
25. Pugliese, 207.
26. Debord, 'Society of the Spectacle (K. Knabb, Trans.),' 8.
27. Pugliese, 'The Tutelary Architecture of Immigration Detention Prisons,' 210.

has now been proposed to be rolled out on a much larger scale.[28] The architecture of these sites echoes many of the features of the immigration detention previously noted, in particular the double effect of simultaneous exposure and enclosure. The way that barracks-based accommodation has been developed also highlights that the distinction between asylum accommodation and immigration detention has begun to collapse. As deterrence and punishment becomes the priority for the government, the distinction between the two begins to fade away.

Manston, an ex-RAF facility located in Kent has been used as a sort of 'holding' centre for migrants who have arrived to the UK on small boats since 2022. Originally, people were to be held for twenty-four hours before being moved on to asylum accommodation, which was often temporary accommodation like hotels because of the lack of more permanent asylum accommodation. It soon became clear that people were being held well beyond the twenty-four-hour period, even weeks beyond the permitted limit.

The overcrowded conditions that migrants were being held in Manston became the subject of many headlines as it became obvious that the state was not moving people out to alternative asylum accommodation in the timeframe that it had set for itself. In a centre that was meant to hold 1600 people, 4000 were being held.[29] In November 2022, Hussein Haseeb Ahmed died while being held in Manston. Negligence by staff as well as the extremely poor conditions in the site appear to have been key factors in his drastic deterioration and ultimate death. Despite the death at Manston and the persistent evidence that military barracks are unsuitable and even dangerous places to hold asylum seekers on a long-term basis, the government remains committed to their use. Most recently, the government has acquired RAF Scampton, associated with the Dambusters raid during the Second World War, as the latest site to be used as accommodation.

The reliance on military barracks to house asylum seekers has come about because of the failure to secure more permanent asylum accommodation. Previously, asylum seekers were dispersed to accommodation that was run by private companies. Owing to mismanagement as well

---

28. 'Asylum Seekers to Be Accommodated on Surplus Military Sites,' GOV.UK, accessed 6 June 2023, https://www.gov.uk/government/news/asylum-seekers-to-be-accommodated-on-surplus-military-sites.
29. 'Manston Asylum Centre Could Be Overwhelmed Again within Weeks, Staff Warn | Manston Asylum Centre | The Guardian,' 30 May 2023, accessed 6 June 2023, https://www.theguardian.com/uk-news/2023/may/30/overcrowding-problems-could-return-at-manston-migrant-centre-staff-warn.

as overall lack of suitable housing, the Home Office is now more reliant on hotels to accommodate asylum seekers. While in the past, hotels were used on a 'contingency' or temporary basis until more long-term dispersal accommodation became available, the lack of available dispersed accommodation means that their use has skyrocketed since the pandemic.[30] In response to this, military barracks are presented as a more cost-efficient way to house asylum seekers in comparison to hotels.[31]

Complaints over the conditions that are experienced by those who are housed there are responded to by the government in a dismissive and callous way where the suffering that is experienced is minimised or even framed as something to be expected or deserved. Chris Philp, the policing minister, speaking to Times Radio about the situation at Manston stated, '[if] people choose to enter a country illegally, and unnecessarily, it is a bit, you know, it's a bit of a cheek to then start complaining about the conditions when you've illegally entered a country without necessity.'[32] Previously, in 2021, Priti Patel, the then-Home Secretary, reacted to protests about conditions in Napier Barracks by stating, 'this site has previously accommodated our brave soldiers and army personnel – it is an insult to say that is it not good enough for these individuals.'[33]

Philp's statement was made sixteen days before the death of Hussein Haseeb Ahmed in Manston, and after there had been reports of serious concerns over the conditions that people were being held.[34] No adequate bedding, clothing, or washing facilities were provided. While the Home Office had been warned in the weeks prior to Ahmed's death

---

30. David Neal, 'An Inspection of Contingency Asylum Accommodation' (Independent Chief Inspector of Borders and Immigration, 2021), https://assets.publishing.service.gov.uk/government/uploads/system/uploads/attachment_data/file/1137444/An_inspection_of_contingency_asylum_accommodation.pdf.
31. 'Asylum Seekers to Be Accommodated on Surplus Military Sites.'
32. Jamie Grierson, 'No 10 Distances Itself from Minister's Remark about Asylum Seekers' "Cheek",' *The Guardian*, 4 November 2022, accessed 13 July 2023, https://www.theguardian.com/uk-news/2022/nov/04/minister-says-bit-of-a-cheek-for-asylum-seekers-to-complain-about-conditions.
33. Jamie Grierson, 'Priti Patel Suggests Fire at Kent Asylum Seeker Site Started Deliberately,' *The Guardian*, 29 January 2021, accessed 13 July 2023, https://www.theguardian.com/uk-news/2021/jan/29/napier-barracks-fire-asylum-seekers-kent.
34. Amelia Gentleman, '"You Walked in and Your Heart Sank": The Shocking inside Story of Manston Detention Centre,' *The Guardian*, 25 March 2023, accessed 13 July 2023, https://www.theguardian.com/uk-news/2023/mar/25/inside-story-of-manston-detention-centre.

of the risk of diphtheria, these warnings were ignored. The Home Office subsequently admitted that Ahmed's death may have been caused by diphtheria.[35]

The suffering that was experienced at Manston, and previously at Napier, was acknowledged by the government, but it was simultaneously presented in a way where the migrants were deserving of this treatment. There was an expectation of 'necessary suffering' that was justified on the basis of so-called 'illegal entry' to the state. In March 2023, months after the death of Ahmed, Robert Jenrick, the Minister for Immigration stated, 'we must not elevate the wellbeing of illegal migrants above those of the British people.'[36] It was the very minimisation of the pain and suffering of migrants being held in these conditions that led directly to the death of Hussein Haseeb Ahmed. In the aftermath however, the Home Office continued to blame asylum seekers by referring to low vaccination rates among the group, as well as their 'decision' to come to the UK.[37]

Graduated Zones of Sovereignty and the New Legal Landscape

The increased use of ex-military barracks to house asylum seekers comes at the same time as the development of drastic new legal measures that are aimed at making it increasingly difficult to claim asylum in the UK. Anyone travelling through a so-called 'safe third country' on their way to the UK faces the prospect of being removed to Rwanda to have their claim processed. Yet despite this agreement being signed with great fanfare in 2022, and the Home Secretary's 2023 visit to Rwanda to tour potential migrant housing, there has yet to be a removal carried out by the British government. Indeed, the Court of Appeal has recently ruled that asylum seekers should not be removed to Rwanda because it does not reach the standard of 'safe country'.[38] Importantly however, the Court did not find the removal of asylum seekers to a third country to have their asylum claim heard to be illegal.

---

35. 'Manston Migrant's Death May Have Been Caused by Diphtheria - Home Office,' *BBC News*, 26 November 2022, accessed 13 July 2023, https://www.bbc.com/news/uk-63766770.
36. Walker and correspondent, 'Asylum Seekers Will Get the Most Basic Housing Possible, Says Robert Jenrick.'
37. 'Manston Migrant's Death May Have Been Caused by Diphtheria - Home Office.'
38. AA v SSHD [2023] EWCA Civ 745. The government has appealed the decision to the Supreme Court and at the time of writing we await that decision.

While these particular types of removals may never come to pass, the legal changes that have been enacted to facilitate potential removals have created new legal landscape for asylum seekers in the UK. While the government has presented the use of military barracks as owing to necessity and financial prudence, the establishment of these spaces is key to facilitating the degradation of asylum law and policy in the UK.

The mentioned practices in military barracks and the comments made by government officials clearly indicate that these spaces are being used as a 'tutelary spectacle.' Military barracks have always been established as spatially distinct from the surrounding area and this has continued as the spaces are now being used for asylum accommodation. In addition to the new use of military barracks, the state is now establishing 'offshore accommodation' for migrants in the form of a barge to be docked off the coast.[39] While the government insists that the use of barge accommodation is necessary because of the lack of available housing for asylum seekers, the cost of leasing and operating the barge would appear to far outstrip the cost of setting up less spectacular accommodation on the mainland. As the Shadow Home Secretary has pointed out: 'this barge is ... still more than twice as expensive as normal asylum accommodation,' as well as only accommodating a tiny proportion of all those in need of accommodation.'[40] In this way, the government responds to imagery of migrants in highly mobile small boats attempting to cross the Channel by transporting them to large fixed floating structures. The message is clear: migrants will try to enter the (territory of the) state by boat, but they will never really be permitted to access the *terra firma* of the state. They are destined to remain on the water but are stripped of their ability to move freely. From the perspective of the government, emplacing asylum seekers in this way also reasserts sovereignty in terms of their control of the borders of the state. The spectacle of hypermobile irregular border crossings is reappropriated by the state, replaced by a static structure, floating off the coast, but within the complete control of the state.

With both the ex-military camp and offshore accommodation, we can see that the state is keen to carve out specific geographical locations where the rules that we generally expect to apply within the British state

---

39. 'Bibby Stockholm: Inside the Giant Barge for 500 Migrants That Just Arrived in Falmouth | The Independent,' accessed 6 June 2023, https://www.independent.co.uk/news/uk/home-news/migrants-giant-barge-asylum-seekers-falmouth-b2335456.html.
40. 'Home Office Confirms Plan to House Asylum Seekers in Giant Barge in Dorset,' Sky News, accessed 6 June 2023, https://news.sky.com/story/home-office-to-unveil-plan-to-house-asylum-seekers-in-giant-barge-in-dorset-12850342.

no longer apply in the same way. It is clear that the circumstances of these types of accommodation physically affect the way in which asylum seekers can move and interact with their surroundings. The physical abstraction of these spaces from mainstream society however also act to facilitate new law. As per the Illegal Migration Act, anyone who enters the state irregularly via a 'safe third country' will automatically face deportation.[41] Given that the government has in theory secured an agreement with Rwanda to send asylum applicants there, there is still uncertainty where applicants can be sent. Therefore, while asylum applicants will be prevented from accessing an asylum procedure in the UK, there is also uncertainty that those applicants can be sent anywhere else. Under the Act, those who would seek asylum will be detained until their removal. The co-development and expansion of the ex-military space as asylum accommodation and the proposed designation of most asylum seekers as falling outside the protection of the Refugee Convention within the UK indicates the possibility that these spaces will take on a new legal character. As already noted, the distinction between asylum accommodation and immigration detention has already begun to significantly break down.

States such as Australia and the US have used former colonial outposts and ex-military facilities, especially on islands, as locations to enforce ambiguity and uncertainty to migrants' legal status.[42] The distance from the mainland state and the invisibilizing effect of holding migrants in offshore contexts helps to enforce these locations as 'graduated zones of sovereignty.' The development of ex-military barracks in the manner described above indicates the development of graduated zones of sovereignty, but within the borders of the state. The use of ex-military barracks and potential use of offshore accommodation could be categorised as 'non-contiguous zones' which are used to 'promote the differential regulation of populations.'[43] The use of military barracks in this way further deepens existing stigma and prejudice associated with asylum seekers. A new spatialized legal status is also created. Under the Illegal Migration Act, the UK government will not accept their status as asylum seekers regardless of their need. Bolstered by the imaginary that they are deportable, the government can potentially detain them indefinitely.[44] With few options to send

---

41. 'Illegal Migration Act' (2023) s. 2.
42. Mountz, 'The Enforcement Archipelago.'
43. Ong, *Neoliberalism as Exception*, 77.
44. Illegal Migration Act, s.12

such asylum seekers to a safe third country, this group will reside in category of deportable in law but not in practice. The sweeping categorisation of asylum seekers arriving in this way means that the scale of detention needed will be unprecedented. Increasing areas will need to be demarcated in order to effectively govern this newly created legal category.

The government has justified the drastic changes to the law on the basis that people who have arrived in the UK via a 'safe third country' and without documentation have acted illegally. This treatment, the UK government asserts, could be avoided if people arrived via 'legal routes.' However, this territorial claim radically misrepresents the legal realities underpinning the international refugee legal order, as well as the specific legal restrictions in the UK. Reference to 'illegality' also allows the government to deliberately conflate the movement of asylum seekers across borders with organized crime gangs engaged in smuggling and trafficking operations. The language of illegality and criminality also appeals the imaginary of the dangerous and hypermobile asylum seeker: both the image of the dangerous single figure illicitly scaling a border fence, and the image of the huge number of migrants, poised to overwhelm the state. All of this however masks what is really going on. By relying on the images of uncontrolled movements, the UK government can characterise these acts as 'illegal,' even as the Refugee Convention specifically singles them out as protected.

Using the Spectacle of the Migrant to Establish Discipline and Mask Legal Realities

The concept of illegality as it relates to irregular migration on small boats to the UK tends to be presented in two ways. First, these movements are presented as illegal because the people crossing the Channel are usually relying on smugglers for the crossing. Second, it is claimed that these movements are illegal because those who are entering the state have not travelled to the state on a visa or another kind of permission. The dual meaning that is attached to the concept of illegality is then mapped on to imagery that is used to cover these kinds of movements in the media. Media articles covering issues like trafficking, smuggling, and irregular movements all tend to use the same imagery of migrants arriving to the state, aboard small boats and clad in lifejackets. The image of the migrants presented in this way then becomes the visual shorthand for a myriad of concepts, many of which are morally reprehensible and cannot be justifiably associated with any individuals depicted.

The distinction between acts of trafficking, smuggling, and crossing a border irregularly is collapsed as they are translated into a single type of image. As trafficking, an act which involves the effective enslavement of people, becomes indistinguishable from crossing a border to flee from persecution, these acts become morally equated. What becomes obfuscated then are the basic tenets of international refugee law. When people arrive to the state without the required paperwork or permissions, this does not automatically mean that they are 'illegal.' International refugee law specifically envisages the situation where someone needs to enter the state without documentation. Because refugee status can only be applied for on the territory of the state where asylum is being sought, Article 31 of the Refugee Convention acknowledges that the person seeking asylum may need to move clandestinely in order to access the state. The Convention therefore acknowledges the immediacy of the need to access asylum as well as the often complete lack of access to such visas. This was also reflected in British legislation, with section 31 of the 1999 Immigration Act establishing a defence against illegal entry where asylum is being sought.

Despite this, the Home Secretary has claimed that asylum seekers should use 'legal routes' to access the UK. There is no way to access an 'asylum visa' to travel to the UK to seek asylum. Similarly, as already noted, asylum must be applied for in the host state. This also means that asylum cannot be accessed via embassies and there is no mechanism in place which would permit that. The only 'legal route' which the Home Secretary could potentially be referring to is that of resettlement. The continual and persistent reference to 'legal routes' as a viable alternative was recently debunked by UNHCR, including with reference to resettlement. The organization clarified that UNHCR cannot be directly approached to process applications for asylum: 'there is no asylum visa or 'queue' for the United Kingdom.'[45] UNHCR further demystified the claim made by the British government that people could simply approach the UNHCR offices in other countries and request resettlement there. UNHCR went on to note that resettlement is only offered on a very limited basis and in partnership with host states, who establish a set number of refugees that they are willing to accept. Within these limitations, resettlement is only offered to people who have already been living as refugees in a state and are particularly

---

45. 'Statement on Asylum Processing and Resettlement via UNHCR,' UNHCR UK, accessed 6 June 2023, https://www.unhcr.org/uk/news/statement-asylum-processing-and-resettlement-unhcr.

at risk there, making integration there impossible. Equally, only those who are unable to return to their home country would be eligible for resettlement. UNHCR notes that this accounts for a tiny proportion of the world's refugees – less than 1%. The UK currently accepts approximately 100 refugees through resettlement per month.

The strength of the Government's arguments about the so-called 'illegality' of movements are premised on the false notion of an available and accessible legal route, which asylum seekers nonetheless reject in order to 'skip' a queue. The imaginary of rejecting a legal route and foregoing the 'very British' activity of queuing is therefore understood as flouting a set of reasonable and proportionate rules. Asylum seekers are portrayed as willingly choosing dangerous and illegal routes. Imaginaries of boat arrivals 'swamping' and 'engulfing' the state—apparently confirmed through the persistent use of images of small boats in the media—allows a sense of crisis around the issue to be cultivated.

This narrative in turn emphasises that the asylum seeker is culpable for their own circumstances as they have embraced criminality and reckless dangerousness over a 'safe and legal route.' Initially, the government emphasised that 'stopping the boats' was being prioritised to protect those who would use smugglers to cross the Channel to seek asylum.[46] Intervening and ceasing these movements 'protected' asylum seekers from smuggling gangs who were preying on vulnerable and desperate asylum seekers. The government therefore posited that by 'breaking the business model' of the smugglers, i.e. by stopping Channel crossings, asylum seekers would be protected and criminal enterprises would be scuppered.[47]

This of course entirely ignores the realities facing asylum seekers already outlined. In the space of a year however, we can see that the narrative about asylum seekers has also dramatically shifted. Where at one point 'stopping the boats' was (perhaps disingenuously) associated with protecting asylum seekers, this framing now appears to be disposed of entirely. In a recent interview, the Home Secretary flatly referred to anyone who travelled to the UK via boats as 'criminals.'[48]

---

46. 'Channel Crossings, Migration and Asylum - Home Affairs Committee.'
47. 'Channel Crossings, Migration and Asylum - Home Affairs Committee.'
48. '"They Are Criminals": Suella Braverman on People Crossing Channel on Small Boats – Video | Politics | The Guardian,' accessed 6 June 2023, https://www.theguardian.com/politics/video/2023/apr/26/they-are-criminals-suella-braverman-on-people-crossing-channel-on-small-boats-video.

It can be argued that the continual reference to arrivals as 'illegal' as well as the presentation of boat arrivals as being fundamentally connected to criminality through the act of smuggling has culminated in asylum seekers now being categorised as 'criminals.'

Further, developing the narrative extended by Pugliese in relation to the concept of 'refugee prisoner,' it is clear that the emphasis on criminality informs and is informed by the telegenic spectacle of small boat arrival to the state. Illegality, which has long been associated with irregular arrivals to the state, has been transmuted into the concept of criminality, thereby overtly signalling the legitimacy of punishment. The consistent increase in the level of punitiveness that is being either enforced or imposed is confirmed and reinforced through the visual language of the same punitiveness.

The visual language of the treatment of asylum seekers at the hands of the British state in these newly hypervisible and tutelary contexts reveals that the British government is testing the lengths that it can take its punitive treatment in the name of 'stopping the boats.' The current emphasis on pushing the spectacle of deterrence is not new, despite the 'newness' of punitive legislation. The shape and content of the British asylum system itself is rooted in the concept of deterrence and suspicion of the legitimacy of asylum claims. The articulation of asylum seekers as 'illegal,' and more recently 'criminals,' builds upon pre-existing tropes of the 'bogus' asylum seeker who is masquerading as someone in need of protection to take advantage of the welfare state.

Imaginaries of Deterrence and 'Law-Creating' Moments

The spectacle of the border is used to further logics of deterrence. The increased hypervisibility of arrivals to the state by small boats has inspired a form of visual dialogue whereby migrants' hypervisible entrance to the state is responded to by hypervisible and spectacular modes of detention and expulsion. This ranges from detention in former military barracks to the so-called Rwanda agreement, to the proposed 'floating prisons.' The spectacle of the border is having an increasingly large impact on the content of asylum law and policy in Britain, and will also inform the trajectory of the same as the public is 'tutored' as to the treatment that asylum seekers and other migrants 'deserve.'

Spectacular punishment as deterrence is not just a characteristic of the current government's policies but has defined the status of the asylum seeker in Britain since the establishment of the category under law. Asylum policy in the UK has been associated with the language of deterrence for decades, dating back to the New Labour era as well as the latter years of their predecessors, the Conservative government in the early 1990s. The ascension of Labour in the late 1990s coincided with a notable rise in the number of people applying for asylum in the UK. 'Fixing' the immigration system therefore became a key feature of Labour policy during its tenure.

As Patricia Hynes notes, while the UK had long been a destination country for people seeking asylum, the only legal categories that existed were 'quota refugees' and 'non-quota refugees.' This referred respectively to refugees who arrived as part of a resettlement scheme and those who arrived spontaneously to the state to seek asylum.[49] The formal legal status of 'asylum seeker' did not exist in statute until the passing of the Asylum and Immigration Appeals Act 1993. As Rosemary Sales pointed out, despite the late establishment of asylum on a statutory footing, it quickly became tied to minimising welfare entitlements that asylum seekers could access.[50]

In the Asylum and Immigration Appeals Act 1996, under the Conservative government, asylum seekers were banned from accessing social welfare benefits. In the debates ahead of the introduction of the legislation, the government was keen to not be seen as a 'soft touch' and wanted to ensure that Britain would be perceived as a 'haven not a honeypot.'[51] As asylum seekers were also not permitted to work, the withdrawal of all benefits, including housing support, would result in most asylum seekers becoming destitute and homeless. Under the legislation, asylum seekers could potentially seek support from local councils; however the rules under which councils were meant to act were unclear. Councils were also not to be provided with additional financial aid to assist asylum seekers eligible for council support.

It was clear that the removal of all support in this way was to stage a drastic form of deterrence, making arriving in the UK as unappealing as possible to those who would seek asylum. The intended effect on asylum seekers who were present at the time in the UK was to deprive them the point that they would remove themselves from the state. The spectre of absolute deprivation, for the government, was key to both removing asylum seekers in the state as well as preventing prospective

---

49. Patricia Hynes, 'Contemporary Compulsory Dispersal and the Absence of Space for the Restoration of Trust,' *Journal of Refugee Studies* 22/1 (2009), 101.
50. Rosemary Sales, 'The Deserving and the Undeserving? Refugees, Asylum Seekers and Welfare in Britain' 22/3 (2002), 462.
51. Dallal Stevens, 'The Asylum and Immigration Act 1996: Erosion of the Right to Seek Asylum,' *The Modern Law Review* 61/2 (1998), 220.

asylum seekers from arriving. The spectacle therefore constitutes two different 'publics'—the media-consuming British public whose gaze and support legitimates punitive legislation, and the asylum-seeking public who are also the target of the spectacular measures.

By taking this 'tough stance' on asylum, the government was effectively abandoning councils working on the frontline of asylum arrivals. While the 1996 Act predated the introduction of the Human Rights Act—a specific domestic human rights framework, the 1996 Act was clearly an attack on human dignity, a concept that that was still protected under British law. As a result, councils (including those run by Conservatives), began to take judicial reviews. While the government sought to cease all support to asylum seekers, councils still had legal obligations to children and vulnerable people.[52]

Despite the Court of Appeal stating that the proposed measures were 'so uncompromisingly draconian in effect that they must be ultra vires,' the 1996 Act was nonetheless rushed through the houses and established in law.[53] While the government was able to effectively overturn the judgment of the Court of Appeal by introducing the 1996 Act, they were still unable to exert the full intended effect. Under the obligations set out in the National Assistance Act 1948, there was still a requirement to provide a certain level of shelter, food, and warmth to asylum seekers. As a result of the obligations established by the National Assistance Act cases, a special accommodation grant was agreed to support asylum seekers.

At the time that the Conservative government tried and failed to cut all support to asylum seekers, a number of those in the Labour opposition called for the restoration of benefits to those awaiting an asylum decision. However, after Labour took power in 1997, it became clear that they nonetheless wished to appear 'tough' on asylum. In the 1998 White Paper, *Fairer Faster Firmer*, the Labour government specifically identified asylum as a route that economic migrants would use to enter the state.[54] The white paper also stated that access to the social welfare system would act as an incentive for them to arrive. Through this formulation, a need was articulated for people seeking protection to be subject to a much more restricted status within the British state.

---

52. Stevens, 'The Asylum and Immigration Act 1996,' 219.
53. Stevens, 'The Asylum and Immigration Act 1996.'
54. Home Office, *Fairer, Faster and Firmer: Modern Approach to Immigration and Asylum*, No. 4018 (Command Paper), 1998.

While the Conservative government began to establish a distinct asylum system with the passing of the Asylum and Immigration Appeals Act in 1993, Labour's 1999 Immigration Act formalised a deterrent-focused reception conditions policy that was firmly rooted in neoliberal principles. This legislation kick-started the reliance of the state on private contractors to provide for asylum seekers. The Labour government circumvented some of the key challenges that the Conservatives had encountered in their attempt to establish a deterrent policy by both fully removing asylum support from the existing benefits system and establishing a formal separate provision for asylum seekers.

This model continues to remain in place since the introduction of the 1999 Act. Under the model created by the Labour government, asylum seekers who are classified as 'destitute'—a legacy treatment of asylum seekers by the previous Conservative government and the National Assistance Act decisions—are dispersed across the country with a view to alleviating pressure on the capital and southern parts of the country. Asylum seekers live in accommodation run by private contractors and receive a small stipend every week to purchase food and other essentials: £45 per week for adults. This money is loaded on to a government-issued debit card every week.

The conditions that asylum seekers must live in under the current policy have been subject to consistent criticism. Little care is taken by the private contractors to ensure the safety of the accommodation. There have been widespread reports of vermin and rot within accommodation provision, as well as inadequate support for vulnerable persons.[55] The decline in the quality of asylum accommodation has contributed to the reliance on hotel accommodation and in turn the push to use military barracks as accommodation.

The operation of asylum accommodation by these companies not only demonstrates a decisive shift to neoliberal governance of asylum reception, where the provision of basic support and care is diverted from local governance to privatized companies, but it also signifies the increasing financialization of asylum. As Lauren Martin and Martina Tazzioli note, large companies who have previously established themselves in other neoliberal care arenas like elder care have shifted to growing their provision for asylum accommodation using a similar model.[56]

---

55. 'Asylum Accommodation Is a Disgrace - Committees - UK Parliament,' accessed 6 June 2023, https://committees.parliament.uk/committee/83/home-affairs-committee/news/100602/asylum-accommodation-is-a-disgrace/.
56. Lauren L Martin and Martina Tazzioli, 'Value Extraction through Refugee

Motivated by profit and potential growth, companies like Clearsprings (which runs the Napier Barracks accommodation for asylum seekers) has pivoted from social care settings to public housing with a view to expanding its portfolio in asylum accommodation.

At this point in time, there are clear parallels between the era in the 1990s which gave birth to the parameters of the UK asylum system as we now understand it, and the current moment where there have been similarly drastic changes in terms of who an asylum seeker is considered to be and how they should be treated as a matter of law and as a matter of governance. Current criticism of the Rwanda plan, the placement of asylum seekers barges, as well as the move under the Illegal Migration Act to exclude anyone arriving via a safe third country from any possible access to the UK are certainly warranted, but perhaps do not reflect on the degree to which the UK asylum system is in fact originated in the idea of deterrence.

Indeed, in the 1990s, the commitment to the concept of deterrence was so extreme that it was only through pushbacks from local councils (including Conservative-run councils) as well as other advocacy organisations through the courts that there was a move away from a policy of total deprivation toward many asylum seekers. By drawing on decades old legislation that reinforced the humanity of those who would be subject to such measures, the category of the 'destitute' asylum seeker came into being. Only by conforming to this categorisation could an asylum seeker access assistance from the state.

What is striking about the descriptions that are used at the time of the formulation of the category of asylum seeker under UK law is how much they are shaped by particular imaginaries about those who seek asylum and how they relate to the state. With the introduction of asylum seeker under law through the 1993 and 1996 Acts, the then Conservative government emphasises the untrustworthiness of the asylum seeker and the fact that the asylum seeker category is necessary in order to tackle the inevitable abuse by those who would apply for refugee status, as well as the (unfounded and unevidenced) assumption that those who would apply for protection would in reality be economic migrants trying to access the welfare system.

Then, as a system is rolled out which would enforce a status of absolute deprivation on many asylum seekers, it is only by categorising asylum seekers as 'destitute' that they can access assistance from the state.

Carcerality: Data, Labour and Financialised Accommodation,' *Environment and Planning D: Society and Space* 41/2 (2023), 195.

Here the imaginary is strongly evoked of an asylum seeker who is abject, begging the assistance of the state lest they literally starve. In this way, by establishing this criterion and preventing access to the labour market, the state has also produced the destitute asylum seeker.

As the asylum reception system evolved into the form used during the 2000s and 2010s, the figure of the asylum seeker shifted from view. The way that the dispersal of asylum seekers has operated in the UK means that the treatment of asylum seekers has been hidden from view. This is not to say that they did not exist anymore, but rather that they did not come spectacularly into view in the same way as when local authorities had a larger role in the administration of asylum accommodation. Separated from the mainstream through private administration in a parallel welfare system, suffering was often invisibilized. At the same time, the imaginary of the unproductive scrounger is perpetuated. As noted however, as the dispersal model of accommodation is used less and 'emergency' accommodation like hotels and military barracks become the norm for asylum accommodation, the asylum seeker returns in a spectacular way.

In the same way that spectacular imaginaries played a key role in the development of the asylum system in the 1990s, the current moment in asylum policy, which is mediated through images of boat arrivals to the state, has sparked a new shift in asylum administration. When the legal status of asylum seeker was formally established under British law, the space in which the concept of asylum could exist began to narrow. Asylum seeking status was firmly established as conditional and unlikely to result in conversion to refugee status (despite evidence to the contrary). This was reinforced through the creation of such deterrent conditions upon arrival that even entering the state to request asylum could result in abject destitution.

Under this current trend in deterrence, the government has more clearly graduated zones of sovereignty that are demonstrably spatialized. Unlike other iterations of graduated zones of sovereignty discussed by Mountz, these are spaces that have been carved out within the borders of the state with the intention of creating a spectacle of deterrence.[57] Since 2022, the Conservative government has introduced legislation that will have the effect of denying a significant proportion of asylum seekers from accessing the asylum process. Once asylum seekers are deemed to have passed through a safe third country on their way to the UK, they may be detained and potentially removed to so-called 'safe third countries' such as Rwanda.

---

57. Mountz, 'The Enforcement Archipelago.'

In anticipation of the large number of people that will face removal under the new rules, the government is preparing to use ex-military barracks to 'provide accommodation at scale.'[58]

These spaces not only provide the government with a location to keep asylum seekers before potential removal, but also physically and spatially embody the 'shrinking of legal space' referred to by Mountz.[59] Examples include the manner in which Australia has used territories and countries located in its orbit to process asylum application that arrive by boat. Under the Refugee Convention, it is envisaged that by presenting oneself at the borders of the state and claiming asylum, a person should be given the opportunity to demonstrate that they meet the refugee definition set out in the Convention. Up to this point, states have drawn on concepts like safe third countries in order to externalize this obligation.

The use of ex-military barracks as pre-removal accommodation is a spectacular reminder of the British state's rejection of a good faith reading of the principle of non-refoulement. This 'accommodation at scale' which effectively amounts to mass-detention pending removal is also a key example of the tutelary spectacle elaborated by Pugliese.

Conclusion

The British state has firmly connected its current attack on asylum to the spectre of the hypervisible boat arrival to the state. Fixating on these hypervisible arrivals, the state seeks to signal that it is spectacularly regaining control over the nature of these arrivals by placing them in facilities like the 'floating prisons' referred to above, as well as military barracks. The emphasis on the establishment of a spectacle of deterrence is less recent, recurring since the creation of the category of the asylum seeker in British law.

As I have shown, there is an overlap between spectacular moments of deterrence and 'law creating moments.' The image and imaginary of the asylum seeker has been a crucial element in the development of asylum policy as we currently understand it. The spectacle thus not only influences and informs the nature of the law, but also effects the way that space is ordered within the borders of the UK. As the government

---

58. 'UK to House Migrants in Ex-Army Barracks, Mulls Use of Barges – POLITICO,' accessed 6 June 2023, https://www.politico.eu/article/uk-plan-house-asylum-seeker-barge-ex-military-base-robert-jenrick/.
59. Mountz, 'The Enforcement Archipelago,' 120.

expands the use of military barracks across the state to house asylum seekers before possibly removing them to Rwanda and potentially other states, graduated zones of sovereignty are created. As those are housed in the barracks will never be able to access to the asylum system, there is also a clear shrinking of the legal space for asylum.

The spectacular nature of the current measures being rolled out by the UK government is presented as the justificatory framework for their punitive nature. As a telegenic spectacle, it also teaches the public that these measures are proportionate and acceptable. Despite this, the previous resistance from local councils as well as the courts to extreme deterrence measures in the 1990s provides some hope for the potential to curtail the current sharp pivot toward punitiveness.

However, the landscape of asylum has changed drastically since the National Assistance Acts cases of the mid-1990s. A great deal of the resistance to deterrence measures in that era were connected to the role that local government played in the provision of assistance under the law. Since then, asylum reception and accommodation has been almost entirely severed from the work of local councils. As the operation of asylum accommodation and reception is now being wholly operated by private contractors, there is not the same interest in the public good and the protection of asylum seekers' rights. Therefore, the possibility of resistance does not exist in the same way as in the 1990s.

As in the 1990s, at the time of writing, Britain currently faces a potential move from Conservative to Labour rule. Hope for a drastic about turn in policy may once again be misplaced. The fundamental concept of deterrence at the heart of asylum policy still remains unchallenged by the current Labour opposition, suggesting that any change in policy to be introduced by Labour may will likely contain more than mere vestiges of the Conservative vision.

It is now therefore crucial to challenge the framing that we have been presented with in the context of asylum and arrivals to the state. The central feature of 'deterrence' that has driven the latest move to restrict access to asylum and perform punishment on asylum seekers is reliant upon a construction of 'illegality' that has been driven by the state. This interpretation of 'illegality' is both legally and morally flawed, yet remains consistent with the government's narrative because 'illegality' has been reduced to an aesthetic. The image of asylum seekers and migrants arriving to the state in small boats has become the visual representation of illegality, regardless of whether those on board are in need of international protection.

As noted, images of migrants and asylum seekers have become shorthand for illegal and criminal activity. As these spectacular images become abstracted from their context and their meaning, the ability to challenge government policy to 'fight illegal migration' in the language of law also diminishes. The reduction of migrants and asylum seekers to mere imagery in this way has been deeply damaging. As I have discussed, these images are not neutral, and are presented to the public in a way that is steeped in political agenda – both that of the government and the media. Now, as imagery can be more easily manipulated, it is imperative that the image itself is critically challenged. This however must not descend into the stereotypical binary of the 'good' as opposed to the 'bad' migrant, but rather reflect the solidarity that should be inherent in holding an oppressive government to account.

5

Aesthetics and the Construction of the 'Grateful Refugee'

CRITICAL PERSPECTIVES FROM LAW AND DESIGN

Christine Schwöbel-Patel and Deger Ozkaramanli

The mass displacement of people remains one of the defining issues of the twenty-first century so far. Displacement can occur through conflict, political dissent, poverty, persecution, or through climate change. The growing numbers (over eighty-nine million displaced people worldwide) and the recognition of this as a 'new normal' poses challenges for the individuals involved as well as on receiving states, origin states, and organisations and agencies of humanitarianism.[1] Particular pressure points depend on the migration routes one investigates, whether this is at or near the border into Europe, Australia's offshore detention of refugees and migrants in Nauru and Papua New Guinea, or migration into North America via sea or land. Although diverse, these pressures have raised common questions on who qualifies as a refugee, possible short-term and long-term solutions to displacement, and discussions regarding symptoms and root causes of displacement and migration. In receiving states, certain images of migration circulate that have tended to prompt a demand for punitive action against migration (against migrants themselves as well as traffickers). Both legal and design professionals and scholars are contributing to the debates and policies that construct and reproduce narratives around migration. In our conversations, we have found that there are certain recurring patterns—or dominant frames—in how our disciplines of law and design construct refugees, in particular around questions of desert that congeal

---

1. 'Global Trends,' UNHCR, accessed 17 April 2023, https://www.unhcr.org/global-trends.html.

in expectations of a 'grateful refugee.' In the following, we explore the commonalities in the framing of refugees in the disciplines of law and design. These commonalities, we find, are not simply incidental; they shine a light on the neoliberal capitalist political project in which the disciplines operate. Having established the commonalities in law and design that indicate legal-material technologies around punitive policies, we ask whether a law-design critical enquiry can be used as a platform for unsettling the recurring construct of a 'grateful refugee'?

Building on Judith Butler's work in *Frames of War*, we argue that representations of refugees are framed by neoliberal market thinking and that these representations themselves have a framing function.[2] We identify the means by which experiential and discursive fields such as design and law create and sustain certain frames. Narratives and imagery of mass displacement do not simply unfold in a world 'out there' with facts ripe for the picking.[3] Instead, narratives and imagery are based on particular epistemic and ideological assumptions. Representations of refugees are constructed by the priorities of a neoliberal capitalist global order; but this is not a unidirectional process. These representations also have a capacity to order the world, to include and exclude people, debates, issues. We agree with Butler that framing is an operation of power. We add to the understanding of this operation of power the legal-material technologies that are operationalised through law and design.

The specific practices of framing which we draw attention to from the perspective of our respective disciplines regards the construction of a simultaneously deferential and entrepreneurial 'grateful refugee.' It is notable, we argue, that 'deferential' and 'entrepreneurial' stand in tension with one another and are even paradoxical. The grateful refugee is expected to be *deferential* to the laws, culture, and even discriminatory practices of the receiving state. At the same time, this idealised and imagined refugee is also *entrepreneurial*, as in, not dependent on state resources and economically productive. We argue that both law and industrial design have a role to play in constructing the idea of a grateful refugee within this neoliberal market-oriented frame. The 'grateful refugee' is constructed in contrast to what Dina Nayeri has described as the 'ungrateful refugee,' who refuses to see

---

2. Judith Butler, *Frames of War: When is Life Grievable* (New York: Verso, 2010).
3. Hilary Charlesworth, 'International Law: A Discipline of Crisis,' *Modern Law Review* 65/3 (2002).

the status of being a refugee as needing to pay off a debt to the hosts.[4] The grateful refugee is a narrow and imagined sub-set of the lived experience of forced displacement. It is on behalf of this notion that inclusions of privileges are determined. In other words, those who have been displaced are measured against the frame of the 'grateful refugee.'

In law, the construction of the 'grateful refugee' operates at the intersection between the permissive and the punitive. We focus in particular on the intersection between International Law, Refugee Law, and International Criminal Law, although these legal regimes are not exhaustive of the frame. These disciplines have come under pressure to respond more adequately to the 'refugee crisis.' The legal and political framing exercises around the definition of refugee, asylum seeker, and migrant are key for determining the fate of individuals as granted either legal protection or legal punishment. As much of the legal response is reactive to what is considered to be a crisis in the West, we find it places pressure on the individual and their behaviour rather than on the states and international legal system to deal with the political, economic, historical, ecological, cultural, and social root causes of the refugee crisis. The response has been a visceral securitization regime, with an emphasis on criminal justice.[5]

While law researchers and professionals strive to define the boundaries of legal protection and legal punishment, design practitioners, particularly in industrial design, have turned their attention to tackling the practical challenges that emerge from large numbers of people moving across borders. Among these challenges are finding or making shelter, addressing language barriers, and securing an income. For instance, What Design Can Do (WDCD)—a platform through which the societal impact of the design discipline is discussed and debated—launched the 2016 WDCD Refugee challenge in collaboration with the United Nations Refugee Agency and the IKEA Foundation. This challenge invited designers to tackle the difficulties faced by millions of refugees in everyday life. In addition, a recently launched initiative 'Good Design for a Bad World' brings together domain experts

---

4. Dina Nayeri, 'The ungrateful refugee: 'We have no debt to repay',' *The Guardian*, 4 April 2017, accessed 17 April 2023, https://www.theguardian.com/world/2017/apr/04/dina-nayeri-ungrateful-refugee.
5. Policing and sanctioning infringements of immigration rules has prompted the use of the portmanteau 'crimmigration.' See Juliet P Stumpf, 'The Crimmigration Crisis: Immigrants, Crime, and Sovereign Power' *American University Law Review* 56 (2006)) 367; Kathleen R Arnold, *Arendt, Agamben and the Issue of Hyper-Legality: In Between the Prisoner-Stateless Nexus* (Oxford: Routledge 2018).

in various fields to reflect on and communicate how design can address global issues such as climate change, refugee crisis, and terrorism.[6] The effort to do 'social good' through design is also evident in the emergence of research areas such as Social Design,[7] Design for Emotional Durability,[8] and the uptake of Participatory Design, which places community interest (vs. monetary gain) at the core of its practices.[9]

Figure 1: Design-Problem-Solving the Refugee Crisis

In our critical analysis, we point to how reactive refugee laws as well as design for refugees are addressing the symptoms and not the root causes of the challenges faced by refugees. This is arguably closely linked to a neoliberal market thinking in practice and the sustaining of rigid disciplinary boundaries in research, which places emphasis on problem-solving at the expense of a structural analysis.

---

6. 'Dezeen and Dutch Design Week launch Good Design for a Bad World Initiative,' Dezeen, accessed 17 April 2023, https://www.dezeen.com/2017/10/02/dezeen-dutch-design-week-launch-good-design-for-a-bad-world-initiative/.
7. Nynke Tromp and Paul Hekkert, Designing for Society: Products and Services for a Better World (London: Bloomsbury, 2018).
8. Jonathan Chapman, 'Design for Emotional Durablity,' *Design Issues* 25/4 (2009).
9. Elizabeth B. N. Sanders and Pieter Jan Stappers, 'Co-creation and the New Landscapes of Design,' *Co-design* 4/1 (2005).

Such market thinking is evident in the construction of a neoliberal subject, the deferential yet entrepreneurial 'grateful refugee.' Gratitude, aligned with a notion of 'desert' and debt, is the defining feature of an idealized archetype of the grateful refugee, constructed to be in a constant state of precarity.[10]

In the following, we first set out representations of refugees and the refugee crisis in law and then in design. Subsequently, we go into further detail on the dilemma presented by the concept of the grateful refugee, who is expected to be both deferential and entrepreneurial. Finally, we consider ways in which the construction of the grateful refugee stereotype can be contested, both in critical orientations to law and design as well as in design solutions.

Representations of Refugees in Law

The legal protection of refugees is regulated in a panoply of domestic and international laws, regulations, and interpretations. The Universal Declaration of Human Rights, a non-binding instrument but an influential one nonetheless, states in Art. 14(1) that 'Everyone has the right to seek and to enjoy in other countries asylum from persecution.' The 1951 Refugee Convention is the United Nations convention which offers protection to refugees, drafted following the huge number of (mainly Jewish and political) refugees in and after the Second World War. It recognizes the need for protection that emerged from the context of certain peoples being forced to leave their homes for fear of persecution and seek refuge elsewhere. The key principle of refugee law, found in Art. 33 of the Refugee Convention, *non-refoulement*, refers to the obligation of states not to *refoule*, or return, a refugee to 'the frontiers of territories where his life or freedom would be threatened on account of his race, religion, nationality, membership of a particular social group or political opinion.'[11]

The Refugee Convention itself is narrow on the question of 'who qualifies as a refugee?,' giving rise to a politics of labels. Prior to a formal determination of refugee status, people moving across borders to seek refuge are referred to as 'asylum seekers.' So long as

---

10. As Butler writes, 'lives are by definition precarious: they can be expunged at will or by accident; their persistence is in no sense guaranteed.' Butler crucially also explains that while all life is equally defined by precariousness, it does not follow that all lives are equally precarious. Butler, *Frames of War*, 25.
11. Refugee Convention 1951, Art. 33(1).

the status determination has not been made, the Convention subscribes a presumption of protection. In international law, refugee status is determined through the United Nations High Commissioner for Refugees (UNHCR) system, the implementation of which lies with individual states. The determination of refugee status is a legalized and bureaucratic process. According to the UNHCR, 'states have the primary responsibility for determining the status of asylum-seekers, but UNHCR may do so where states are unable or unwilling.'[12] National refugee policy, it should be said, often contests or circumvents international legal obligations under the 1951 Refugee Convention in order to create punitive or preventative environments for migrants.[13]

Although this representation of international law appears *prima facie* as a protective measure, international law also entails exclusionary features. Take for instance the significance of territorial boundaries, and borders as their legal manifestation, under international law. Many territorial disputes concerning ethnic tensions and resources in the Global South date back to the period of colonialism in particular in the nineteenth century, when up to eighty percent of the world was colonized. As colonized states were claiming independence in the process referred to as decolonization in the mid-twentieth century, territorial boundaries were, under the international legal principle of *uti possidetis*, declared as fixed. The imperial borders, marked by imperial powers through drawing lines on a map, remain the same. Rather than a break with colonial dependencies, independence often proved to be about the continuation of dependencies; mostly pertaining to trade. The so-called Westphalian (European) international order assumes a centralized state authority which exercises power over its citizens. Such arrangements around territory and sovereignty have been interpreted as requiring strict delimitations between citizens and non-citizens and their respective rights and responsibilities. This delimitation in law can become punitive if stress is put on the system, such as experienced in the refugee crisis. The very statist system itself is therefore not only a form of protection, but a means for exclusion.

A further basis of exclusion is predicated on the narrow premise of protection under the international refugee law regime. The basis of protection through law is, as mentioned above, granted on the basis of *persecution*. However, with internal conflict increasing, climate

---

12. 'Refugee Status Determination,' UNHCR, accessed 17 April 2023, http://www.unhcr.org/uk/refugee-status-determination.html.
13. Thomas Gammeltoft-Hansen, 'International Refugee Law and Refugee Policy: The Case of Deterrence Politics,' *Journal of Refugee Studies* 27/4 (2014).

change impacting on living conditions, and a global political economy that is skewed in favour of the Global North, there are increasing flows of people who are seeking refuge, but do not necessarily fit the requirement of being persecuted. Such exclusions and categorisations prepare the ground for a narrow understanding of protection, which is enmeshed with laws and policies of securitization. This in turn fires up a public notion of exclusion, exploited by some politicians and news outlets through inflammatory language.

As the pressure has grown through refugee applications being the norm rather than the exception, the legal provisions in the West have moved from protection to securitization, evidenced in particular by the detention of migrants often in devastating conditions.[14] As the pressure has grown politically with receiving states claiming they are unable to absorb the large and unabating flows of people, a public debate in Western receiving states around 'bogus' asylum seekers has emerged, who arrive not because of persecution (those who are persecuted are protected under law) but because they want to make better lives for themselves. There is growing demand not only to have legal assurance that these so-called 'bogus' asylum seekers are 'sent back,' but also to criminalise them. This framing around asylum and immigration inclusions and exclusions highlights the nature of the 'crisis' depending on which part of the world one is in. What states in the Global North view as a 'crisis' tends to be that which poses a threat to peace and security in the Global North. This has provided fertile ground for distinctions between undeserving migrants (illegals) and deserving refugees (legals). The political and public pressure is brought into the legal realm through a more punitive system of securitization, which fixes the debate and public imagination on a criminal justice lens. Criminalization is employed both for 'bogus' asylum seekers as well as for traffickers, i.e. those assisting migrants, including for economic gain.[15]

A framing of the legal dimension through the extreme poles of innocence on the one hand and criminalisation on the other is linked to punitive regimes for exerting agency. Refugees are often expected

---

14. At the US border to Mexico, the detention of children separated from their parents caused outrage and concern. The holding of children in the offshore detention facilities of Australia has also sparked concern among humanitarian organizations and parts of the public.
15. The simultaneous penalising of immigrants and traffickers is illustrated in the UK's recent Nationality and Borders Act 2022. For a comment, see Emilie McDonnell, 'The UK's Securitisation and Criminalisation of Migration and Asylum,' *Verfassungsblog*, 11 November 2021, accessed 17 April 2023, https://verfassungsblog.de/os2-uk/.

to remain *deferential*, even passive. For example, a refugee's desire to work, as an example of exerting agency, is often an excluding factor from refugee status. If they decide to work, they are at risk of falling into the muddy regulative waters of economic migrants. Indeed, many refugees are denied the right to work, particularly in the so-called 'humanitarian silos,' the areas and states outside of warzones which deal with the first emergency response. The reward for passivity (waiting for status determination) is arguably reifying societal expectations of refugees who give up their foreign identities and submit to the ethical and legal frameworks of their destination countries without questioning. It also concerns a deferential attitude, where abuse and rejection are expected to be endured.

The expected passivity of the grateful refugee, who is not a drain on state resources, is curiously and paradoxically pitted against pressures of *entrepreneurship*. Whilst passivity is expected when it comes to demands on the host state, activity is rewarded for the entrepreneurial refugee, who makes something out of his or her situation. The entrepreneurial stories are constructed as heroic resourcefulness and savviness. The passivity in the public sphere and agency in the private sphere is hardened through an international legal refugee regime which places a great onus on humanitarian agencies (rather than state agencies).[16] Humanitarian agencies, which receive a large amount of funding from donors of the Global North, in turn construct their refugee images and narratives to coincide with the constructed notion of the grateful refugee.

The international legal move towards securitization at the interface between international criminal law and refugee law is as much defined by the securitization measures as by that which is *not* regulated and debated. Omissions include a workable and interconnected regime which is sensitive to the causalities between migrant flows, climate change, conflict, neocolonialism, and neoliberalism. Rather, international law, including refugee law, has adopted a problem-solving attitude towards the refugee crisis. This includes interpretations of the Refugee Convention, discussions on whether the Convention (or the discipline) requires a modest overhaul, and the role which humanitarian agencies should be playing. Securitization is part of a reactive problem-solving approach that requires political support only so long as the attention of the distracted masses can be arrested with the problem.

---

16. Caroline Wanjiku Kihato, Loren B. Landau, 'Stealth Humanitarianism: Negotiating Politics, Precarity and Performance Management in Protecting the Urban Displaced,' *Journal of Refugee Studies* 30/3 (2017).

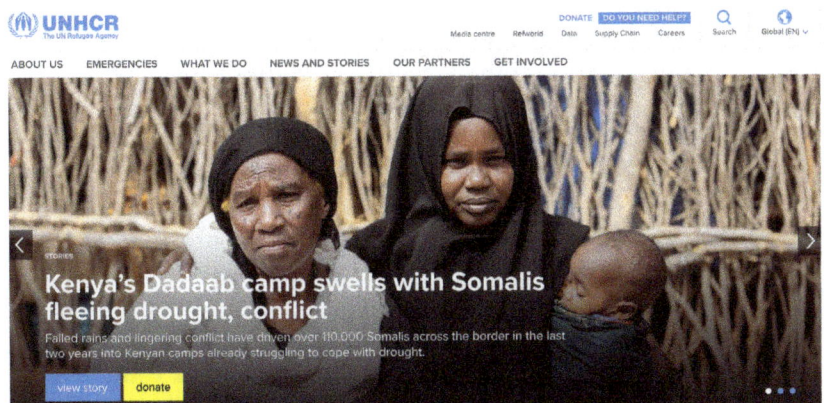

Figure 2: UNHCR website home page 1 (Screenshot 2023)

UNHCR's Global Appeal for 2023

The Global Appeal is UNHCR's annual publication describing its plans for the coming year and the outlook for forcibly displaced and stateless people in 2023.

Figure 3: UNHCR website home page 2 (Screenshot 2023)

This short-term spectacularized narrative has fostered an aesthetics replete with stereotypes, both in regard to victims of conflict (the 'ideal victim' in international criminal law) as well as those uprooted, mostly during or after conflict (the 'grateful refugee').[17] The aesthetics of the 'grateful refugee' privileges images of women and children vis-à-vis men. Images of women and children in rags, unwashed, or in make-shift shelter are common refugee images. Men tend to only be included in the images and rhetoric of protected refugees if they are aesthetically feminized by carrying children and looking forlorn. For instance, the UNHCR homepage has three images representative of this stereotype: first, an image of two Black women and a baby in a rural setting, looking passively at the camera; second, a man with a turban and beard holding a baby outside of an UNHCR tent; and third, three young women of various ethnic backgrounds laughing, holding mobile phones, sitting at a table. This last image is under the rubric of 'Information for refugees, asylum-seekers and stateless persons.' Here we see the two conflicting images of the deferential (Figure 2 and Figure 3) and the entrepreneurial (Figure 4) playing out.

The notion that women and child refugees are more marketable than men as the 'faces of humanitarianism,' is politically and socially precluding men from the privilege of protection, unless these men are carers. An assumption is created that if they leave the realm of care, they enter the realm of criminality. However, when it comes to conflict zones, men are often the ones most at risk. As Kate Evans demonstrates in Figure 5, 'When home is a war zone, for men 'of fighting age,' the choice is conscription or extermination.'[18] And yet, the display of agency of these young men—moving from conflict to a safer place—often deems them 'bogus.'

Women and children, although more readily considered as deserving of protection, are equally confined to passivity if they wish to retain their privileges. The conditions placed aesthetically on refugees is then to be understood as a political move from protection to precariousness whereby precariousness 'is not simply an existential condition of individuals, but rather a social condition from which certain clear political demands and principles emerge.'[19]

---

17. See Christine Schwöbel-Patel, 'Spectacle in International Criminal Law: The Fundraising Image of Victimhood,' *London Review of International Law* 4/2 (2016).
18. Kate Evans, *Threads: From the Refugee Crisis* (London: Verso, 2017).
19. Butler, *Frames of War*, xxv.

Aesthetics and the Construction of the 'Grateful Refugee'

Information for refugees, asylum-seekers and stateless persons

Visit our Help site to find information about asylum procedures, your rights and duties and many more topics.

Figure 4: UNHCR website home page 3 (Screenshot 2023)

Figure 5: From the book 'Threads: From the Refugee Crisis' by Kate Evans. (image from: http://www.cartoonkate.co.uk/threads-the-calais-cartoon/)

In the spirit of transcending one's discipline and entering into productive discussions with other disciplines, we find it important to highlight that the problem-solving approach favoured by law is serving in particular the interests of lawyers. The problem-solving attitude to highlighting the enforceability of certain rights obscures the view to the root causes of conflict. Many international lawyers 'have the self-image of problem solvers and cool professional realists imbued with humanitarian motives.'[20] Responding to crises enhances an international lawyer's relevance and places them within a self-perceived progress narrative in which international law is a means to bring peace, security, human rights, and democracy.[21] We suggest that this desire for relevance, expressed through a problem-solving framing, can also do harm; by eliding the root causes of conflict and the lived experiences of those who are in the frame as 'the problem' and causing 'the crisis.'

Representations of Refugees in Design

Designers have also turned their attention to migration and the so-called refugee crisis. Design, particularly human-centred design, has historically focused on understanding and addressing people's unfulfilled wants and needs through creating new products and services.[22] Creative problem-solving plays an important role in this process as successful products often fulfil numerous design requirements such as feasibility, functionality, efficiency, comfort, ease of use, and aesthetic and emotional appeal. As consumer markets get increasingly saturated with more of the same products, terms such as competitive advantage, innovation, unique selling point, and market success dominate design discourse.

More recently, design has moved beyond being concerned solely with the creation of tangible outcomes. In addition to products and services, the methods of design have received increased attention as an alternative mode of business development and managing innovation.[23] According to 'design thinking' advocates Tim Brown and Roger Martin,

---

20. Anne Orford, 'Muscular Humanities: reading the narratives of the new interventions,' *European Journal of International Law* 10/4 (1999), 699.
21. Anne Orford, *Reading Humanitarian Intervention: Human Rights and the Use of Force in International Law* (Cambridge: Cambridge University Press, 2009).
22. N. F. M. Roozenburg and J. Eekels, *Product Design: Fundamentals and Methods*, vol. 2 (Chichester: Wiley-Blackwell, 1995).
23. Roger Martin, *The Design of Business: Why Design Thinking Is the Next Competitive Advantage* (Brighton, MASS: Harvard Business Review Press, 2010).

the way designers organize their processes implies an iterative process of inspiration, ideation, and implementation, integrating 'the needs of people, the possibilities of technology, and the requirements for business success.'[24]

Finally, design has become increasingly sensitive to societal challenges and the role the discipline can play in contributing to social welfare.[25] Some of the new and emerging approaches in this direction are DesignX,[26] which proposes guidelines to navigate the complexity of socio-technical challenges; Systemic Design,[27] which urges designers to think of societal challenges in a systemic manner and to employ transdisciplinary research; and Transition Design, which focuses on so-called 'wicked problems' such as climate change, loss of biodiversity, depletion of natural resources, and the widening gap between rich and poor.[28] The increasing interest in the social dimensions of design have also led to a new breed of 'social' designers who aspire to use their skills and training for societal impact. For instance, Richard van der Laken, the founder of the What Design Can Do (WDCD) platform, claimed that 'designers cannot just stand by and watch as the refugee crisis unfolds' and explained the aim of the 2016 WDCD Refugee Challenge as follows:

> what we hope to achieve is an improvement, however small, to the lives of millions of people. And to restore some of the self-esteem of people who are forced to wait years for asylum in foreign countries, without permission to work, sometimes without access to education, and often limited in their social lives.[29]

To better understand the problematics of this positioning, let us first examine design methods, i.e. how designers do what they do. When dealing

---

24. 'About IDEO,' IDEO, accessed 17 April 2023, http://www.ideo.com/about/.
25. Victor Margolin and Sylvia Margolin, 'A "Social Model" of Design: Issues of Practice and Research,' *Design Issues*, 18/4 (2002).
26. D. A. Norman and P. J. Stappers, 'DesignX: complex sociotechnical systems,' *She Ji: The Journal of Design, Economics, and Innovation*, 1/2 (2015).
27. M. van der Bijl-Brouwer and M. and Bridget Malcolm, 'Systemic Design Principles in Social Innovation: A Study of Expert Practices and Design Rationales,' *She Ji: The Journal of Design, Economics, and Innovation*, 6/3 (2020).
28. Terry Irwin, 'Transition design: A Proposal for a New Area of Design Practice, Study, and Research,' *Design and Culture* 7/2 (2015).
29. Richard van der Laken, 'Designers cannot just stand by and watch as the Refugee Crisis Unfolds,' *Dezeen*, 29 April 2016, accessed 17 April 2023, https://www.dezeen.com/2016/04/29/richard-van-der-laken-opinion-what-design-can-do-refugee-challenge-role-designers-humanitarian-design/.

with open and complex problems, designers typically work through iterative cycles of problem framing and solution finding.[30] As design problems are 'ill-structured' or 'wicked' (i.e. they can be interpreted in multiple possible ways giving rise to multiple appropriate solutions as opposed to a 'right' or a 'wrong' solution), a logical step in the design process is to elaborately define the lens through which design can tackle the problem at hand.[31] This is called problem framing. In Kees Dorst's definition, "Framing' is a term commonly used within design literature for the creation of a (novel) standpoint from which a problematic situation can be tackled.'[32] Problem framing is not a straightforward process as it involves reflective cycles of moving towards a solution and reflecting on the outcome guided by perception, appreciation, language and active manipulation of the design situation and its materials.[33] The framing of the design problem consequently defines the qualities of the design outcome as it forms a concrete starting point for where to channel one's skills and resources.

This is where the core of the challenge for design lies: to recognise that the way one 'frames' the design problem—i.e. what gets addressed as part of the problem, and what remains unaddressed—is a political choice guided by one's moral ideals or, as Donald Schön put it, by one's 'structures of belief, perception, and appreciation.' If, in this framing, too much emphasis is placed on market-oriented success criteria (e.g. creativity, innovation, user-friendliness) instead of society-oriented success criteria (e.g. equality, inclusivity, justice), proposed design solutions, while being original, useful, and feasible, may risk unintended consequences (e.g. reinforcing stereotypical images or serving capitalist agendas). We illustrate this point through two design examples borrowed from the website of the 2016 WDCD Refugee Challenge competition.

In Figure 6, 'Reframe Refugees' is one of the five shortlisted designs of the WDCD Refugee Challenge.[34] It is an online platform that enables

---

30. Kees Dorst and Nigel Cross, 'Creativity in the Design Process: Co-evolution of Problem–Solution,' *Design Studies* 22/5 (2001).
31. Herbert A. Simon, 'The Structure of Ill Structured Problems,' *Artificial Intelligence* 4/3–4 (1973).
32. Kees Dorst, 'The Core of 'Design Thinking' and its Application,' *Design Studies* 32/6 (2011), 525.
33. Donald A Schön, 'Designing as reflective conversation with the materials of a design situation,' *Knowledge-based Systems* 5/1 (1992).
34. 'Reframe Refugees: Digital Platform for New Storytelling,' What Design Can Do, accessed 17 April 2023, https://www.whatdesigncando.com/project/reframe-refugees/.

refugees to sell their own photographs to media companies to raise money for selected charities. The designers of 'Reframe Refugees' have placed self-representation and empowerment at the core of this design concept, which has attracted many positive comments from the public, including refugees themselves.

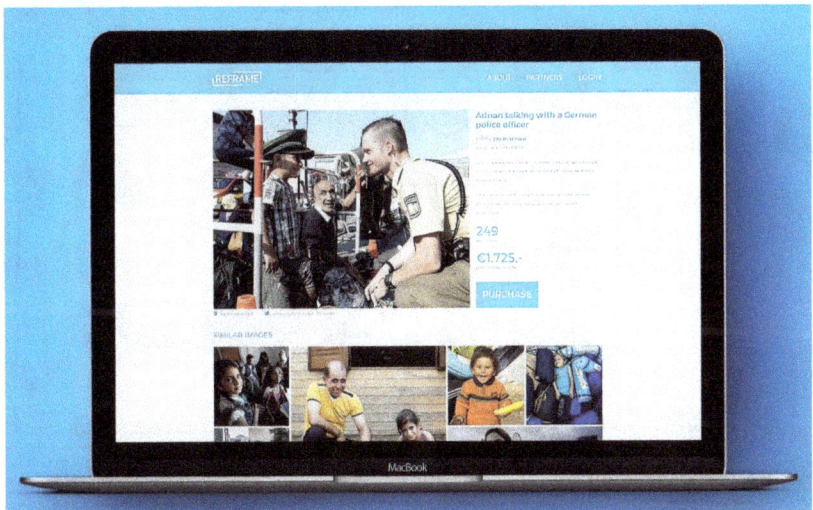

Figure 6: Reframe Refugees by Marie-Louise Diekema and Tim Olland (https://www.whatdesigncando.com/project/reframe-refugees/)

Although self-representation can be a powerful stance in combating stereotypical representations of refugees, the hidden assumption here seems to be that refugees are aware of and ready to challenge their own stereotypical representations in powerful media channels, which may or may not hold true for distressed communities. The expectation is that they would do this through creating a sub-culture that extends the much-criticised selfie culture in society. The concept also falls short of explaining how it would establish the necessary collaborations with non-governmental organizations and media channels for it to work.

Another example that raises critical questions is Mezzahome in Figure 8. Mezzahome is a structurally and experientially sound design solution that consists of a modular furniture system to be placed in abandoned buildings for shelter. It successfully envisions the challenges of not having shelter and offers the basic spatial necessities for everyday living. What grabs attention here are the form-giving choices, which suggest aesthetics of an IKEA-style home combined with the odd orientalized soft furnishings. This points to a superficial interpretation

Figure 7: Reframing the Refugee Experience

Figure 8: Mezzahome by Ke Tian Tay (https://www.dezeen. com/2016/06/25/what-design-can-do-refugee-challenge- 25-shortlisted-projects-improve-refugees-lives/)

of a culture and highlights the importance of real empathy-work in design, similar to the work of anthropologists. Moreover, implementing a design concept such as Mezzahome in real life can potentially neutralize the urgency and depth of the forced displacement issue. Designing a temporary, IKEA-inspired shelter for refugees is, in a way, agreeing to isolate refugees from host states and creating a new citizenship status, whilst attributing western values to their living conditions. In sum, critical examination of these design concepts, which were proposed to alleviate the hardships of being a refugee, reveal that they address the symptoms of the refugee crisis instead of its root causes. We do not wish to misinterpret these design concepts, neither do we claim that they are unaspiring.

To a certain extent, these design concepts do provide incremental improvements in the everyday life quality of a refugee. At the same time, some of the concepts raise critical questions, mask implicit assumptions, and often propagate stereotypical representations of refugees.

Together with critics such as Ruben Pater, an Amsterdam-based designer, researcher and the author of the book *Politics of Design*, we argue that 'treating the refugee crisis as a design problem is problematic.'[35] Pater's reluctance to position design as the 'solution' to such a complex societal issue deserves attention for several reasons. Addressing the refugee crisis through design requires structural thinking and collaboration among governments, non-profit organisations, experts across a variety of disciplines, and the migrants themselves. As Pater emphasizes: 'design may be able to come up with clever products or enlightening ideas, but only governments and NGOs can provide refugees with the resources, infrastructure, and laws that are needed in the long run.'[36]

For design to have a meaningful contribution in the social realm, it must move away from problem-solving paradigms prevalent in technical disciplines and incorporate a humanities-oriented thinking—more specifically, political, and ethical theory—as an explicit ingredient in its theory and methodologies. With this theoretical renovation will come elements of critique that will equip designers with at least a 'beginners' mindset to think and operate outside of market structures.

---

35. Ruben Pater, 'Treating the refugee crisis as a design problem is problematic,' *Dezeen*, 21 April 2016, accessed 17 April 2023, https://www.dezeen.com/2016/04/21/ruben-pater-opinion-what-design-can-do-refugee-crisis-problematic-design/.
36. Pater, 'Treating the refugee crisis.'

The Dilemma of the 'Grateful Refugee'

As introduced above, we have observed that both lawyers and designers are aesthetically framing the debate on the refugee crisis through the construction and imagination of a certain *type* of refugee. Importantly, this is not a happenstance, or a strange coincidence of disciplinary overlap. Rather, this is because of the neoliberal structures in which the disciplines operate. Framing refugees as 'grateful refugees,' and in turn letting this frame do the work of obscuring structural harm, is a legal-material technology employed in the neoliberal order. The stereotype of the 'grateful refugee,' framed as needing to be both deferential and entrepreneurial, is the corresponding dilemma to what has been referred to as 'Schrödinger's immigrant' who is 'simultaneously stealing your job and too lazy to work' (Figure 9), epitomizing the *un*grateful refugee. The ungrateful refugee exercises agency through labour and making demands on state resources. These two features are connected to anti-immigrant and anti-refugee sentiments and were circulated as a meme by those less hostile to immigrants in an effort to demonstrate the dilemma in which immigrants find themselves.

Figure 9: Schrödinger's immigrant meme

Exerting agency in the public sphere means to participate in public life. Public life comes with certain public assurances; depending on the governance form, some more or fewer assurances are provided. Examples of this are the guarantee of basic rights such as the right to assembly or the provision of welfare or social support. To participate in public life also means to participate in the labour force, and generally to be able to claim certain benefits from this productivity, guaranteed by the state. Refugees, however, are mostly not permitted to participate in public life. They remain placed in the space of emergency which is deemed to exclude agency. Instead, they are dependent on the confusing and often dysfunctional network of governmental and non-governmental support. In addition, they are deemed not yet to have accumulated sufficient trust for the reciprocal relationship of public life. Refugees in the public sphere are expected to remain passive; such passivity here means to observe the obligations but not reap any benefits from public life. Refugees are expected to strictly observe the laws, norms, and customs, even the ones which discriminate against them, whilst making no claims on state provision. The mere *promise* of future public benefits (of any kind) is regarded as an act of benevolence from the side of the state.

The deferential individual wanting to gain or maintain refugee status is moreover faced with a critical dilemma: ideal refugees are not only expected to be deferential and therefore passive, but they are also expected to demonstrate agency through entrepreneurship. Whilst being deferential to the receiving state, the refugee is expected to improve their situation, ideally through contributing to the market economy without taking up employment which could be reserved for a citizen-worker. Refugees must therefore be economically active (inventive) in previously unchartered market territories. Ideally, this type of new business is the business of refugees problem-solving for themselves, precluding the need of any form of state (public) involvement. This idea of self-maximising human capital is key to the making of neoliberal subjectivity. Crucially, exerting agency exclusively in the private sphere means that the refugee bears the risks of failure themselves.

Such expectations of entrepreneurship must be understood in the context of the predominant economic model of neoliberal capitalism. Here, the state's welfare provisions are wound back in favour of competitive market models which allow for the movement of capital, particularly across borders. The state steps in mostly to protect capital movements, not human movements. Entrepreneurship is allowed to flourish as an individualized form of risk which may wield rewards for the market but requires no or few guarantees from the side of the state. Entrepreneurs themselves tend to focus on problem-solving industries.

Entrepreneurial refugees, who only exert agency in the private sphere, are depoliticised and often reimagined as 'stakeholders' rather than political subjects.³⁷ Structural questions are accordingly blended out. Such blending out is exemplified in the images of the UNHCR (Figures 2 and 3), which excludes from the frame visual markers of origin or destination. Mostly, the displaced are always already in the borderlands: in a refugee camp, on a boat, on the move with their few possessions. Such visual placing in a space of flux blends out questions pertaining to the socio-economic conditions of their origin country or the root causes (colonial or post-colonial) of the conflict they may have escaped. Blending out prevents furthermore enquiries into resource conflicts between states and corporations, enquiries into equitable redistribution of resource gains, the racialized order of those most affected by climate catastrophe, or current exploitative global value chains. The entrepreneurial refugee therefore also acts out of gratitude: adding to the economy without demanding from it, which stems from the idea of giving something back. The attitude of 'gratitude.' i.e. deference and entrepreneurialism, has moreover been embodied and naturalized by refugees, as exemplified in the following quotation by Nayeri, who labelled herself the 'ungrateful refugee':

> afraid for my future, I decided that everyone was right: if I failed to stir up in myself enough gratefulness, or if I failed to properly display it, I would lose all that I had gained, this western freedom, the promise of secular schools and uncensored books.³⁸

Gratitude of refugees towards the host state is a recurring theme in the (conservative-corporate) media. The media has popularized this idea and aesthetic and has helped legitimize the current order through popular assent. However, the dilemma of the 'deferential and entrepreneurial' grateful refugee has shifting goalposts, often depending on the level of anti-immigrant sentiment in receiving states. As Lisa Malkki observes, the constructed notion of a refugee adds up to 'an ideal figure of which any actual refugees were always imperfect instantiations,'³⁹ The level of anti-immigrant sentiment is itself a phenomenon which arguably comes with feelings of having been overlooked in the rapid pace of globalisation in its neoliberal instantiation.

---

37. Guy S Goodwin-Gill, 'The Dynamic of International Refugee Law,' *International Journal of Refugee Law* 25/4 (2013), 651–666.
38. Nayeri, 'The Ungrateful Refugee.'
39. Lisa Malkki, 'Speechless Emissaries: Refugees, Humanitarianism, and Dehistoricization,' *Cultural Anthropology* 11/3 (1996), 337–404, 385.

The sites of framing, then, are to be found at an institutional level as well as at the level of the cultivation and maintenance of popular assent. When it comes to refugees, the framing capacity refers to the construction of delimitations in the experiential and discursive fields regarding 'whose life *is* a life,' as Butler observes, 'and whose life is effectively transformed into an instrument, a target, or a number, or is effaced with only a trace remaining or none at all.'[40]

Figure 10: *The Deferential and Entrepreneurial Refugee*

Framing refugees in this narrow and myopic way obscures the frequent complicity of receiving states in the plight of refugees. Both Syria and Libya are origin states of refugees; both are countries in which Western military intervention has occurred, creating dire prospects for those who dare to stay.

Contesting the Figure of the 'Grateful Refugee'

Butler suggests that critical analysis helps us 'to learn to see the frame that blinds us to what we see.'[41] An attention to the framing capacities

---

40. Butler, *Frames of War*, ix, x.
41. Butler, *Frames of War*, 100.

of law and design therefore includes an opening towards the political, economic, historical, ecological, cultural, and social root causes of the issues dealt with. In design, this is commonly an iterative process composed of two main steps: the identification of the problem space through asking questions (i.e., problem framing) and the exploration of the solution space through generating preliminary design ideas (i.e., solution finding). Traditionally, the evolution of the problem and solution go hand in hand in design processes, where the development of solutions adds to the understanding of the problem until 'the feeling of having grasped the core of the problem' is reached.[42] As critique is about raising questions, the interest in critical design practices lies with *lingering* in the problem space. The goal here is to approach the problem from interdisciplinary perspectives and find alternative ways of framing the problem through critical thinking and reflective questioning (e.g., does the problem involve capitalist agendas and power struggles? Am I interpreting this problem through the lens of western values?). These questions are likely to evoke numerous dilemmas, which may generate discomfort. As suggested by Kees Dorst and Nigel Cross, the feeling of grasping the core of the problem may in fact never be achieved.[43] As a result, lingering in the problem space can be characterised by finding comfort in the discomfort of surfacing dilemmas fuelled by critical thinking, reflection, and interdisciplinary collaboration. In law, this lingering in the problem space is occupied by long-standing critical legal studies debates, postcolonial, decolonial, gender, queer, Marxist, and anarchist studies, as well as other scholarly and activist traditions on the Left.

A number of design approaches, such as Critical and Speculative Design or Adversarial Design, place critique and critical problem framing (vs. creative problem-solving) at the centre of their activities.[44] These approaches, despite important nuances in their practices, converge at the main aim of raising questions and stimulating critical reflection and debate among designers and users alike, about the often implicit

---

42. Kees Dorst and Nigel Cross, 'Creativity in the design process: Co-evolution of problem–solution,' *Design Studies*, 22/5 (2001), 425–437.
43. Dorst and Cross, 'Creativity.'
44. Anthony Dunne and Fiona Raby, Speculative everything: design, fiction, and social dreaming (MIT press, 2013)
Carl DiSalvo, Adversarial Design (MIT Press, 2015).

values and assumptions that drive the agenda of existing design practices.[45] Much like critical law scholars, their tools act as 'inward-looking' mechanisms that question and critique the state of existing design practices. A lingering in the problem space that is open to inter- and trans-disciplinarity could draw attention to some of the frames which commonly blind us. We might take inspiration from movements that have aimed to transcend disciplines altogether in favour of creating broader debates focusing on structural issues.[46] From our experience, critical designers and critics of law share a common purpose in raising discussion and contesting the ethical and legal frameworks that provide or deny refugees agency and protection.

Dilemmas and contradictions are useful starting points for creative thinking as they trigger the imagination to envision novel scenarios of resolving or accepting the respective dilemma or contradiction.[47] In law, these are often referred to as the 'hard cases' in which certain important societal values are weighed against each other. When faced with dilemmas, the most intuitive move is to resolve the dilemma through searching for solutions that would remedy the conflicting motives or values that underlie the dilemma or contradiction. However, dilemmas and contradictions are situated phenomena influenced—and even imposed—by socio-cultural factors or historical-material circumstances.[48] When dilemmas and contradictions are recognized as socially and materially constructed phenomena, a critical design or a critical legal move would be to expose the factors underlying this construction (here, for example, neoliberal subjectivity). This can consequently serve to raise awareness about the lack of truthful or realistic representations of refugees and the unease such truthful representations may bring. It also shifts the lens away from representation on an individual level and shifts the view to representations of structural violence.

---

45. Matthew Malpass. *Critical Design in Context: History, Theory, and Practices* (London: Bloomsbury Publishing, 2017).
46. We might take some inspiration from the so-called Situationist International movement of the late 1950s, early 1960s, which wanted to transcend disciplines and create provocative 'situations' in which the current ideology became apparent and turned on itself (what they termed *détournement*). Frances Stracey, Constructed Situations: A New History of the Situationist International (London: Pluto Press, 2014).
47. Deger Ozkaramanli, 'Me against myself: Addressing personal dilemmas through design' (PhD thesis, Delft University of Technology, 2017).
48. Michael Billig, et al., *Ideological Dilemmas: A Social Psychology of Everyday Thinking* (London: Sage Publications, 1988).

*Figure 11: Photo of 25m^2 Syria Project.
https://www.dezeen.com/2016/11/08/ikea-red-cross-
design-syrian-apartment-replica-flagship-store-norway-pol/*

Re-framing the Problem Space

A possible example of a critical design project that demonstrates 'lingering in the problem space' is the joint initiative between the Red Cross, Norway and IKEA. A replica of a Syrian home was designed in store to create a stark contrast between a cosy idea of a Western house and a house affected by the horrors of war. Maja Folgero of the campaign stated in an interview with the *Independent*: 'placing a Syrian home next to all the Scandinavian homes was obviously a brave move from the warehouse, but it made it clearer than any TV commercial how crucial it is to be confronted with some of these questions in a consumerist setting.'[49]

Lingering in the problem space does not preclude problem-solving. An example of problem-solving that includes a structural critique can be seen in Kat Jungnickel's work on the history of women's cycle wear

---

49. 'Ikea builds Syrian home replica in store to show horrors of war,' *The Independent*, 10 November 2016, accessed 17 April 2023, https://www.independent.co.uk/news/world/middle-east/ikea-builds-syrian-home-replica-in-store-to-show-horrors-of-war-a7409896.html.

in relation to questions of women's mobility and public space in late nineteenth century Britain.[50] In the 1890s, cycling became popular with the middle and upper classes in Britain. However, there were social, political, and material challenges for women. Apart from bicycles being designed for the male frame, the restrictive and demure clothing of these Victorian women prevented them from cycling. Jungnickel discovered sewing patterns from the 1890s in which women decided to overcome the restrictions of their mobility through ingenious designs. One of these sewing patterns includes a pulley system at the front and back of the skirt, which enables easier cycling, even if it did expose the women's bloomers (Figure 12).

Figure 12: Sewing Pattern for Pulley Cycling Skirt (Jungnickel, Bikes and Bloomers)

Women designers were also part of wider discussions about the dress reform at the time known as the rational dress movement, an early feminist movement in the US and Britain. This movement was sparked by (mostly working) women who proposed, designed, and wore more comfortable and practical clothing and was closely connected to debates on women's suffrage. This type of problem-solving is interesting for this project as it places an emphasis on enabling mobility through design and technology while foregrounding agency in the public sphere.

---

50. Kat Jungnickel, *Bikes and Bloomers* (London: Goldsmiths Press, 2020).

Conclusion

We have considered how representations of the refugee, and the so-called refugee crisis, have been constructed in design and law. Representations of refugees are not only constructed to reflect the world in which we live, they are also ordering of the world. We have relied on Butler's concept of 'framing' to make this point with regards to legal-material technologies. The concept of framing appealed to us because it is a means of envisioning a phenomenon present in both our disciplines. The narrowing of the frame, according in particular to pressures of a type of market-oriented thinking, has revealed a narrow definition of a 'grateful refugee' who is placed in the dilemma of being expected to at once be deferential and entrepreneurial.

6

International Trials and Justice for Victims

A VIEW FROM PRACTICE

Ruby Mae Axelson and Wayne Jordash

Those who make their living in the international courts will often and loudly claim to be acting on behalf of the 'victims.' The notion of victims in need of justice is seen as the very foundation upon which international criminal justice has been built. This collective—faceless and amorphous though it is—has come to represent all that is true and righteous in international criminal justice.

'Victims' were ostensibly invoked in the UN Security Council resolutions leading to the establishment of the UN-sponsored tribunals that speak of the need to end impunity for atrocity crimes and to restore peace.[1] The 'victims' are presented in the annual reports to the UN Security Council as a measure of the tribunals' success, proclaiming that trials have been completed and justice delivered.[2] Similarly, the Preamble to the Rome Statute of the International Criminal Court (Rome Statute) invokes the 'children, women and men' who have 'been victims of unimaginable atrocities that deeply shock the conscience of humanity.'[3]

---

1. UN Security Council, Resolution 827 (1993), UN Doc. S/RES/827 (1993); UN Security Council, Resolution 955 (1994), UN Doc. S/RES/955 (1994); UN Security Council, Resolution 1315 (2000), UN Doc. S/RES/1315 (2000); UN General Assembly, Resolution 57/228, UN Doc. A/RES/57/228 (2003).
2. See Seventh Annual Report of the International Residual Mechanism for Criminal Tribunals, UN Doc. A/74/267–S/2019/622 (2019); Twelfth Annual Report of the International Tribunal for the Former Yugoslavia, UN Doc. A/60/267 – S/2005/532 (2005); Tenth Annual Report of the International Tribunal for the Former Yugoslavia, UN Doc. A/58/297 – S/2003/829 (2003); Sixth Annual Report of the International Tribunal for the Former Yugoslavia, UN Doc. A/54/187 – S/1999/846 (1999).
3. Rome Statute of the International Criminal Court (last amended 2010) (adopted

In just under thirty years, modern international criminal law has created a system of international justice that confidently proclaims to address the needs of victims. At its most reductive, international trials have equated the convictions of senior political or civilian leaders and the passing of lengthy prison sentences with accountability and justice for victims. So the mantra goes: without convictions, there can be no justice and without justice, there can be no peace.

And yet, there remains a dissonance between the way in which victims are visualized and represented by stakeholders in the international justice system and the stereotyping, marginalization, and disempowerment that is often experienced by victims during and as a consequence of international trials. This dissonance is certainly visible in the evolution of the various means by which the International Criminal Court (ICC) attempts to accommodate or serve victims, including its system of participation and reparations for victims, which increasingly appear unable to meet victims' expectations of justice within the structural constraints of individual criminal responsibility.

This dissonance raises the question whether the justice delivered in international criminal trials is the justice required or wanted by victims. Relatedly, whether international criminal law upholds a specific representation of 'the victim' and their needs merely to justify their chosen action in the international justice sphere? More specifically, it raises the question whether the rapid monopolization of international criminal justice since the 1990s has sought to standardise the Western-centric notion of criminal law and retribution (apparently, on behalf of victims) to the detriment of other more desirable forms of justice. This includes those more focused on restoration or transformation of a victim's lived experience. Can the measures 'welded' onto international criminal law—including victim participation and victim representation—truly live up to the proclaimed aim of embedding the voices and reflecting the needs of victims, or do they merely act to reproduce the hegemony of a chosen form of criminal trial?

Part one of this chapter considers how international criminal justice has represented the role of victims in international trials. This section examines how the role assigned to 'the victims' as the *raison d'être* of international criminal justice simultaneously works to uphold the authority of international criminal trials by shielding courts and tribunals from justified criticism and to remove their individuality

---

17 July 1998, entered into force 1 July 2002) 2187 UNTS 38544 (Rome Statute), Preamble.

and ability to demand forms of justice that accord to their needs. Part two examines more closely whether the systems of victim participation and reparations at the ICC have led to a transformation of the role of victims in international criminal justice. Whilst the introduction of these mechanisms has been hailed as a positive step towards more meaningful justice for victims, this chapter concludes that, while wedded to the strictures of retributive criminal trials, the voices and interests of victims remain on the periphery of international criminal trials. Only a limited opportunity exists for the international community to look beyond the assumed orthodoxies of individual criminal responsibility to what justice for victims might truly look like.

The Role and Representation of Victims in International Criminal Law

Positioned as the *raison d'être* of international criminal justice, victims are represented as an almost mythical collective on whose behalf justice is fought for and delivered through international criminal trials. The international community encourages a view of international justice as the fortress inside of which victims can seek protection, as the last bulwark against the abandonment of a cruel and heartless world. We are told it is only through international criminal trials that victims of atrocity crimes can receive justice and sustainable peace can be achieved.

Prosecutions that have occurred in the international sphere are frequently initiated 'on behalf of' or 'for the benefit' of victims,[4] and positioned as a means to end the ravages of war. Accordingly, victims play a vital role in both the rhetoric and the authority of international criminal trials,[5] by 'giving purpose to the *entire* machinery of international criminal justice.'[6]

On the most grandiose of occasions, prosecutors and judges will invoke religious rhetoric, marking the victim as holy and the accused as the embodiment of evil that may only be stopped through the force of international criminal law and the holy retribution of convictions

---

4. Mariana Pena and Gaelle Carayon, 'Is the ICC Making the Most of Victim Participation?,' *The International Journal of Transitional Justice* 7/3 (2013), 518.
5. Peter Dixon and Chris Tenove, 'International Criminal Justice as a Transnational Field: Rules, Authority and Victims,' *The International Journal of Transitional Justice* 7 (2013), 408.
6. Sara Kendall and Sarah Nouwen, 'Representational Practices at the International Criminal Court: The Gap between Juridified and Abstract Victimhood,' *Law and Contemporary Problems* 76 (2014), 253.

and sentences. This was demonstrated in the dissenting opinion of Judges Gelaga King and Kambada at the Special Court for Sierra Leone (SCSL), in which they concluded the AFRC/RUF joint criminal enterprise (JCE) continued to exist until at least February 1999. After citing to evidence of civilian amputations, the Judges found it necessary to reflect on the following words:

> Blessed is the man that walketh not in the counsel of the ungodly, nor standeth in the way of sinners, nor sitteth in the seat of the scornful. But his delight is in the law of the Lord; and in his law doth he meditate day and night. And he shall be like a tree planted by the rivers of water, that bringeth forth his fruit in due season; his leaf also shall not whither; and whatsoever he doeth shall prosper. The ungodly are not so: but are like the chaff which the wind driveth away…For the Lord knoweth the way of the righteous: but the way of the ungodly shall perish.[7]

Such positioning of 'the victims' as an abstract entity, for whose benefit justice is rendered, enables courts and tribunals to shield themselves from criticism. Prosecutors invoke justice for victims after losing cases, using them to excuse poor results or legitimate acquittals, or to place undue and unfair pressure on the institutions to overturn acquittals on appeal.

For example, after Momcilo Perišić was acquitted by the International Criminal Tribunal for the former Yugoslavia (ICTY) Appeals Chamber, the Prosecutor invoked the power of victimhood to complain about the result, stating that 'the erroneous reversal of Mr Perišić's lawful convictions and twenty-seven year sentence must be corrected to redress the grave injustice caused to the tens of thousands of men, women, and children killed or injured in Sarajevo and Srebrenica and to their families.'[8] Similarly, in the Appeal Hearings in the Stanišić and Simatović case at the ICTY, the Prosecution claimed that 'the Chamber failed to deliver the justice that was the aim of this retrial, to the international community and, most importantly, to the victims.'[9] In 2023, despite being twice acquitted of participation

---

7. *Prosecutor v. Sesay et. al.* (Dissenting Opinion of Justice Gelaga King and Justice Jon Kamanda on Prosecution's First Ground of Appeal (Appeal Judgment)) SCSL-04-15-A (26 October 2009), para. 18, citing The Holy Bible, Psalm 1.
8. 'Statement of Prosecutor Serge Brammertz in relation to the motion for reconsideration submitted by the Prosecution in the Perišić case,' ICTY, 3 February 2014, accessed 1 June 2023, http://www.icty.org/en/press/statement-prosecutor-serge-brammertz-relation-motion-reconsideration-submitted-prosecution.
9. 'Stanišić & Simatović (MICT-15-96 A) - Appeals hearing - 25 January 2023

in a JCE by two Trial Chambers over a twenty year process, the second Appeals Chamber claimed to have 'rectified' previous mistakes and imposed a JCE conviction.[10] Justice was now apparently done. According to Prosecutor Serge Brammertz, the trial record 'demonstrates that the international community, when united, can deliver justice to the victims and hold the most senior perpetrators responsible for their crimes.'[11] Notwithstanding that the trial process lasted for a quarter of the accused's lives and that Appeals Chambers is not a trier of fact, it was sufficient that the Court had shown victims could receive the 'justice' that is seemingly inherent in any conviction.

Moreover, as the ICC struggles through its recurring crisis of legitimacy—much of it caused by its selectivity and failure to ensure effective investigations and prosecutions—it is common to hear the Prosecutors defend their record with plaintive declarations that they are acting on behalf of victims. In response to the growing claim that the ICC was selectively targeting the African continent, the previous Chief Prosecutor, Fatou Bensouda, stated:

> If we are thinking about the victims of these crimes, the victims of these atrocities who are also vulnerable African victims, then we would not think about targeting Africans. We will be thinking about, working for and supporting the victims of these crimes.[12]

Criticism surrounding selective justice continues to plague the ICC, despite these proclamations on victimhood. Investigations into war

---

(3/3),' *YouTube*, 25 January 2023, accessed 1 June 2023, https://www.youtube.com/watch?v=XYNum-3re9E&ab_channel=IRMCT.

10. *Prosecutor v Stanišić & Simatović* (Appeal Judgment) MICT-15-96 A (31 May 2023), para. 419–512.

11. 'Demonstrates that the international community, when united, can deliver justice to the victims and hold the most senior perpetrators responsible for their crimes. Today, we should remember the victims and survivors. And we should recognize the courage of the witnesses who participated in this and other trials. This marks the final ICTY case. However, there are still thousands of war crimes suspects throughout the countries of the former Yugoslavia who remain to be prosecuted. We will continue our intensive efforts to provide support and assistance to national counterparts to ensure that more justice is achieved for more victims.' at 'The IRMCT Office of the Prosecutor (OTP) takes note of today's appeal judgment in the Stanišić and Simatović case,' *IRMCT*, 21 May 2023, accessed 1 June 2023, https://www.irmct.org/en/news/irmct-office-prosecutor-otp-takes-note-todays-appeal-judgment-stanisic-and-simatovic-case.

12. Peter Clottey, 'ICC Prosecutor Hails US International Justice Role,' *VOA News*, 4 April 2013, accessed 1 June 2023, https://www.voanews.com/a/icc-prosecutor-hails-us-international-justice-role/1635160.html.

crimes committed in Afghanistan by the United States and Afghan National Security Forces were deprioritised in favour of crimes allegedly committed by the Taliban and the Islamic State-Khorasan Province (IS-K) due to 'limited resources,'[13] while investigations in Palestine[14] and Nigeria[15] amongst others appear to languish. In relation to Palestine, the ICC Prosecutor assures us of his determination to 'meet our shared aspiration to advance justice for all victims,'[16] and yet the Palestine investigation remains not only the least funded investigation in 2023 but delayed to the point of statis.[17] It seems not all victims (or accused) are treated equally. But when it comes to rhetorically invoking abstract victims, the 'rights of victims' are called upon to justify delays, even whilst the delays are the predictable result of funding decisions.

In stark contrast to these legitimacy crises, the situation in Ukraine has been hailed as inducing a 'revitalization of international criminal justice.'[18] Certainly, the atrocities in Ukraine have led to a rapid response rarely seen in the international justice community. After a unique multilateral referral of the Situation in Ukraine to the ICC

---

13. 'Statement of the Prosecutor of the International Criminal Court, Karim A. A. Khan QC, following the application for an expedited order under article 18(2) seeking authorization to resume investigations in the Situation in Afghanistan,' *International Criminal Court*, 27 September 2021, accessed 1 June 2023, https://www.icc-cpi.int/news/statement-prosecutor-international-criminal-court-karim-khan-qc-following-application.
14. On 2 March 2021, the Prosecutor announced the opening of the investigation into the Situation in the State of Palestine. No warrants of arrest have been issued to date: 'State of Palestine,' International Criminal Court, accessed 11 July 2023, https://www.icc-cpi.int/palestine.
15. On 11 December 2020, the Prosecutor announced the completion of the preliminary examination of the situation in Nigeria, having concluded there was a reasonable basis to believe that war crimes and crimes against humanity were committed. To date, the Prosecution has not requested authorization from the Pre-Trial Chamber to open an investigation: 'Preliminary Examination Nigeria,' International Criminal Court, accessed 11 July 2023, https://www.icc-cpi.int/nigeria.
16. ICC Office of the Prosecutor, 'Letter to Special Procedures mandate-holders United Nations Human Rights Special Procedures in Response to Joint Letter,' *OHCHR*, 12 May 2023, accessed 1 June 2023, https://www.ohchr.org/sites/default/files/documents/issues/culturalrights/activities/CPI-answer-State-Palestine-12May2023.pdf.
17. ICC Assembly of State Parties, 'Proposed Programme Budget for 2023 of the International Criminal Court' ICC-ASP/21/10 (19 August 2022), Annex XII, accessed 11 July 2023, https://asp.icc-cpi.int/sites/asp/files/2022-08/ICC-ASP-21-10-ENG.pdf.
18. Sergey Vasiliev, 'Watershed Moment or Same Old? Ukraine and the Future of International Criminal Justice,' *Journal of International Criminal Justice* 20/4 (2022), accessed 1 June 2023, https://academic.oup.com/jicj/article/20/4/893/6827886#389803402.

Prosecutor by 43 States,[19] an investigation was speedily opened on 2 March 2022. While many other ICC investigations seem to move forward at glacial pace, on 17 March 2023 the first warrants of arrest were issued against the Russian President, Vladimir Putin, and the Commissioner for Children's Rights in the Office of the President of the Russian Federation, Maria Alekseyevna.[20] Moreover, States Parties have infused the ICC Prosecutor's Office with additional 'voluntary' funds 'earmarked' specifically for Ukraine.[21] In 2023, Ukraine will receive over four and half times Palestine's allocated funds and over double those allocated to the long awaited Afghanistan Situation.[22]

While the spectre of selectivity is hardly a new concern, the Ukrainian anomaly (if that is what it is) has thrown old problems into sharp relief. Why are some victims treated as more deserving of justice than others? And why, despite its mandate, do 'only rebels, the vanquished and defeated, rogue States and scapegoats appear to be in the crosshairs of international criminal justice?'[23] Unable, or perhaps unwilling, to grapple with such pivotal questions, international prosecutors instead bolster their legitimacy with promises to 'show the victims and survivors from Kyiv to Cox's Bazar, from Kharkiv to Khartoum, international justice is on their side.'[24] Undoubtedly justice is on the side of some victims, but equally

---

19. See 'Ukraine,' International Criminal Court, accessed 11 July 2023, https://www.icc-cpi.int/situations/ukraine.
20. 'Situation in Ukraine: ICC judges issue arrest warrants against Vladimir Vladimirovich Putin and Maria Alekseyevna Lvova-Belova,' *International Criminal Court*, 17 March 2023, accessed 1 June 2023, https://www.icc-cpi.int/news/situation-ukraine-icc-judges-issue-arrest-warrants-against-vladimir-vladimirovich-putin-and.
21. 'The ICC at 20: Double standards have no place in international justice,' *Amnesty International*, 1 July 2022, accessed 1 June 2023, https://www.amnesty.org/en/latest/news/2022/07/the-icc-at-20-double-standards-have-no-place-in-international-justice/.
22. ICC Assembly of State Parties, 'Proposed Programme Budget for 2023 of the International Criminal Court' ICC-ASP/21/10 (19 August 2022), Annex XII, Budget allocation per active investigation in Major Programme II (in thousands of euros): Afghanistan (EUR 1,791.7); Palestine (EUR 944.1); Ukraine (EUR 4,449.8), accessed 11 July 2023, https://asp.icc-cpi.int/sites/asp/files/2022-08/ICC-ASP-21-10-ENG.pdf.
23. Morten Bergsmo, Mark Klamberg, Kjersti Lohne and Christopher B. Mahony eds., *Power in International Criminal Justice* (Brussels: Torkel Opsahl Academic EPublisher, 2020), accessed 1 June 2023, https://www.legal-tools.org/doc/ankji8/pdf, 624.
24. ICC Office of the Prosecutor, 'Prosecutor Karim A. A. Khan KC addressed a UN meeting on the Situation in Ukraine, The Hague,' *Youtube*, 22 February 2023, accessed 1 June 2023, https://www.youtube.com/watch?v=IPTzzDjCE6Y.

the practice of the ICC has left the 'promise of 'justice for all' unfulfilled.'[25]

Instead of equality and equity for all, the representation of victims in international criminal justice moreover tends to remove a victim's individuality, transforming them into a collective which in turn becomes a homogenous entity on whose behalf the international system is entitled to speak.[26] Depicting 'victims' as a legitimising tool of the international criminal courts and tribunals provides the international community with the ability or cover to act (or not act) whilst painting the victims as helpless and in need of salvation, reinforcing not just their (perceived) passivity but also their dependence upon those deemed agents of change.[27]

International legal scholar Martti Koskenniemi, in his habitual flourish, has observed that the 'victim' is considered 'worthy of humanitarian support as long as he remains a helpless victim – but turns into a danger the moment he seeks to liberate himself.'[28] Indeed, conceiving of the 'victims' as an amorphous and helpless group is an effective tool: it 'suppresses or deprioritises other understandings of the victim as demanding, for example, compensation, or political participation, or non-retributive measures.'[29] In contrast to the *raison d'etre* claim, namely that international criminal tribunals exist to provide justice for victims, victims arguably remain on the periphery of modern international criminal law *in practice*. As Peter Dixon and Chris Tenove suggest, enduring tensions between victims and international criminal justice exist because victims are central to the authority of international criminal justice, but the construction of international criminal justice inhibits their participation and ability to mobilise that authority themselves.[30]

Of course, it is well known that in international criminal law the more the system reflects the adversarial system, the more the role of victims is limited to participation only as a witness. At the ad hoc tribunals,

---

25. Vasiliev, 'Watershed Moment or Same Old?.'
26. Kendall and Nouwen, 'Representational Practices at the International Criminal Court,' 254.
27. Kendall and Nouwen, 'Representational Practices at the International Criminal Court,' 256.
28. Martti Koskenniemi, 'The Lady Doth Protest Too Much': Kosovo, and the Turn to Ethics in International Law,' *Modern Law Review* 65/2 (2002), 173–174.
29. Laurel E. Fletcher, 'Refracted Justice: The Imagined Victims and the International Criminal Court,' in *Contested Justice: The Politics and Practice of the International Criminal Court Interventions*, ed. Kendall de Vos (Cambridge: Cambridge University Press, 2014), 305–306.
30. Dixon and Tenove, 'International criminal Justice as a transnational field,' 411.

this was the limit of their participatory role. Victims had no right to make submissions let alone obtain reparations for any harm done. Naturally, this led to criticisms of a failure to give victims any independent voice during the proceedings, where their own interests, and not only those they were called to serve, could be addressed.[31] At worst, this kind of incongruity led to gross appropriation and ultimately abuse.

The first months of proceedings before the SCSL exemplify this appropriation and abuse. In an attempt to garner international interest for the forthcoming Revolutionary United Front Trial, the SCSL Prosecution handpicked 'impact witnesses' to show the gathered media the 'evil' of the accused and the virtue of their own 'holy' mission. It was by no means for the purpose of providing these victims with a chance to tell their stories in a supportive environment, to seek closure or reparation (or even to serve some peripheral forensic purpose). Instead, they were called to testify merely to display their tragic circumstances: a mere catwalk of the most egregious crimes and grotesque injuries for those attending the SCSL amphitheatre to boo and hiss at the accused as in Roman days of old.

Whilst this was of course an extreme example, the fact that it could be sanctioned as late as 2004 tells its own eloquent tale of the role of victims in international criminal justice and their consequential disappointment and frustration with international justice as a whole.[32] No wonder many victims and affected populations (purportedly served by the ICTR, ICTY and SCSL) considered the tribunals at best as irrelevant, and at worst as 'a wasteful parody of justice.'[33]

A Closer Look at Victims at the ICC: Transformation or Business as Usual?

Has the ICC, with its undoubtedly greater will to consider victims' concerns and to recognise the importance of more their meaningful involvement in international trials,[34] contributed to a meaningful change for victims of mass atrocity? Indeed, the Rome Statute heralded a new era in international criminal justice and, for the first time, included provisions for the participation and reparation of victims, breaking

---

31. Pena and Carayon, 'Is the ICC Making the Most of Victim Participation?,' 521.
32. Pena and Carayon, 'Is the ICC Making the Most of Victim Participation?,' 521.
33. Godfrey M. Musila, *Rethinking International Criminal Law: Restorative Justice and the Rights of Victims in the International Criminal Court* (Saarbrücken: Lap Lambert, 2010).
34. Pena and Carayon, 'Is the ICC Making the Most of Victim Participation?,' 519.

the mould of purely retributive justice seen in the ad hoc tribunals. However, questions remain as to whether these provisions have been able to produce a system of justice in tune with the needs of victims that provides them with real agency.

Victim Participation

The introduction of victim participation in international criminal proceedings through Article 68(3) of the Rome Statute—which allows for the 'views and concerns' of victims 'to be presented and considered at stages of the proceedings determined to be appropriate by the Court'[35]—flows from increased awareness that judgments and prosecutions per se are not sufficient to redress victims' suffering.[36] What is more, instead of having a solely punitive objective, justice should be restorative and participation in the justice process can be an important factor in victims' healing and rehabilitation.[37] The introduction of direct participation of victims in proceedings has in general been hailed as a progressive step for international criminal justice.[38]

However, despite the optimism that was evident after the inclusion of victim participation in the Rome Statute, the last decade of trials at the ICC have witnessed a gradual rowing back on the promise of a more meaningful role for victims.

At the most basic level, it has become increasingly clear that the inevitable narrowing of the scope of victimhood to fit within the contours (and purported purpose) of criminal trials has resulted in very limited numbers of victims participating in trials. 'Victims' are defined in Rule 85 of the Rules of Procedure and Evidence as 'natural persons who have suffered harm as a result of the commission of any crime within the jurisdiction of the Court.' Article 68(3) of the Rome Statute

---

35. The ICC Rules of Procedure and Evidence further expand the rights of the victims to include the right to representation, the right to directly participate in the proceedings and the right to question witnesses during trial: *See* ICC Rules of Procedure and Evidence, ICC-ASP/1/3 and Corr.1 (2002) (ICC Rules of Procedure and Evidence), Rules 90–91.
36. Pena and Carayon, 'Is the ICC Making the Most of Victim Participation?,' 522.
37. Pena and Carayon, 'Is the ICC Making the Most of Victim Participation?,' 522. See also, *Prosecutor v. Katanga and Ngudjolo* (Decision on the Set of Procedural Rights Attached to Procedural Status of Victims at the Pre-Trial Stage of a Case) ICC-01/04-01/07-474 (13 May 2008), paras 31–36.
38. See Antonio Cassese, 'The Statute of the International Criminal Court: Some Preliminary Reflections,' *European Journal of International Law* 144/10 (1999), 167–168.

further states that the 'views and concerns' of victims may be presented 'where the personal interests of the victims are affected.' Importantly, the harm suffered and the personal interests affected 'must be linked with the charges confirmed against the accused.'[39]

This selectivity has led to criticism that 'vanishingly few get a chance to participate' at the ICC since the opportunity is restricted to those affected by the specific crimes brought forward at the discretion of the Prosecutor and, of those who are granted participant status, only a handful are able to appear in trial proceedings.[40] For example, in the *Ongwen* trial, a total of 4,095 victims participated (currently the largest number in any trial before the ICC) but only seven victims testified in court.[41]

While understandable in the context of criminal trials relating to armed conflicts and mass atrocities, where a plethora of crimes are committed by numerous actors, it appears arbitrary to exclude all those unable to establish a link between the harm they personally suffered, and the selected crimes charged against the accused in the case. For example, in future proceedings relating to the Afghanistan situation an arbitrary distinction will arise between victims of charged crimes committed by the Taliban and IS-K who will have the right to participate, and victims of crimes committed by the US or Afghan National Security Forces who will not. In what meaningful forum, one must ask, will these victims' 'views and concerns' be heard?

In the *Lubanga* case, victims from the Democratic Republic of Congo who were able to participate were limited to those harmed by the charged crimes, namely the enlistment, conscription, and use of child soldiers. Notably, this excluded the participation of victims of sexual violence which, despite calls from non-governmental organizations and victim's groups, had not been charged.[42] During the trial, the legal

---

39. See *Prosecutor v Thomas Lubanga Dyilo* (Judgment on the appeals of the Prosecutor and Mr Thomas Lubanga Dyilo against the "Decision on Sentence pursuant to Article 76 of the Statute") ICC-01/04-01/06-3122 (1 December 2014) paras. 2, 62, 64–5.
40. Chris Tenove, 'Victim Participation at the ICC – What's the Deal?,' *Justice in Conflict*, 22 November 2013, accessed 1 June 2023, https://justiceinconflict.org/2013/11/22/victim-participation-at-the-icc-whats-the-deal/.
41. *Prosecutor v Ongwen* (Judgment) ICC-02/04-01/15 (4 February 2021), paras 20, 25.
42. Advocats Sans Frontieres et al., 'DR Congo: ICC Charges Raise Concern, Joint letter to the Chief Prosecutor of the International Criminal Court,' *Human Rights Watch*, 31 July 2006, accessed 1 June 2023 https://www.hrw.org/news/2006/07/31/dr-congo-icc-charges-raise-concern; Pena and Carayon, 'Is the ICC Making the Most

representatives of the victims filed a Joint Application to amend the legal characterization of the facts to include crimes of sexual slavery and inhuman or cruel treatment,[43] contending that a large number of witnesses had already testified to the incidence of these crimes.[44] Despite such arguments, no amendments to the charges were made.[45] Whilst this may have been justifiable in terms of fair trial rights—the charges having been omitted at the outset of the trial[46]—the need to show causality between the harm suffered and the crimes charged remained an insuperable problem for these victims.[47]

Moreover, even for those victims who can participate the reality is that such participation is often 'narrow, limited and offer[ing] little opportunity for agency.'[48] Ex-ICC Judge Christine van den Wyngaert concluded that 'victims who expect to find a forum where they could personally and publicly express their grief and thus have a platform to expose their feelings will probably be disappointed.'[49] In the Kenyatta case, the Pre-Trial Chamber excluded the charge of sexual violence for acts of forced circumcision in favour of charges for the same conduct under 'other inhumane acts.'[50] The Chamber reasoned that 'not every

---

of Victim Participation?,' 529.

43. *Prosecutor v Lubanga* (Joint Application of the Legal Representatives of the Victims for the Implementation of the Procedure under Regulation 55 of the Regulations of the Court) ICC-01/04-01/06-1891-tENG (22 May 2009), paras 4, 18–23, 24–42.

44. *Prosecutor v Lubanga* (Joint Application of the Legal Representatives of the Victims for the Implementation of the Procedure under Regulation 55 of the Regulations of the Court) ICC-01/04-01/06-1891-tENG (22 May 2009), para. 15.

45. *Prosecutor v Lubanga* (Decision on the Legal Representatives' Joint Submissions concerning the AC's Decision on 8 December 2009 on Regulation 55 of the Regulations of the Court) ICC-01/04-01/06 (8 January 2010), paras 34–38; See also, *Prosecutor v Lubanga* (Judgment on the Appeals of Mr Lubanga Dyilo and the Prosecutor against the Decision of the Trial Chamber I of 14 July 2009 Entitled 'Decision Giving Notice to the Parties and Participants that the Legal Characterization of the Facts May Be Subject to Change in Accordance with Regulation 55(2) of the Regulations of the Court) ICC-01/04-01/06-2205 (8 December 2009), paras 109–111.

46. *Prosecutor v Lubanga* (Decision on the Confirmation of Charges) ICC-01/04-01/06 (29 January 2007).

47. Veena Suresh, 'The Victims' Court? An Analysis of the Participation of Victims of Sexual Violence in International Criminal Proceedings,' *Groningen Journal of International Law* 8/2 (2021), 252.

48. Tenove 'Victim Participation at the ICC – What's the Deal?.'

49. Christine Van den Wyngaert, 'Victims before International Criminal Courts: Some Views and Concerns of an ICC Trial Judge,' *Case Western Reserve Journal of International Law* 44/475 (2011), 489.

50. *Prosecutor v Kenyatta* (Decision on the Confirmation of the Charges) ICC-01/09-02/11-382-Red (29 January 2012). See also, *Prosecutor v Muthaura, Kenyatta*

act of violence which targets parts of the body commonly associated with sexuality should be considered an act of sexual violence.'[51] It considered instead that charges of 'other inhumane acts' were more appropriate since 'the acts were motivated by ethnic prejudice and intended to demonstrate cultural superiority of one tribe over the other.'[52] However, these decisions sit squarely at odds with the views of the victims who filed observations (in subsequent litigation on the reclassification of crimes) arguing that the Pre-Trial Chamber had 'relied on an outdated conceptualization of sexual violence; namely, that such acts are purely about sex and not about the complex power dynamics at play.'[53] They highlighted that these acts of violence had 'a detrimental effect on them physically and psychologically, including on their ability to have sexual intercourse' and 'a severe effect on [their] masculinity and sense of manhood.'[54]

Eventually, by 2016, all cases in the *Kenya situation* had collapsed,[55] leaving victims with 'no truth, accountability or reparation from the court' after years of proceedings and nearly ten years after the crimes were committed.[56] The Victim's Response to the Prosecution's withdrawal of charges against Kenyatta spoke of 'anger, betrayal and disbelief at the prospect that they to be totally abandoned by the ICC.'[57]

---

and Ali (Decision on the Prosecutor's Application for Summonses to Appear) ICC-01/09-02/11 (8 March 2011), para. 27.
51. *Prosecutor v Kenyatta* (Decision on the Confirmation of the Charges) ICC-01/09-02/11-382-Red (29 January 2012), para. 265.
52. *Prosecutor v Kenyatta* (Decision on the Confirmation of the Charges) ICC-01/09-02/11-382-Red (29 January 2012), para. 266.
53. *Prosecutor v Kenyatta* (Victim's Observations on the 'Prosecution's application for notice to be given under Regulation 55(2) with respect to certain crimes charged') ICC-01/09-02/11-458 (24 July 2012), para. 12.
54. *Prosecutor v Kenyatta* (Victim's Observations on the 'Prosecution's application for notice to be given under Regulation 55(2) with respect to certain crimes charged') ICC-01/09-02/11-458 (24 July 2012), para. 14.
55. *Prosecutor v Kenyatta* (Victim's Response Prosecution Notice of Withdrawal of Charges against Uhuru Muigai Kenyatta) ICC-01/09-02/11 (9 December 2014), para. 7.
56. Chris Tenove, 'International Criminal Justice and the Empowerment or Disempowerment of Victims,' citing *Prosecutor v Kenyatta* (Victims' Response to the "Prosecution's Notice of Withdrawal of the Charges against Uhuru Muigai Kenyatta") ICC-01/09-02/11-984 (9 December 2014), accessed 1 June 2023, https://www.legal-tools.org/doc/d87801.
57. *Prosecutor v Kenyatta* (Victims' Response to the "Prosecution's Notice of Withdrawal of the Charges against Uhuru Muigai Kenyatta") ICC-01/09-02/11-984 (9 December 2014), para. 7.

They argued that the Prosecution had failed to comply with obligations set out under Article 54(1) of the Rome Statute and asked the Chamber to direct the Prosecutor to take measures to ensure the effectiveness of her investigation.[58] The Chamber declined.[59] These trials serve as a stark reminder of the failings of the ICC, and perhaps international criminal law processes more generally, to adequately contend with the views of victims and, ultimately, their ability to have their voices heard let alone actualized.

Indeed, whilst resources and time constraints have been used to justify the reduced numbers of victims able to participate in ICC cases,[60] these trends also speak to a broader marginalization of victims in trials focused on individual criminal accountability. Despite advances in the ICC and a general acceptance that the ad hoc tribunals' treatment of victims left much to be desired, there remains a considerable gap between the (limited) role that victims play in international criminal proceedings due to the 'juridification' of victimhood and the continued 'presentation of 'The Victims' as the *raison d'être* of international criminal law.'[61]

Victim Reparations

In a step away from the traditionally punitive focus of international criminal law, Article 75 of the Rome Statute provides for a system for victims to receive reparations. Certainly, the inclusion of a form of restorative justice in the Rome Statute aligns closely with the priorities expressed by many victims of mass violence.[62] This represents a welcome retreat from the sole focus on criminal punishment as the main or only method of achieving justice for victims. Reparations can create a more victim-focused justice by prioritising material needs as well as granting recognition of their being active participants in the justice meted out by criminal trials. The ICC claims that the dual focus

---

58. *Situation in the Republic of Kenya* (Victims' request for review of Prosecution's decision to cease active investigation) ICC-01/09-154 (3 August 2015), paras 55–86.
59. *Situation in the Republic of Kenya*, para. 13.
60. REDRESS, Representing Victims before the ICC: Recommendations on the Legal Representation System (2015), 8; see *Prosecutor v Ongwen* (Decision on contested victims' applications for participation, legal representation of victims and their procedural rights) ICC-02/04-01/15-350 (27 November 2015), para. 20.
61. Kendall and Nouwen, 'Representational Practices at the International Criminal Court,' 7–8; 30.
62. Dixon and Tenove, 'International Criminal Justice as a Transnational Field,' 409.

on retributive and restorative justice will enable it to not only 'bring criminals to justice but also to help the victims themselves rebuild their lives.'[63]

To date, the Court has issued orders for reparations in three cases against persons convicted of international crimes, namely in the cases of *Lubanga*,[64] *Katanga*,[65] and *Al Mahdi*.[66] However, the reality of the reparation orders and their ability to truly align with the priorities of victims or to deliver victim-focused justice must be examined. As found by the 2023 Independent Expert Review of the ICC and the Rome Statute System, meaningful reparations are gravely impacted by the 'Court's conceptual and procedural processes for reparations' which are 'laden with complexity and uncertainty.'[67]

Perhaps most immediately apparent, the system's ability to provide reparations for victims is significantly curtailed by delays and financial constraints. The excessive length of the reparation process has led to (justifiable) criticism that victims must 'wait a lifetime' for resolution.[68] For example, in the *Lubanga* case, whilst the accused was released on 15 March 2020 after serving fourteen years in prison,[69]

---

63. ICC, 'Victims and Witnesses,' (ICC-CPI/Ron Haviv/VII), accessed 1 June 2023, https://www.icc-cpi.int/en_menus/icc/structure%20of%20the%20court/victims/Pages/victims%20and%20witnesses.aspx.
64. *Prosecutor v Lubanga* (Order for Reparations) ICC-01/04-01/06-3129-AnxA (3 March 2015).
65. *Prosecutor v Katanga* (Order for Reparations pursuant to Article 75 of the Statute) ICC-01/04-01/07 (24 March 2017).
66. *Prosecutor v Al Mahdi* (Reparations Order) ICC-01/12-01/15 (17 August 2017). In the *Ntaganda case,* reparations proceedings are ongoing after the Appeals Chamber reversed the findings of the Trial Chamber and ordered the Trial Chamber to issue a new reparations order: *Prosecutor v Ntaganda* (Judgment on the appeals against the decision of Trial Chamber VI of 8 March 2021 entitled "Reparations Order") ICC-01/04-02/06 A4-A5 (12 September 2022). See also, 'What we do,' *Trust Fund for Victims*, accessed 1 June 2023, https://www.trustfundforvictims.org/en/what-we-do/reparation-orders.
67. 'Independent Expert Review of the International Criminal Court and the Rome Statute System Final Report' (30 September 2020), accessed 1 June 2023, https://asp.icc-cpi.int/sites/asp/files/asp_docs/ASP19/IER-Final-Report-ENG.pdf, para. 879, *citing* Alina Balta, Manon Bax, Rianne Letschert, 'Trial and (Potential) Error: Conflicting Visions on Reparations within the ICC System,' *International Criminal Justice Review* 29/3 (2019), 221–248.
68. 'Independent Expert Review of the International Criminal Court and the Rome Statute System Final Report' (30 September 2020), accessed 1 June 2023, https://asp.icc-cpi.int/sites/asp/files/asp_docs/ASP19/IER-Final-Report-ENG.pdf, para. 889.
69. 'Lubanga Case,' *International Criminal Court*, accessed 1 June 2023, https://www.icc-cpi.int/drc/lubanga.

the implementation of reparations is still ongoing.[70] In the *Ongwen* case, a coalition of ten civil society organizations filed *amicus* submissions noting previous (unrelated) proceedings had been marred with delays and underperformance and requesting that the Court ensure the timely implementation of reparations and the dignity and centrality of victims.[71] However, over two years since Dominic Ongwen was convicted and over eighteen years since the crimes were committed, the Court is yet to issue a Decision on Reparations in this case.

As for funding constraints, these are equally problematic. In both the *Lubanga* and *Al Madhi* cases, the Trust Fund for Victims (TFV) faces 'grave challenges' due to their incapacity to implement. The TVF has called upon individuals, institutions, and State parties to support the implementation of reparations through significant financial contributions to the Fund.[72]

Alongside these practical concerns, more fundamental procedural impediments exist within the reparations system. Critically, in ordering reparations, the Court can only 'make an order directly *against a convicted person* specifying appropriate reparations *to, or in respect of, victims*.'[73] In practice, this means that reparations may only be granted to victims 'who suffered harm as a result of the commission of the crimes of which [the accused] was found guilty.'[74] As a consequence of these provisions, to receive reparations the crimes which the victims

---

70. 'Independent Expert Review of the International Criminal Court and the Rome Statute System Final Report' (30 September 2020), accessed 1 June 2023, https://asp.icc-cpi.int/sites/asp/files/asp_docs/ASP19/IER-Final-Report-ENG.pdf, para. 880.
71. *Prosecutor v Ongwen* (Amicus Curiae brief pursuant to article 75 of the Statute and Rule 103 of the Rules of Procedure and Evidence) ICC-02/04-01/15 (4 February 2022), para. 12.
72. 'Report to the ASP on the projects and the activities of the Board of Directors of the Trust Fund for Victims for the period 1 July 2018 to 30 June 2019,' ICC-ASP/18/14 (2019), para. 120. In the *Lubanga* case, the TFV has asked for contributions amounting to EUR 4.25 million. 'The Lubanga Case,' *Trust Fund for Victims*, accessed 1 June 2023, https://www.trustfundforvictims.org/what-we-do/reparation-orders/lubanga. In the *Al Mahdi* case, the TFV has asked for contributions amounting to EUR 1.35 million. 'The Al Mahdi Case,' *Trust Fund for Victims*, accessed 1 June 2023, https://www.trustfundforvictims.org/what-we-do/reparation-orders/al-madhi.
73. Rome Statute, Article 75(2), emphasis added.
74. *Prosecutor v Lubanga* (Appeal against Trial Chamber I's Decision establishing the principles and procedures to be applied to reparations of 7 August 2012) ICC-01/04-01/06-2909-tENG (24 August 2012), para. 211. See also, *Prosecutor v Katanga* (Order for Reparations pursuant to Article 75 of the Statute) ICC-01/04-01/07-3728-tENG (24 March 2017), para. 37; *Prosecutor v Al Mahdi* (Reparations Order) ICC-01/12-01/15-236 (17 August 2017), para. 42.

suffered must have been charged *and* successfully prosecuted, and the victim must provide sufficient evidence of their harm.[75] In the *Lubanga* case, this meant that only victims of the crime of enlistment and conscription of child soldiers were eligible for reparations. Those victims of other crimes committed by Lubanga's forces, as well as victims who suffered from crimes committed by the child soldiers, were unable to request let alone establish their right to reparation.[76] Similarly, in the *Katanga* case, some Applicants claimed for sexual and gender-based violence crimes which occurred during the attack on Bogoro in the Ituri Province of the DRC, but the Chamber concluded that it was not in a 'position to determine that that harm was a consequence of one or more of the crimes of which Mr Katanga was convicted.'[77]

Of course, in situations where there are usually a large number of victims and where charges before the ICC are often 'highly selective, discretionary, and even idiosyncratic,'[78] this leads to 'inequality between victims, by anchoring Court-order reparations only on the crimes for which conviction against an accused person has been entered, and not on the totality of the crimes charged or perpetrated in a situation.'[79] As Luke Moffett notes, the restrictions placed on the eligibility of victims for reparations 'is contrary to the nature of reparations, which are intended to be victim-centred in responding to their harm, rather than being dependent on the identification, prosecution or conviction of an accused.'[80]

Moreover, there have been concerns that the modalities of reparations ordered have not reflected the needs and expectations of victims,

---

75. Luke Moffett, 'Reparative Complementarity: Ensuring an Effective Remedy for Victims in the Reparation Regime of the International Criminal Court,' *International Journal of Human Rights* 17/3 (2013), 375. See *Prosecutor v Katanga* (Order for Reparations pursuant to Article 75 of the Statute) ICC-01/04-01/07-3728-tENG (24 March 2017), para. 31; *Prosecutor v Lubanga* (Appeal against Trial Chamber I's Decision establishing the principles and procedures to be applied to reparations of 7 August 2012) ICC-01/04-01/06-2909-tENG (24 August 2012), paras 1, 32.
76. Luke Moffett, 'Reparative Complementarity,' 375.
77. *Prosecutor v Katanga* (Order for Reparations pursuant to Article 75 of the Statute) ICC-01/04-01/07-3728-tENG (24 March 2017), para. 179.
78. Frédéric Mégret, 'Reparations before the ICC: The Need for Pragmatism and Creativity,' in *Contemporary Issues Facing the International Criminal Court*, ed. Richard Steinberg (Leiden: Brill Nijhoff, 2016), 256.
79. 'Independent Expert Review of the International Criminal Court and the Rome Statute System Final Report' (30 September 2020), accessed 1 June 2023, https://asp.icc-cpi.int/sites/asp/files/asp_docs/ASP19/IER-Final-Report-ENG.pdf, para. 885.
80. Luke Moffett, 'Reparations for victims at the International Criminal Court: a new way forward?,' *The International Journal of Human Rights* 21/9 (2017), 1207.

although there is some indication that the Court has been receptive to criticisms in this regard. In the *Lubanga* case, when determining the type of reparations to be ordered (reparations either on an individualized basis, a collective basis, or both),[81] the Trial Chamber exclusively adopted collective reparations, emphasizing that collective awards would have 'greater utility' and reduce the administrative costs associated with individual awards.[82] Although this approach 'was visibly geared towards facilitating swift collective reparation through the Trust Fund,'[83] it nonetheless caused significant disappointment among victims, and the legal representatives of both groups of victims subsequently appealed the decision.[84] However, the Appeals Chamber dismissed the appeal rejecting the notion that individual awards must be granted.[85] This was despite the victims clearly favouring individual reparations and advocating that awards should take into account the particular need of individual victims for economic and psychological assistance.[86]

In the *Katanga* and *Al Madhi* cases, the Court appears to have moved beyond reparations solely on a collective basis to recognize individualized reparations.[87] In the *Katanga* case, in addition to collective reparations in the form of support for housing-income-generating

---

81. Rules of Procedure and Evidence, Rule 91(1).
82. *Prosecutor v Lubanga* (Decision establishing the principles and procedures to be applied to reparations) ICC-01/04-01/06-2904 (7 August 2012), para. 274.
83. Carsten Stahn, 'Reparative Justice after the Lubanga Appeal Judgement: New Prospect for Expressivism and Participatory Justice or 'Jurified Victimhood' by Other Means,' *Journal of International Criminal Justice* 13/8 (2015), 812.
84. *Prosecutor v Lubanga* (Appeal against Trial Chamber I's Decision Establishing the Principles and Procedures to Be Applied to Reparation of 7 August 2012) ICC-01/04-01/06, V01 team of legal representatives (3 September 2012); *Prosecutor v Lubanga* (Appeal against Trial Chamber I's Decision Establishing the Principles and Procedures to be Applied to Reparations of 7 August 2012)ICC-01/04-01/06, Office of Public Counsel for Victims/V02 team of legal representatives (24 August 2012).
85. *Prosecutor v Lubanga* (Judgment on the appeals against the "Decision establishing the principles and procedures to be applied to reparations" of 7 August 2012 with AMENDED order for reparations (Annex A) and public annexes 1 and 2) ICC-01/04-01/06 A A 2 A 3 (3 March 2015), paras 152, 155.
86. *Prosecutor v Lubanga* (Observations on the Sentence and Reparations by Victims (V01 Group)) ICC-01/04-01/06-2864 (18 April 2012), paras 24–27. See also, Sharon Nakandha, 'ICC Makes Progress on Reparations for Victims in Lubanga Case,' *International Justice Monitor*, 27 October 2016, accessed 1 June 2023, https://www.ijmonitor.org/2016/10/icc-makes-progress-on-reparations-for-victims-in-lubanga-case/.
87. Luke Moffett, 'Reparations for victims at the International Criminal Court,' 1208.

activity, education, and psychological support,[88] the Chamber ordered each victim to receive a symbolic award of USD 250 compensation.[89] It explicitly recognized the need to 'heed the expectations and needs voiced by the victims'[90] and that 'individual reparations are important to the victims' and might 'afford personal and symbolic acknowledgement of the harm suffered.'[91] Similarly, in the *Al Mahdi* case, the Chamber ordered individual reparations for those whose livelihoods exclusively depended upon the Protected Buildings destroyed by Al Mahdi in addition to collective reparations,[92] and for 'the mental pain and anguish of those whose ancestors' burial sites were damaged in the attack.'[93]

Despite an apparent shift towards the provision of individual *and* collective reparations, it remains to be seen whether this approach will continue in cases with far greater numbers of victims and, if so, how the TFV will be able to fulfil the orders considering its grave financial and capacity shortfall. Indeed, in the *Katanga* case the fact that the Trial Chamber found the figure of 297 victims eligible for reparations to be 'a figure which makes individual awards feasible'[94] demonstrates that management and budgetary constraints remain at the forefront of the Court's mind.

A broader notion of 'victims' (for the purpose of reparations) would of course almost inevitably impact the rights of the accused. It would be unfair for an order for reparations to be made against the accused for crimes not established against him or her.[95] Whilst this makes 'legal sense' in the context of individual criminal responsibility, it also brings into focus once again the dissonance between victim-centred justice

---

88. Prosecutor v Katanga (Order for Reparations pursuant to Article 75 of the Statute) ICC-01/04-01/07-3728-tENG (24 March 2017), para. 305.
89. Prosecutor v Katanga (Order for Reparations pursuant to Article 75 of the Statute) ICC-01/04-01/07-3728-tENG (24 March 2017), para. 300.
90. *Prosecutor v Katanga* (Order for Reparations pursuant to Article 75 of the Statute) ICC-01/04-01/07-3728-tENG (24 March 2017), para. 266.
91. *Prosecutor v Katanga* (Order for Reparations pursuant to Article 75 of the Statute) ICC-01/04-01/07-3728-tENG (24 March 2017), para. 285.
92. *Prosecutor v Al Mahdi* (Reparations Order) ICC-01/12-01/15-236 (17 August 2017), para. 83.
93. *Prosecutor v Al Mahdi* (Reparations Order) ICC-01/12-01/15-236 (17 August 2017), para. 90.
94. *Prosecutor v Katanga* (Order for Reparations pursuant to Article 75 of the Statute) ICC-01/04-01/07-3728-tENG (24 March 2017), para. 287.
95. *Prosecutor v. Katanga*, Order for Reparations pursuant to Article 75 of the Statute, ICC-01/04-01/07-3728-tENG, 24 March 2017, para. 31.

and the realities of international criminal justice.[96] The inextricable connection of the ICC reparations system with a criminal trial will continue to restrict their effectiveness in remedying victims' harm.[97] In sum, despite good intentions, Moffett's characterization of the reparation system as 'grossly inadequate' to address reparations for victims of mass atrocity remains convincing.[98] Reparations appear destined to be little more than an 'add-on' to the overall trial process[99] and in the end make limited contribution to meaningful justice for victims of international crimes.

Conclusion

Faced with criticism that international criminal law has traditionally been unable to provide meaningful justice to victims, efforts have been made to ensure greater participation and remedy for victims of international crimes. However, there remains a dissonance between the representation of 'the victims' by the international community, on the one hand, and the actual role that victims are afforded within international trials on the other.

The presumption that the role of international criminal law is to deliver justice *to* the victims through accountability and punishment continues to be all pervasive. Despite claims that the role of international justice 'is to investigate and prosecute those most responsible for the world's gravest crimes, where no-one else is doing justice for the victims,'[100] there is much to doubt that claim.[101] The road to hell is, of course, paved with good intentions. As has been seen, in practice this representation of the victims—as an amorphous group in need of 'justice' which can only be provided for by the international courts in

---

96. Luke Moffett, 'Reparations for victims at the International Criminal Court,' 1207.
97. Luke Moffett, 'Reparative Complementarity,' 369.
98. Luke Moffett, 'Reparations for victims at the International Criminal Court,' 1206.
99. Luke Moffett, 'Reparations for victims at the International Criminal Court,' 1207.
100. 'Nairobi, Statement by the Prosecutor of the International Criminal Court Mrs. Fatou Bensouda,' *ICC*, 22 October 2012, accessed 1 June 2023, https://www.icc-cpi.int/Pages/item.aspx?name=otpstatement221012&ln=en.
101. 'Statement to the Press by the Prosecutor of the International Criminal Court (Abidjan, Côte d'Ivoire, 20 July 2013),' in *ICC Weekly Updates 22 July 201 –20 August 2013, International Criminal Court*, accessed 1 June 2023, https://www.icc-cpi.int/iccdocs/PIDS/wu/ED181_ENG.pdf.

the form of convictions and punishment—is a long way from being shown to be true. If it is not true, then what are the dangers inherent in this? At the very least, the consistent appropriation of victims' voices and claims to be acting on 'their' behalf to deliver justice remains inconsistent with victim interests in practice. At worst, it shields international courts from justified criticism and removes the agency of victims to demand justice more attuned to their needs.

As the brief analysis provided in this chapter has shown, the gap between the claims made and the rights afforded to victims, including extremely limited participation at the ICC and the painfully slow and inadequate economic or community reparation, means that these measures are at best an appendage to the ICC's form of retributive justice. Whilst wedded to the strictures of criminal justice, the systems of victim participation and reparations do not serve the interests of victims in any meaningful sense, or at least only a select few. In this way, we must take 'seriously the need for a radical departure'[102] from the current system.

Perhaps it is time to look beyond the orthodoxies of individual criminal responsibility, and question how justice might really empower the individual and collective agency of victims and embed their voices, interests, and needs. A better approach might be to decouple these systems from international criminal trials and invest greater attention and resources into locally owned, victim-centred mechanisms which prioritize all forms of restorative and transformative justice. Whilst 'criminal courtrooms' continue to 'dominate the discourse and architecture of post-conflict justice'[103], we must contemplate these alternative ways to better provide the justice victims desire within the international system. Most importantly, international law practitioners and academics must learn to avoid imposing *our* values concerning justice onto the 'international' sphere. We must examine how justice might more effectively meet the varied and diverse expectations of those who have been directly or indirectly impacted by mass atrocities. Until we really ask these questions to both ourselves and others, and be prepared to question our beloved retributive orthodoxies, international justice will never work out how to deliver justice to victims.

---

102. Christine Schwöbel-Patel, *Marketing Global Justice - The Political Economy of International Criminal Law* (Cambridge: Cambridge University Press, 2021) 242.
103. Mark Drumbl, 'International Justice Outside of Criminal Courtrooms and Jailhouses,' in *Arcs of Global Justice: Essays in Honour of William A. Schabas*, ed. Margaret M. deGuzman and Diane Marie Amann (Washington & Lee Legal Studies Paper No. 2018-01, January 2018), 397.

7

The International Justice Robe

Terry Duffy

Figure 1: The International Justice Robe

Figure 2: Painting The International Justice Robe

The International Justice Robe portrays a powerful message.

There are several details to take note of: The underlying painting expresses and symbolises the torment of torture, anger, and bloodshed experienced when innocent lives are lost. The painting shows the initial thought process of the artwork; the journey taken on how to portray victims and their stories. It provides the canvass for the images, showing the layers and symbolic colours, in particular the colour red representing bloodshed. Applied to the painting is the photomontage. These images are for most people counter-aesthetic, disturbing to view and consider. It is significant that the montage is crowned by a set of broken scales underneath which can be seen those suffering from war crimes.

THE INTERNATIONAL JUSTICE ROBE   139

Figure 3: The International Justice Robe on a Mannequin (Back)

Figure 4: The International Justice Robe on a Mannequin (Front)

PART 2

COUNTER-AESTHETICS OF INTERNATIONAL JUSTICE

8

Counter-Aesthetics of International Justice

Christine Schwöbel-Patel and Robert Knox

A central insight that we have taken from critical and radical writings on aesthetics is that the dominant aesthetic never goes unchallenged. As the embodiment of both a dominant style *and* particular political-economic project, dominant aesthetics are frequently contested by alternative, disruptive, and oppositional forms of aesthetics, which challenge both the form and content of the dominant aesthetic. Accordingly, following discussions of 'hegemony' and 'counter-hegemony,' we have grouped such approaches together under the term 'counter-aesthetics' of international justice.

Because of the inescapable connection between 'form' and 'content' in the dominant aesthetic, *transformation* is a crucial element of our understanding of counter-aesthetics. Engaging with counter-aesthetics necessarily means going beyond critique for its own sake, and instead focuses on the transformation of social relations. If our approach to the aesthetics of international justice means examining how these aesthetics are both produced by and sustain oppressive and exploitative social relations, then our approach to counter-aesthetics focuses on how aesthetics are produced by the opposition to such social relations, and might contribute to their overthrow. In this way, we understand transformation as a political intervention, with struggles being played out in the terrain of reform and revolution;[1] or, if you prefer, strategy and tactics.[2] At the same time, we must therefore enquire as to how such projects might be reappropriated, repurposed, or recuperated by the very systems they seek to contest.

---

1. Rosa Luxemburg, *Reform or Revolution* (London: Militant Publications, 1986).
2. Robert Knox, 'Strategy and Tactics,' *Finnish Yearbook of International Law* 21 (2010).

In the context of international justice, therefore, counter-aesthetics is concerned with shifting the dominant gaze or frame, without necessarily committing to its redemption. Critically, our vision and practice of a counter-aesthetics of international justice are inspired and guided by the political economy critique that we also emphasized in our aesthetic enquiries. This means that a counter-aesthetics framing of international justice is materially informed and foregrounds the social relations around capital accumulation. In this way, our understanding of the counter-aesthetic of international justice embraces a broad range of struggles that seek to contest the current social order. The struggles of racialized people, Indigenous decolonial, and feminist liberation struggles all fall under this category, as do abolitionist feminist, Marxist, anti-imperialist, eco-socialist and anarchist lenses – and all the spaces in which they overlap and create a progressive tension.

Counter-aesthetics, how we understand it, somewhat obviously, is conceptualized as reaching beyond 'high art' Western-dominated forms. The movement and struggles we are inspired by have attempted to contest and overcome the dominant liberal-internationalist aesthetics, which is not necessarily about being true to 'high' art, but certainly arrives at questions of representation with certain aesthetic preconceptions as discussed in the first part of this volume. Drawing on such contestations, we propose three techniques of counter-aesthetics: (a) rupture, the process of breaking from the familiar; (b) *détournement*, the process of diversion, especially from a capitalist viewpoint; and (c) solidarity aesthetics, the forms of representation that make an intervention explicitly for the interests of the oppressed. As in our introductory framing chapter, we provide an overview of these techniques, exemplifying them through the medium of (ICL) film. We then situate the contributions in the second part in one of the three tactics.

Before setting out the distinctions between our proposed techniques, a few words on how they overlap and inform each other. A very fitting example of such an overlap of techniques is expressed in the cover art of this collection. On the cover is a poster, created for the Organization of Solidarity of the Peoples of Africa, Asia, and Latin America (OSPAAL) by Cuban graphic designer and artist Alfredo Rostgaard in 1968. OSPAAL was founded in Havana, Cuba as an organization to fight imperialism and unite liberation struggles, especially across the three continents of the Global South. The most important gathering of state and liberation movement delegates took place in Havana at the Tricontinental conference in 1966, which spurred a host of political, intellectual, and artistic outputs.

In the top panel of the artwork for the cover of this book, we see a Zaire banknote, which would have been issued under the leadership of Joseph Mobutu whose face is depicted on the note. Mobuto renamed the Congo to Zaire as part of a pro-African move. However, all is not as it seems with this ostensible act of self-determination. Mobuto was recruited, supported, and funded by the CIA to take power in the Congo. As such, the second panel depicts a US dollar note behind the peeled-back Zaire banknote. Mobuto was deployed to take power from Patrice Lumumba, the first Congolese elected prime minister after independence from the Belgian colonial masters. Lumumba had become a threat to US (and Western hegemonic) power because he wanted to take control of the country's minerals. After failing to secure assistance from the United Nations to expel the Belgians, Lumumba sought help from the Soviet Union. The planned nationalization of the vast mineral resources in combination with a Soviet alliance prompted a plan by the United Nations, the USA, and Belgium to assassinate Lumumba. He was assassinated in 1961. In the third and last panel on the poster, we see the next layer being peeled back, showing a picture of Lumumba as he was captured by Mobuto's soldiers. The layering of the three panels as bank notes is arguably a form of rupture, in that it gestures towards political interests behind currency and its use. In our everyday dealings with bank notes—particularly in everyday purchases—we are not usually confronted with the political economy of the currency with which we are dealing. Next, the tactic of *détournement* can be spotted in the poster's use of layering and collage. The French word *détournement* means deflection, diversion, rerouting, distortion, misuse, misappropriation, hijacking, or otherwise turning something aside from its normal course or purpose. The reading of new and radical content through techniques of collage can be seen in the peeling back of the bank notes. Finally, an aesthetic of solidarity perhaps needs no further explanation: the seeming act of self-determination and pro-Africanism in the Zaire bank note is revealed to be connected to counter-revolutionary forces. The complicity with Western finance proves to be a renewed form of oppression of the Congolese people. Indeed, after taking power, and already at the time of the poster's conceptualization, Mobuto ran the Congo very much in the same way as the brutal Belgian colonizer King Leopold II, as 'a personal wealth machine.'[3] Having acknowledged and demonstrated how all three techniques can be effectively used

---

3. Siddharth Kara, *Cobalt Red: How the Blood of the Congo Powers our Lives* (New York: St. Martin's Press, 2023), 112.

in one counter-aesthetic, let us now set out the three techniques of counter-aesthetics in turn, applying them more directly to international criminal justice.

Rupture

Rupture as a form of counter-aesthetics has the purpose of making the familiar strange. It exposes hidden assumptions, distributions of power, biases, and inequalities. Such exposure happens through moments of reflexiveness. An example of rupture, beyond what has already been gestured to in the poster art, can be found in the work of German poet and playwright Bertolt Brecht. Working in Berlin of the 1920s, Brecht began experimenting with alternative forms of theatre. Together with theatre director Erwin Piscator, Brecht invented the 'episches Theatre' (epic theatre), which aimed to move away from hero narratives and instead portray social conflicts such as war, revolution, and economic and social injustice.

Brecht's work offers guidance on a radical content and form of counter-aesthetics that is attendant to class relations and critical of art being an elite undertaking. Brecht devised what he called a 'Verfremdungseffekt' (estrangement/alienation effect) when staging his plays. The goal of this technique was, in Brecht's words, 'to act in such a manner that the spectator is prevented from feeling his way into the characters' and instead force the spectators to actively and consciously engage with the issues presented to them.[4] Estrangement in Brecht's works was affected in a variety of ways. Songs or comments to the audience—the breaking of the fourth wall—would interrupt the narrative, rupturing the illusion, and prevent the audience from immersing themselves in theatrical fiction.[5] The play *Der Gute Mensch von Sezuan* (*The Good Person of Szechwan*) ends with a direct address to the audience, pointing out that the open-endedness of the play is 'not the right kind of ending' as one would surely rather have a 'golden legend'; instead we have the 'disappointment of many questions' and no answers.[6] The estrangement devised by Brecht did not only take place in the narrative but also took place in the stage design. There was no regular backdrop with which to lead the audience into a different

---

4. Bertolt Brecht, 'On Chinese Acting,' The Tulane Drama Review, 6/1 (1961), 130.
5. Bertolt Brecht, 'Kleines Organon für das Theater,' in Bertolt Brecht, *Gesammelte Werke 16 / Schriften zum Theater 2* (Frankfurt: Suhrkamp Verlag, 1967).
6. Bertolt Brecht, *Der Gute Mensch von Sezuan* (Frankfurt: Suhrkamp Verlag, 1964).

world: instead, wires were exposed and the structure of the stage was kept visible rather than hidden. Ultimately, then, Brecht aimed for a critical audience through these techniques of estrangement, similar to an audience of satire which could be moved to action rather than remaining passive consumers of entertainment.

Rupture in international justice might be exemplified in mockumentaries (a portmanteau of 'mock' and 'documentary') critical of development institutions and celebrity humanitarianism. 'The Samaritans' is a 2014 mockumentary set in Kenya and created by a Kenya-based production company, chronicling the work of the fictitious NGO sardonically named 'Aid for Aid.'[7] The characters are immediately recognizable to those who have encountered international development and aid work, including the white male suited director who compensates for his inexperience and lack of knowledge with exaggerated confidence and clichéd one-liners. The trailer for the show captures these stereotypes exceedingly well, ending with a Black female office worker saying to the NGO director with concern: 'We mustn't lose sight of what is important here.' The white director then turns to the camera in a break of the fourth wall, stating 'Saving Africa?'[8]

A critical, 'estranged' audience of international justice might be able to appreciate that the stories presented on victims, Africa, and the legal profession are often emotionally manipulative.[9] Certainly, as a reflexive and critical audience, being forced to resist this presents us with a sense of discomfort and, possibly, reluctance, as it highlights our own manipulation, easy association with stereotypes, and complicity in reproducing them.[10]

In the opening chapter to this volume (Chapter 2), we see behind the scenes of an ICC institutional film through Sofia Stolk's deft making visible of frames, tracking the camera's zooming in and zooming out, and emotive musical accompaniments. This contribution highlights that

---

7. Caitlin L Chandler, 'The first Kenyan mockumentary about NGO's,' *Africa is a country*, 2 October 2014, 30 June 2023, https://africasacountry.com/2014/02/kenyas-first-mockumentary-takes-on-the-ngo-world.
8. 'The Samaritans Teaser,' Xeinium Productions, 2 October 2015, accessed 30 June 2023, https://www.youtube.com/watch?v=0cn-kvOqLyg.
9. For an example of applying this form of rupture to international criminal justice mooting, see Christine Schwöbel-Patel and Wouter Werner, 'A Brechtian Way of Mooting,' *Ejil:Talk!*, 24 October 2022, accessed 11 July 2023, https://www.ejiltalk.org/a-brechtian-way-of-mooting/.
10. See Christine Schwöbel-Patel and Wouter Werner, 'Screen' in *International Law's Objects*, eds. Jessie Hohmann and Daniel Joyce (Oxford: Oxford University Press, 2018).

the distinction between aesthetics and counter-aesthetics as we have set them out is a fickle one. It both opens our eyes to what we see and how our gaze is directed (aesthetics), and at the same time makes the familiar strange (counter-aesthetics). Anastasia Tataryn (Chapter 9) engages the rupture tactic through anarchic thinking in combination with the praxis of contemporary dance choreography. Applying anarchic thinking to 'Justice' breaks with what she terms the 'choreography' of international criminal law. A freeing from the modern legal frame, including a freeing from the aesthetic/counter-aesthetic binary, occurs through anarchic thinking as a theoretical lens and through contemporary dance choreography as praxis. Randle DeFalco (Chapter 10) engages the tactic of rupture in his contribution through a more normative frame, asking the reader to consider atrocities as public health catastrophes. This both highlights the normalization of visceral violence aesthetics as the dominant aesthetics of international criminal justice and proposes a break with this aesthetic in favour of alternative readings. In his reflection 'Violence' (Chapter 11), Jo Frank offers a challenge to the narrative that individual violence—particularly domestic violence—is assumed to be more readily expressed and visible than structural violence. Language falls short. Through the form of theses and extensive footnotes, the language genre for violence, as well as theories on it, is made strange. Through this, the experienced violence is brought closer to the reader. Justice remains removed and even impossible. The words are pregnant with an absence of empowerment.

Despite its aptness as a counter-aesthetic tactic, there is a notable downside to this form of counter-aesthetics: it assumes an 'ironic spectator' as someone who is informed, engaged, and often also privileged.[11] The emphasis for the tactic of rupture is on de-centering taken-for-granted privilege; it is less aimed at evoking empathy or relating experiences of suffering with other experiences.

Détournement

Détournement is a technique which arguably operates in a similarly ironic fashion, although with the aim of creating alternative aesthetic forms through subversion and the reorganization of aesthetic material. The term was initially coined by the Letterist International in the 1950s, the predecessor grouping to the Situationist International (SI), which

---

11. Lilie Chouliaraki, *The Ironic Spectator: Solidarity in the Age of Post-Humanitarianism* (London: Polity Press, 2012).

was a Paris-based collective of (mainly Marxist) radical artists and cultural theorists. Perhaps the most famous figure in the SI was the previously mentioned Guy Debord. In *The Society of the Spectacle*, Debord notes that 'diversion leads to the subversion of past critical conclusions which were frozen into respectable truths, namely transformed into lies.'[12] *Détournement* is often described as the turning of expressions of the capitalist system and its media culture against itself. For Debord, since everything that needs to be said has already been said, *détournement* is not a way of creating new content per se as it is much more a technique of reorganizing, cutting up, and collage.

> Plagiarism is necessary. Progress implies it. It embraces an author's phrase, makes use of his expressions, erases a false idea, and replaces it with the right idea.[13]

A key element here is playfulness. Indeed, play was regarded as an important part of a *détourned* society which refused to be commoditized. Hence *détournement* as a technique is playful, momentary, and a patchwork of materials and methods.[14] The SI created *détourned* films, including a film adaption of Debord's *The Society of the Spectacle* which resulted in a delirious collage of image and film snippets.[15] The film *Can Dialectics Break Bricks?* is a 1973 film by the SI that claims to be the very first entirely *détourned* film. The Kung-Fu film *Crush* is dubbed over it by the filmmakers to include dialogue on questions of class and revolution. Collage is also the creative means employed in Tom Phillips's *A Humument*, a project he began in 1966. In this book, Phillips used painting, montage, and cut-up techniques to create an entirely new book from an obscure Victorian romance *A Human Document*.[16] In the 1990s and the early-2000s, *détournement* became closely associated with the anti-globalization movement, particularly in the tactic of 'culture jamming' or subvertizing. Here, activists take corporate advertisements and subvert them, whilst mimicking their form as closely as possible.[17] In a recent example from September 2022, climate activists filled advertising

---

12. Guy Debord, *The Society of the Spectacle*, trans. Kenn Knabb (Berkeley: Bureau of Public Secrets, 2014), para. 206.
13. Debord, *The Society of the Spectacle*, para. 207.
14. McKenzie Wark, *50 Years of Recuperation of the Situationist International* (Princeton, MA: Princeton Architectural Press, 2008), 11.
15. *La Société du Spectacle*. Directed by Guy Debord, 1973.
16. Tom Phillips, *A Humument: A Treated Victorian Novel* (London: Thames & Hudson, 2016).
17. See Naomi Klein, *No Logo* (London: Flamingo, 2000) 284-315.

spaces with *détourned* adverts for the airline industry, pointing out the environmental damage caused by flying whilst otherwise mimicking the style and form of a standard advert.[18]

In international law, Valentin Jeutner has employed software to rearrange words and letters from judgments, treaties, and journal articles in a small volume titled *Lex machina*. The outcome is simultaneously disorientating and gripping. In the spirit of the SI's playfulness, it is humorous although not overtly political. One example of collage is the inclusion of multiple translations of Article 1 of the Statute of the International Court of Justice,[19] which translates from English to Mandarin Chinese to Spanish to Hindi to various other languages and back to English as: 'the International Court of Justice, established under the United Nations Code of Ethics, is a United States Central Court operating under this article.'[20]

Gerry Simpson's humorous parables (Chapter 12) arguably engage the tactic of *détournement* as envisaged by the Letterist International through their playfulness. Of course, there is something deeply disturbing about play and humour when we are considering mass crimes; and yet, it is also—because of its seemingly oxymoronic nature—especially compelling. The parables are a collage of historical facts (several about the infamously unfunny Nazi Adolf Eichmann), literary excerpts on humour, and personal reflections. What is it that the reader learns from these parables? We leave it up to you to decide. In an overtly political style, that perhaps sits at the juncture between *détournement* and solidarity aesthetics, Alex Batesmith (Chapter 13) describes the way in which Theary Seng, a victim-survivor of the Khmer Rouge regime in Cambodia, refused the victim aesthetics presented by the hybrid tribunal the Extraordinary Chambers in the Courts of Cambodia (ECCC). In an act of turning the marketized form of justice against itself, and in refusing the passive victim archetype, Seng developed so-called 'Poetic Justice Products' on her website to engage public debate both playfully and provocatively.

In a similar vein to the tactic of rupture, *détournement* has its limitations in assuming an already critical or politicized audience, and perhaps also a privileged audience. Perhaps as a consequence of this,

---

18. https://www.theguardian.com/environment/2022/sep/22/activists-subvert-poster-sites-aviation-ad-industries-airline-emissions-climate-crisis
19. Art. 1 StICJ reads: ...
20. Valentin Jeutner, *Lex machina: Unlikely encounters of international law and technology* (Lund: Media-Tryck Lund University Sweden, 2020) 75.

détournement does not lend itself to the creation of political *agency*, dwelling primarily in the negative criticism of the existing order without providing a sense of political alternatives, or serving as a 'call to action.' This likewise sits in contrast to the final type of counter-aesthetics we would like to propose as a tactic: solidarity aesthetics.

Solidarity Aesthetics

Solidarity as a counter-aesthetic concerns the depiction of individuals as active agents making their own destiny, often portraying them as heroic. This is asserted against those depictions and stereotypes of the 'masses' or the oppressed as essentially powerless and in need of outside help. As such, there is a focus on people's collective action and political organization, in particular a sensibility that connects a lack of privilege to other people's lack of privilege in an internationalist sense. Crucially, it also involves open partisanship, in essence taking the side of the downtrodden. This aesthetic has less in common with the counter-aesthetics of rupture and *détournement* as we have described them. The first two tactics are relatively 'auteur' driven. The aesthetic choices occur at an 'editing' level, either by drawing attention to the constructed nature of the dominant gaze (the look 'behind the scenes') or by 'editing' an existing aesthetic (the diversion of the gaze through layering and collage). One of the central things that both of these techniques seek to enact is consciously and openly politicize the aesthetic. There is a sense in which they are therefore openly political themselves. But, whilst the classic examples were always linked with an explicitly left-wing politics (Brecht, Debord, etc.), that is not necessarily the case. Here we can think about *Lex machina* and its use of international law and technology: the outcome can gesture towards a political aspect, but, although we can appreciate its playfulness, we are not the wiser about the politics of it. A solidarity aesthetic however aims to be explicitly political.

There are a number of classic documentaries in this solidarity aesthetic style. One of the most important of these is *The Battle of Chile*, directed by Patricio Guzmán, which chronicles the political tensions in Chile throughout 1973. In some respects it is an aesthetically traditional documentary: talking heads, interviews, a narrative arc. But what it chooses as its subjects—crowds, factory floors, direct confrontation—is more unusual. It is likewise a more 'live action' style, in the thick of the action (famously one cameraman filmed his own death). Similarly, Ken Loach's documentary period, including *A Question of Leadership*, discloses such a sense of being in the thick of the action. It is important to note that the style of these cannot simply be characterized as 'realism'; the aesthetic precisely depicts the people 'in movement' as something almost superhuman. It is an attempt to capture the power of radical agency to break through the mundane. In the OSPAAL poster art, we find something similar, namely people in the midst of political struggle. This includes colourful graphic images of Black women bearing arms, pop art depictions of liberation struggle figures, and, as in our cover art, an arresting mix of styles and colours.

The solidarity aesthetic is, then, in stark contrast to the way in which international justice tends to disempower people and re-cast them as 'victims' who need to be saved by the international institutions. The way a racialized, infantilized, and feminized victimhood aesthetic is achieved here is through interviewing individuals in isolation, often disfigured and disabled, and generally removed from any social context. Or, if groups of people are depicted, they are formless masses *asking* for things. This maneuver also has the political consequence of allowing international institutions to not 'take sides' in a political sense because what they are doing is intervening into a 'humanitarian situation.' Employing in part a solidarity aesthetics in the international criminal justice documentary genre is Klaartje Quirijns's *Peace versus Justice*, which follows the Northern Ugandan struggle for peace processes. Here, the efforts of the international prosecutor are portrayed as a hindrance rather than as assistance in the conflict. Quirijns gives a voice to the female politician at the forefront of this political struggle. The storytelling here decentres the ICC and its actors to make space for the people depicted largely as 'victims' to become active subjects. In sum, this documentary style is more about representing ICL's *effects* and charting the situation.

One aspect of solidarity that we have considered in this collection is the challenging of hegemonic forms of representation, including in academic knowledge production. Solidarity aesthetics often distance themselves from what is considered higher art forms such as paintings, sculptures, or classical dance. One of the art forms we have chosen to highlight in this collection is the comic, fitting nicely alongside the poster art already described. As Peter Quach (comic co-creator of *Pinan*, Chapter 14) puts it: 'for a long time (and still in some quarters), the medium of comics as a whole was looked down upon as a lesser art form compared to other media such as painting or sculpture.' And yet, he continues, 'comics are not only a valid medium, but also might offer a worldview free of the burdens and assumptions that have accumulated in other media around what counts as a valid object of art and who counts as an artist.' It is no coincidence that we have included an interview with cartoonist Kate Evans (Chapter 15) as well as commissioned cartoons in the chapter contribution of Christine Schwöbel-Patel and Deger Ozkaramanli (Chapter 5).

Of course, solidarity aesthetics is vulnerable to criticism as the relatively 'straightforward' style can amount to its cooptation. Indeed, those previously radical political movements or governments that have collapsed into authoritarianism have often maintained the same 'solidarity' aesthetic, using this to buttress their claims to popular support.

Recuperation/Conclusion

In this section, we have attempted to think through several 'modes' of counter-aesthetic, which have—and might—inform oppositional movements. These tactics recognize the idea that aesthetics is always political, but that the dominant aesthetic is *depoliticizing*, or rather, naturalizes a particular politics as normal and neutral. Accordingly, when we engage in questions of aesthetics we need to pay attention to the content of what we do but also the form. These two are inextricably linked, and both are politically relevant. Every counter-aesthetic approach explicitly foregrounds its own politics to consciously think through what makes it a *counter*-aesthetic (both in form and content): 'rupture' exposes the politics of the existing order by making it strange; '*détournement*' uses the power of the existing order and tries to turn it against itself, working through the cracks and contradictions; 'solidarity aesthetics' opposes the existing order by posing an alternative vision of those it disempowers. All are thus connected by being consciously political.

At the same time, however, we have demonstrated that each of these techniques are ultimately vulnerable to being incorporated into a politics supportive of the existing order. The spectacle—like capitalism itself—has a seemingly unlimited capacity to incorporate that which appears oppositional to it into its own logic. The seeming subversion of an advertising campaign can suddenly simply become such a campaign, self-awareness is frequently now a deliberate tactic of marketing, every attempt at subversion can become its opposite. As noted above, this is clear in each of the modes of counter-aesthetic that we have discussed.

Rupture is arguably easily recuperable, the sly nod and a wink is not necessarily a break with the spectacle. *Détournement* can slide into recuperation by normalizing the aesthetic it seems to criticize. Furthermore, as we have already noted, it remains questionable how both rupture and *détournement* can mobilize people.

Solidarity's aesthetic can be coopted and can be used to glorify or justify the mobilization of 'the masses' by oppressive regimes. For Debord, an important aspect of *détournement*, to avoid recuperation, was to remain protean and flexible. These tactics cannot therefore be thought of as fixed techniques, but rather different components of an overall aesthetic strategy which necessarily goes beyond isolated aesthetic production. Counter-aesthetics is only meaningful as a product of existing political movements and organization, avoiding recuperation or insignificance by being framed through a wider political project.

9

Provocation and Possibility in Counter-Aesthetics

Anastasia Tataryn

Hope is the opposite of security. It is the opposite of naïve optimism. The category of danger is always within it. Hope is not confidence.[1]

Thinking anarchically poses a challenge to the juridification of international problems. Juridification involves applying a prescriptive frame, i.e. the modern legal frame which includes international criminal law and justice, to contexts according to predetermined categories of recognition. Within this legal frame, and the practise of international law, a stage is set for the enactment and performance of Justice. Law and Justice are bestowed onto victims and perpetrators through the choreography of international criminal law and legal trials, as well as the marketized melodrama of violence commonplace in legal discourses and public (including media) imaginations. The choreography of international criminal law orbits a promise of Justice, heralding resolution from within the modern legal frame. While the power of the aesthetic often lies in it being experiential, felt, and subjective, the aesthetic of law has become emblematic of the order and security that Law and Justice are believed to provide.[2] Law's aesthetic, and Justice as the

---

1. Ernst Bloch quoted in Athena Athanasiou, 'At Odds with the Temporalities of the Im-possible; or, What Critical Theory Can (Still) Do,' *Critical Times* 3/2 (2020).
2. I am informed here by the work of Peter Fitzpatrick in the *Mythology of Modern Law* (Abington: Routledge, 1992) and other critical legal scholars whose work has explored the (false) primacy of modern law (see Susan Marks, 'Human rights and root causes,' *Modern Law Review* 74/ 1 (2011); Duncan Kennedy, *The Critique of Adjudication* (Cambridge: Harvard University Press, 1998)). Modern law is a product of a particular historical and cultural movement. Law claims universality (rule of law,

resolution brought about by Law, is indistinguishable from the presentation of law's infrastructure, both spatial and temporal. Similarly, what may be considered a *counter*-aesthetic ironically reveals not only the predictability but expectation of a normative aesthetic—even if ostensibly 'counter.' To contrast the potential for a normative binary of aesthetic versus *counter*-aesthetic, I explore anarchic thinking not only as a theoretical lens but tangibly as a practice in contemporary dance choreography. As a difference, not only a counter-aesthetic to classical dance, contemporary dance choreography can provide an example of a practice, or praxis, of anarchic thinking. Anarchic thinking is not a refusal of a frame, neither is it an oppositional binary. Indeed, I explore *choreography*, not random acts of physical movement. The difference explored through thinking anarchically within and through contemporary dance choreography offers an experience of resistance that radically challenges normative frames of intelligibility.

Choreographer Crystal Pite's *Body and Soul* and *Tempest Replica* offer a site through which to explore the provocative question, what is it that can be pursued, as a challenge, through bringing attention to counter-aesthetics? Is a counter-aesthetic designed to—or prepared to—disrupt the choreography that asserts a normative Justice in international law? Thinking anarchically does not suggest ignoring or destroying all power and authority. In fact, this critical approach does not attempt to dismantle or deny that there is or will always be a choreographer, a frame, or a limit.[3] Rather an anarchic possibility as a counter-aesthetic is a rupture that explores power and authority as contingent and non-universal. For this, I turn to Hélène Cixous' *écriture féminine* to consider possibilities where Law and Justice are aesthetics in and of themselves, existing among multiple possible aesthetics of law and justice.

Aesthetics and Counter-Aesthetics of International Criminal Law

When we think about challenging victim stereotyping and deconstructing an aesthetic or counter-aesthetic, what is it that we are aiming for?

---

justice, etc.) yet law as we know it within the liberal, Western, legal tradition is historically specific. See Katrina Forrester, *In the Shadow of Justice* (Princeton, NJ: Princeton University Press, 2019),

3. For a more detailed exploration of law as a limit, see Anastasia Tataryn, *Law, Migration and Precarious Labour: Ecotechnics of the Social* (Oxford: Routledge, 2021) and Jean-Luc Nancy, *Experience of Freedom* trans. Bridget McDonald (Sunford: Stanford University Press, 1993).

Authors included in this collection have identified that there is a problem or impasse understood as the over-juridification of life. Namely, where the infrastructure of law (lawyers, law-makers, judges and the institutions they work for) acts *as if* the legal architecture (including trials, judgements, public shaming, sanctions, prison or rehabilitation) could repair wrongs or bring an end to violence and atrocity. This legal architecture relies on prescribed or predetemined roles and rituals that represent rights and wrongs, horrors and resolution, *as if* law and justice—the former bringing about the latter—was able to capture the experiences and realities of life in war or extremes of violence in order to repair wrongs. As Sofia Stolk writes in this volume, the aesthetical devices engaged to narrate victimhood are built on a hierarchy of power and privilege, where lived experiences are interpreted through the vocabulary of those presiding in the halls, offices, and promotional materials of Law. Every tear, every bead of sweat, is made to work for its worth in Justice; a value, the *worthiness* of a victim for instance, measured by a globalized regime of modern Law. Suffering is put to work for a purpose, an outcome that is judged according to the Laws of the ones that wield the hand of Justice in the International Criminal Court, tribunals and, of course, the international media. The actors of Law are referred to below as the Suited Ones, the ones that wear the suits of Law and Justice; not only the robed lawyers and judges of international law, but all the bodies working and moving within the bureaucracies of Law and Justice. These are the persons familiar and ostensibly comfortable with the vocabularies and discourses of Law and Justice; those who are privileged by the aesthetics of law and occupy the spaces of clean, sterile, 'normal' Justice. It seems to suit them well, the lawyers, judges, and policy makers: they report to governments, funders, the IMF, the World Bank, the US, the UK, to the suited vocabulary of sweat-less, tear-less justice. Unless the adjudicator of this justice is a woman, in which case a single tear may be acceptable, if not appropriate.

Questioning the dominant aesthetic of international law's justice and questioning its counter-aesthetic aims for a break, a difference, and thereby a challenge to the norm. Exploring the power of dominant aesthetics rattles against the comfort of those who weild power within Law's discourses and aesthetic. Against the juridification of international conflict and violence we look for counter-representations to challenge, provoke, overturn or jolt. But counter-representation and critique itself has been capitalized to a form of its own resistance-aesthetic: the hipster, the activist, the Che Guevara quote, the defiant fist in the air, the survivor, the child solider, the dark-skinned figure whose eyes stare directly into the camera lens and make the viewer squirm in their seat with a privileged, purchased discomfort. The Suited Ones in the courts of Justice and offices of Law may condone this resistance. They applaud its honesty, its rawness, its confrontation with 'truth,' 'experience,' and thus encourage its display. Why not? It is marketable, consumable, and even more so when these representations continue to emphasise the contrast between the horrors of violence and the pristine halls of Justice where the Suited Ones appear as the saviours.[4] Misery not only sells, it converts people to the cause of Justice, reasserting a familiar counter-aesthetic as an acceptable binary to the aesthetic. And the Suited Ones can benevolently and sympathetically offer a platform, a podium, a speech at the UN to peasants and activists alike. But most of all the resistance counter-aesthetic gives the Suited Ones, the tearless, sweatless ones, the one thing they need: relevance.[5]

In the choreography of Law and Justice the Suited Ones perform rules, rituals, paradoxes, absurdities, and melodramas.[6] These tropes are known. They have become so familiar as to seem natural or normal in the realm of International Law, particularly the adjudication of international criminal law. Law's justice in courtrooms around the world, moreover, repeats a performance that has been taught, rehearsed, and refined in law schools and law practice for decades, if not centuries.[7] What choreography then is a counter-aesthetic? On the one hand, a counter-aesthetic can equally emerge from the same performance: the 'counter' can provide a contrast as that which needs to be brought within the ambit of Justice. In other words, tamed, such as the grieving mother that needs Justice to bring closure to death, or the 'wild' child soldiers that must be taken from the jungle to have their AK-47s replaced with schoolbooks. On the other hand, a counter-aesthetic

---

4. Popular saviours at that, where popularity is assessed by increased hits on the ICC website and growing numbers of followers on Twitter feeds.
5. As Yoriko Otomo writes, 'the greatest is fear of non-existence,' that is, fear of irrelevance or the disappearance of the subject of human history. Yoriko Otomo, *Unconditional Life: The Postwar International Law Settlement* (Oxford: Oxford University Press, 2016), 89.
6. See Sofia Stolk, 'A Solemn Tale of Horror' (PhD thesis, Vrije Universiteit Amsterdam, 2017).
7. Laurie Levenson, 'Courtroom Demeanor: The Theater of the Courtroom,' *Minnesota Law Review* 582 (2008), accessed 13 July 2021, https://scholarship.law.umn.edu/mlr/582; Duncan Kennedy, *A Critique of Adjudication* (Cambridge, MASS: Harvard University Press, 1998); Peter Goodrich, 'Inutilious Propaedeutics: Performances in Theatre and Law,' *Social & Legal Studies* 29/4 (2020), accessed 13 July 2021, doi:10.1177/0964663919900270.

such as the one I explore through anarchic thinking can be a deep resistance to power. The 'counter' opens space for opposition, disruption, and difference. As Yoriko Otomo writes, law, and international law in particular, is 'fundamentally concerned with the construction and anchoring of value.'[8] Here, value and relevance come from bringing down or enforcing judgement—*as if* law could restore order.[9] The acts of judgement, the trial, the performance of choreographed rituals in the courtrooms and offices of Law—the aesthetic of Justice—create a tangible site and a reality wherein justice can be materialized or made to exist. The resolution found within the same structures that construct the oppositional conflicts in the first place.[10] So, what is it that can be aimed for as a challenge in bringing attention to aesthetics or counter-aesthetics?

Anarchic Bodies

Athena Athanasiou takes up a similar question within critical theory by asking what, now, in our twenty-first century can critical theory still do? Her response looks to the possibility of the impossible. Rather than a mere philosophical exercise, the im/possible is a pursuit of the 'other,' the 'counter'; it is exploring the 'aporetic performative power underlying the uncanny utopian implication of going on ... towards an impossible, unsettled, and indeterminate elsewhere.'[11] Aesthetics plays a key role in reminding us that the impossible surrounds us in the 'out-of-placeness enacted by the knowledges, desires, and troubling affects of displaced and spaced-out bodies.'[12] Bodies 'bear witness to political despair and dispossession,'[13] before and beyond the normative aesthetics prescribed by Law and Justice.

Saul Newman explores the experience of anarchy, which is not a nihilistic move, but a freeing moment, that 'frees action from its telos.'[14] This kind of 'ontological anarchy' has no predetermined end(s), unlike the anarchism proposed by writers such as Kropotkin

---

8. Otomo, *Unconditional Life*, 16.
9. Judgement, with reference to psychoanalysis, can be understood as: 'falling in love with the fantasy that the law returns life to its origin, and fulfils an originary loss.' Otomo, *Unconditional Life*, 17.
10. See Makau Mutua, 'Savages, Victims, and Saviors: The Metaphor of Human Rights,' *Harvard International Law Journal* 42/201 (2001).
11. Athanasiou, 'At Odds,' 258–9.
12. Athanasiou, 'At Odds,' 267.
13. Athanasiou, 'At Odds,' 261.
14. Saul Newman, *PostAnarchism* (Cambridge: Polity Press, 2016), 10.

and Proudhon who sought to substitute one political authority with an alternative other.[15] Ontological anarchy suggests anarchistic thinking as movement, opening onto a counter-aesthetic that dislodges from the very framework of analysis towards the other-already-happening. In refusing to have as an end goal the move from one form (political authority, societal organization) to another, ontological anarchy accepts that there is no end in sight. Rather, attention is constantly returning to the movement that is already taking place. This movement is not made to conform to a binary of good versus evil, or law versus lawlessness, or order versus chaos. Thinking anarchically rather seeks to see life before it is translated or structured by Law: the modern legal order, legal modernity and it's categories, vocabularies and frames. The language of law—be it the frame of the trial or the language of victimhood and criminality via individual perpetrators—ostensibly universalizes and reigns judgement of good and evil on each case and on each singular body. Yet before these experiences are captured within the language of law there is messiness, complexity, and a multiplicity of variables, contingencies, and actors. There is life lived parallel to the law that resists the very temporality and judgement that the Law claims to authoritatively wield.[16] This life parallel to law offers the possibility of alternative expressions, whether of grief, tragedy, or structural and institutional complicity in atrocity and violence. An experience of anarchy, moreover, is a turbulent experience of love and compassion, one that can never be captured into Law or Justice. It demands a different aesthetical experience all together: one that can seem, as Athanasiou states above, impossible. The counter-aesthetic of expression, experience, and emotion, not just of those who have physically or tangibly suffered an identified violence, but the expression, experience, and emotion of all of us is perhaps the greatest counter-aesthetic to the Suited Ones continuing the rituals of Law and Justice.

---

15. Saul Newman, 'Postanarchism today: Anarchism and political theory,' in *The Anarchist Imagination,* ed. Carl Levy and Saul Newman (London: Routledge, 2019), 83.

16. See Elena Loizidou, 'Love, Law, Anarchism,' in *Law and Philosophical Theory: Critical Intersections,* ed. Thanos Zartaloudis (Maryland: Rowan & Littlefield Publishers, 2018). Loizidou quotes Goldman: 'anarchism, a movement that aims at the social, political, economic and spiritual emancipation of the human race-without a ruler-no master and no ought-living life without 'oughts,' from Emma Goldman, 'Marriage and Love,' in *Anarchism and Other Essays* (New York: Dover Publications, 1969), 227.

Thinking anarchically is not only counter-aesthetic. Thinking anarchichally is not about replacing one aesthetic with another or denying the inevitability of a frame, i.e. a determination or choreography.[17] Thinking anarchically suggests an opening onto a multiplicity of expression that challenges the status quo of stagnant power and the manufactured hubris and superiority of international law. Anarchic thinking therefore urges a plurality of experiences and emotions as an 'ethical point of departure' resisting the finality or necessity of existing power structures.[18] As an illustration of thinking anarchically—not to ignore or destroy power and authority, but to expose its contingent, non-universal nature and, ultimately, to explore the dominant normative order as an aesthetic in and of itself, as one of multiple possible aesthetics—I turn to the works of choreographer Crystal Pite: *Tempest Replica* (2011) and *Body and Soul* (2019).

Vital Conflict

Pite describes her choreography as the only way she has found to grapple the world in its current form. For Pite, the body in motion is a resistance to death, but as such the body in motion is constantly in vital conflict.[19] The tension between conflicting energies and movement within the body are the origin of expression and communication. This vital conflict extends beyond the body to form the body of art that Pite produces. Pite's choreography follows a circular, infinite, flow: conflict and tension that leads to release and resolution yet only to circle back to conflict. Like the anarchist subject that is in constant questioning, Pite's bodies are in perpetual turbulence and ambivalence, seizing and releasing. The viewer, or audience, sees muscles, arms, legs, heads, expressing the infinite motion of life. For instance, we see the sea; then a heartbeat. The movements are rehersed, yes, and Pite is a choreographer. But the purpose or aim is anarchic: to open rather than to close, to question rather than to answer.[20]

---

17. See ecotechnics in Tataryn, *Law, Migration, and Precarious Labour*, 4–7.
18. Saul Newman, 'Postanarchism today,' in Levy and Newman, *The Anarchist Imagination*, 82.
19. 'Crystal Pite: Conflict is Vital,' Creative Mornings HQ, accessed 13 July 2021, https://www.youtube.com/watch?v=QG5S31Q7DPM.
20. Here Judith Butler's work becomes prescient, which Mona Lloyd describes as posing questions in the place of normative assertions 'to open a field rather than close it.' Mona Lloyd, *Judith Butler* (Cambridge: Polity Press, 2007), 22.

In *Tempest Replica*, created for her Canadian dance company, Kidd Pivot confronts themes from Shakespeare's The Tempest through two parallel worlds. The first represents a minimalist narrative of the tale of the magician Prospero and his creations. The second consists of portraits of the characters and their relationships, represented through physical (bodily) language.[21] Through these parallel worlds, in Pite's words, 'the choreography becomes more than just a dance between two people – rather, it is imbued with a story we have all shared.'[22] This story of 'relationships between the civilized and the wild echo the tension between the conscious and the unconscious, the instinct and the intellect.'[23] The audience and dancers are united in an experience of a familiar, shared emotion without having to put it to words or explain it—the entire experience is *felt*. Meanwhile, there is no singular claim or experience that the *Tempest Replica* espouses. There is no central common cause, nor any affirmation of a specific emotion or response. Rather, the experience of the movement is meant to 'move' people; to give body to a shared concern or experience. The emotion, ex-pression, is not made intelligible within the normative, expected, and comfortable aesthetic frame.

To extrapolate this to law, these are experiences that are *not juridified* by the normative frame of modern law. While the law, in aiming to control the aesthetics of justice, advertises itself through aesthetics and counter-aesthetics of victims, perpetrators, and the suited arbiters of Justice, Pite's choreography feels through the conflict without an end goal or mandate. The circular, infinite flow of tension and release speaks to a justice that cannot be captured in the halls of Justice. The non-juridified body poses the fundamental challenge to the normative aesthetic of international law and justice.

Pite's 2019 piece for the Paris Opera Ballet, entitled *Body and Soul*, offers no solution or resolution within its performance – like *Tempest Replica*.[24] There is only the opening of emotion and an invitation to *feel* with the performers, to feel through the movement as two contrasting ideas—bodies, groups—collide from a desire for connectedness. *Body and Soul* begins as a series of duets between beings that are in connection and conflict.[25] This movement is accompanied by a voice,

---

21. 'Kidd Pivot: Works – The Tempest Replica,' Kidd Pivot, accessed 13 July 2021, https://kiddpivot.org/works/the-tempest-replica/
22. 'Kidd Pivot: Works – The Tempest Replica.'
23. 'Kidd Pivot: Works – The Tempest Replica.'
24. 'Crystal Pite: Body and Soul,' Foundation BNP Paribas, accessed 13 July 2021, https://youtu.be/GXGzJpv-9tg.
25. See clip 'Body and Soul (Lenore Baulac & Hugo Marchand)' 2019, accessed 13

unemotionally, narrating the movement: 'right, left, left, right, arm up, head down.' This builds to include: groups against each other; groups against one; one emerging from group. Couples in movement express conflict, love, loss, mourning, and anger, all brought together by and through the rhythm of a heartbeat. This rhythm returns later, not so clearly as a beating heart, but as the sea, that is unruly, chaotic, but ever rhythmic.

Pite's choreography says everything without saying anything. Bodies in white and black, falling, swaying, becoming the ocean, violent, soothing, searching, loosing, failing. Arms, fingers, palms, pulsing in unison; a heartbeat, ominous and elemental. In one scene a *pas de deux* involves two figures connecting, melting into each other, and then, abruptly, the music cuts. Lights down. Over.[26] To the audience expecting classical dance, the abrupt, elemental choreography can be jarring, uncomfortable, and unsettling. *Body and Soul* is divided into three parts, the third of which was the most unsettling, even disliked outright by reviewers as detailed below. While the first two parts include dancers in couples and groups wearing suits, heavy black coats, or body-suits—all in black or white—in part three, dancers emerge in alien, Stranger Things-esque prosthetics and oily bodysuits. Insect-like the dancers move to a soundtrack that emits non-human words, staccato-ed incomprehensible dialogue. The beautiful, lithe dancers of parts one and two remain lithe and beautiful, only unrecognizable, alien, covered in black slick. Curiously, it is also the first and only time we see dancers in pointe shoes, the footwear classically expected of ballet dancers. The alien insect ballerinas perform with the same voice-narrated choreography, growing in numbers, delicately repeating in unison what was previously seen expressed by 'relatable' dancers' bodies.

Parts one and two present us with recognizable bodies, albeit in contemporary dance form rather than classical ballet. The bodies perform in struggle and movement but nevertheless as Suited Ones. Part three, however, banishes recognition. The audience is disoriented. Yet the alien insect-like beings conform to the same movements and themes as the former two parts. As part three develops, it suggests a shared existence, bizarrely concluding with a 1970s disco-like finale with the dancers in slick alien body suits, pincher prosthetics, and pod headgear. In the experience of watching *Body and Soul*, the repetitive movements

---

July 2021, https://youtu.be/1rA6E9IpVGA
26. 'Body and Soul, by Crystal Pite – Teaser' Paris Opera, accessed 13 July 2021, https://youtu.be/6L16YOXFRCo

performed by the Suited dancers display what an audience expects to see of a dancer's body and costume. This may feel acceptable, even aesthetically pleasing and appropriate. When otherwise costumed in part three, the audience experience changes. When contained, audiences can deal with some discomfort in dance, such as androgony or bare-feet rather than pointe shoes. But take these 'etoiles of the Paris Opera Ballet' and put them into pod headgear, prosthetic limbs, and oily black unitards, and the reception is not quite the same. A New York Times Review of *Body and Soul* illustrates how our difficulty with aesthetics or attempts at counter-aesthetics provoke distain and dismissal: we do not like it.[27] It makes us uncomfortable. It bewilders us. Confuses and unsettles. It is preferable to have the Suited Ones steer us towards the normative zone of comfort, predictability, and contained anguish. Here, our emotions—whether mourning, fear, excitement, or sympathy—may follow a script through which our emotions may be formed and guided. It is under these contained circumstances that the Law acts so that Justice may prevail.

Relating *Body and Soul* to international law and justice begs us to question, what is the aesthetic of conflict? An aesthetic of agony? What is the aesthetic of despair without redemption? Modern law has developed *as if* there was a proper way to contain, determine, and frame the experiences of violence, agony, and suffering. The juridification of international conflict—or the creation of conflict which is then adjudicated in the halls of Justice by the Suited Ones—relies on the myth that conflict, agony, despair, and redemption can be legally remedied. Yet is there space in Justice to feel unfairness, violence, or loss as an experience of the irresolution and infinite circularity of conflict? The circularity would leave no option but to confront the impossibility of Justice where all one can do is repeat the same movements; whispered, murky, increasingly coordinated, syncopated. Pite's creations are forever bodies in tension and conflict, but rife with beauty, life, and emotion. In opening up to thinking anarchically, are we prepared to forfite the myth of Law and Justice, and question the privileged Suited Ones when we disrupt the normative frames of their choreography?

'écriture féminine'

In 1976, Hélène Cixous wrote a counter-aesthetic, *écriture féminine*, to contrast the dominant symbolic discourse that underpins Western

---

27. Roslyn Sulcas, 'Review: Crystal Pite's Disjointed 'Body and Soul' in Paris,' *New York Times*, 27 October 2019, accessed 13 July 2021, https://www.nytimes.com/2019/10/27/arts/dance/crystal-pite-body-and-soul-review.html.

thought. As a feminist scholar, she observed that symbolic masculine discourse is a metaphysical construct that serves to define humanness. Notions of property, individual subjectivity, autonomy, rationality, and capacity are upheld against a 'feminine' one, not necessarily limited to biology but one that represents the detriment or what is lacking in the (male) human. The metaphysics founding the international domain (in international law, the idea of the 'international')[28] and, relatedly, the idea of the human, deny alternative bodies and expressions of being by subjugating these alternatives as 'savage,' 'primitive,'[29] and 'feminine': hysterical, emotional, traumatized, irrational, dependent. As other contributions to this volume have demonstrated, tropes of these other-bodies persist in the construction of victimhood: victims, including 'the refugee,' who lack full subjectivity and humanness. In other words, they are the bodies the Suited Ones look down upon to bestow Law and Justice.

Cixous, in resistance to this pervasive norm that has defined (legal and cultural) modernity instead writes the 'feminine.' Writing the feminine, *écriture féminine*, is for Cixous best embodied as laughter, the laugh of the Medusa. The Medusa, for Cixous, is not to be feared: 'you only have to look at the Medusa straight on to see her. And she's not deadly. She's beautiful and she's laughing.'[30] Against the fear of irrelevance carried by the Suited Ones, wherein there exists an unspoken acknowledgement that Law and Justice cannot return us to an original position and restore Order, écriture feminine writes the body in all its messiness, indeterminacy, and beauty.

Re-visiting Cixous's writing in our present day brings to light that a counter-aesthetic to the juridification of international problems, or to the aesthetic of Law and Justice that reign in international legal arenas, is not a creation of something new but involves recognising what is 'behind the curtain.' What already exists yet is ignored, silenced, or devalued. Introducing abnormality, messiness, disability, or disfunction, challenges the symbolic discourse of what is normal, ordered,

---

28. See Peter Fitzpatrick, *Modernism and the Grounds of Law* (Cambridge: Cambridge University Press, 2001) for a critique of Vitoria and Grotius as the founders of international law and claims to law's universal and global presence. See also, Anastasia Tataryn and Erdem Ertürk, 'Unrecognised States: The Necessary Affirmation of the Event of International Law,' *Law and Critique* 31 (2021).
29. See Catherine E Walsh, 'Insurgency and Decolonial Prospect, Praxis, and Project,' in Walter D Mignolo and Catherine E Walsh, *On Decoloniality* (Durham: Duke University Press, 2018), 33.
30. Hélène Cixous, 'The Laugh of the Medusa,' trans. Keith Cohen and Paula Cohen, *Signs* 1/4 (1976), 885.

and functional. Not as an end to constitute another replacement aesthetic, but rather opening onto realities, experiences, and lives being lived according to a multiplicity of different discourses. Cixous's articulation of *écriture féminine* parallels the aesthetics of thinking anarchically:

> it is impossible to define a feminine practice of writing, and this is an impossibility that will remain, for this practice can never be theorized, enclosed, coded—which doesn't mean that it doesn't exist. ... It will be conceived of only by subjects who are breakers of automatisms, by peripheral figures that no authority can ever subjugate.[31]

The writing of feminine writing revels in that dimension of life and living that 'exceeds and resists' the symbolic control of the masculine.[32]

In her book *Unconditional Life*, Otomo enacts the counter-aesthetic of *écriture féminine* as anarchic thinking in international law. Otomo suggests that some of the impasses and struggles faced by jurists of international law—in the encounter between Law and the impossibility of any originary return to humanness or restorations, of Justice—can be thought of as a phenomenon akin to 'hysteria.' Hysteria, according to Sigmund Freud, was the archetypal feminine malaise. Rather than either embrace hysteria as a revolutionary potential or discount it as an illness within international legal thought, Otomo suggests thinking through the impasses of international law using écriture féminine. In her own work, she demonstrates an anarchic thinking of international law[33] as a poetic reflection on the origins of international law.[34] This takes the form of a re-writing of events through a feminine perspective on the signing of the Treaty of Westphalia. Within this poem, Otomo's *écriture féminine* reflects on the 'virtues' of international law. For Otomo, this 'means moving away from the idea that virtue is to be measured in terms of international law's ability to preserve the inviolability of the state or its bodies,'[35] towards thinking of international law's cases and applications as attentive to the particularities of history, relationality, and materiality.[36] Such an attentiveness to the vital and impossible

---

31. Cixous, 'Laugh of the Medusa,' 883.
32. Saul Newman describes the 'anarchic dimension to life' as that which 'exceeds and resists this control [of the masculine].' Newman, *PostAnarchism*, 18.
33. This is my observation of her work, not a phrase or description Otomo uses herself.
34. See Otomo, *Unconditional Life*, 135–144.
35. Otomo, *Unconditional Life*, 144.
36. In her Epilogue, Otomo 'urges readers to embrace a poetics that resists the

conflict of bodies in movement is necessary everywhere, whether in choreography of dance or choreography of international law, in order to comprehend the possibility of a counter-aesthetic to international justice. A counter-aesthetic therefore needs to be a deep, foundational critique and refusal of the normative frame. By refusing the primacy of and false claim to normality or naturalness[37], we open onto other vocabularies of emotion, experience, and expression.[38] Such refusal does not deny that there will be a frame but fundamentally resists the singular exclusivity of Law and Justice as manifest in the modern Western, liberal legal frame.

Conclusion

An anarchical thinking, or thinking anarchically, is manifest in movement, dance, as well as counter-aesthetical movements in philosophy and literature, such as *écriture féminine*. These 'movements' of thought and embodiment of conflict dismantle normative frames of conceptualizing violence, victimhood, and justice. The vital conflict of bodies in motion, like the indeterminacy and groundlessness that comes with letting go of the modern—Western, liberal, colonial, patriarchal—belief that there is one able, clean, functional, and secure space of order and justice, exposes the limitations of Law and Justice.

Law does not move people. A singular Justice cannot be found within Law. The Justice of the Suited Ones is a predetermined and performed Justice that has already declared *them* the saviours. The justice of the body and soul, however, is an anarchic justice. In 1934, Simone Weil wrote that workers need poetry more than bread. Law needs poetry more than judgement. The world needs expression and movement, more than salvation or Suited saviours. In exploring aesthetics and counter-aesthetics, a singular resolution or an alternative consensus is not going to serve the multiplicity of experience and expression needed to grapple with the vital conflict of Law and Justice. Rather, the radical anarchic potential lies in our openness to ceaseless and conflictual movement, expressed through plural aesthetical choreographies and forms.

---

violent binaries engendered by existing forms of legal syntax.' Otomo, *Unconditional Life*, 160.
37. On false contingency, see Susan Marks, 'False contingency,' *Current Legal Problems* 62/1 (2009).
38. See Mignolo and Walsh, *On Decolonality*. See also Tataryn, *Law, Migration, and Precarious Labour*.

10

Recasting Atrocities as Public Health Catastrophes

Randle DeFalco

Dominant shared understandings of genocide, crimes against humanity, and war crimes remain grounded in an aesthetics of horrific spectacle.[1] This emphasis on spectacular harms helps obscure the culpability and potential criminality of equivalently severe harms brought about through slow and attritive forms of harm causation that may be aesthetically unspectacular in nature. The emphasis on spectacle also helps to perpetuate oversimplified, decontextualized understandings of even the most aesthetically paradigmatic atrocities. Moreover, what harms are recognized as potential international crimes dictates what individuals are viewed as potential victims and/or perpetrators. Victims tend to be framed as hapless, feminized individuals defined wholly by their victim status.[2] Perpetrators, meanwhile, are presented as sophisticated 'beasts' or 'savages' in need of civilizing.[3] These simplistic representations of victims, perpetrators, and atrocities themselves, combine to transform complex situations involving varying motivations and culpabilities, and overlapping structural and direct forms of violence, into relatively straightforward (and highly marketable) dramas of good and evil.[4]

---

1. Randle C. DeFalco, *Invisible Atrocities: The Aesthetic Biases of International Criminal Justice* (New York: Cambridge University Press, 2022).
2. Christine Schwöbel-Patel, 'Spectacle in International Criminal Law: The Fundraising Image of Victimhood,' *London Review of International Law* 4/2 (2016).
3. Sofia Stolk, 'A Sophisticated Beast? On the Construction of an 'Ideal' Perpetrator in the Opening Statements of International Criminal Trials,' *European Journal of International Law* 29/3 (2018).
4. For an account of this highlight successful 'cross-fertilization' of marketing a brand of 'global justice' grounded in international criminal law, see Christine Schwöbel-Patel, *Marketing Global Justice: The Political Economy of International Criminal*

The visibility of harm, culpability, and victimhood are all mediated through this myopic focus on the spectacular at the expense of the everyday in this dominant atrocity aesthetic of horrific spectacle. Decades of victimization suffered by Rohingya populations in Myanmar, for example, are ignored in favor of a narrow focus on relatively recent spectacular forms of targeted violence.[5] Settler colonial atrocities in places such as Canada were largely ignored despite overwhelming evidence—until the spectacle of unearthing mass graves of children on the former grounds of residential schools.[6] Meanwhile, even these aesthetically paradigmatic forms of atrocity violence remain largely dehistoricized and decontextualized.[7] The spectre of colonialism remains outside the gaze of the law and connections with ongoing violence and oppression are ignored. The burning of Rohingya villages is not connected to Burmese and British imperialism in the Rakhine region and decades of active persecution are set aside as the prelude to contemporary eruptions of shocking violence. Deaths of Indigenous children at residential schools in settler colonial nations such as Canada are not connected to continuing forms of oppression such as poverty, over-carceration, and extreme precarity afflicting Indigenous communities today.[8]

This chapter considers whether efforts to conceptualize atrocity crimes as public health catastrophes might provide a useful tactic to combat the dominant horrific spectacle model of atrocity described

---

Law (New York: Cambridge University Press, 2021), 60–95.
5. See Randle C. DeFalco, 'Time and the Visibility of Slow Atrocity Violence,' *International Criminal Law Review* 21 (2021), 922–26.
6. See Pauline Wakeham, 'The Slow Violence of Settler Colonialism: Genocide, Attrition, and the Long Emergency of Invasion,' *Journal of Genocide Research* 24/3 (2021); Kiera L. Ladner, 'Political Genocide: Killing Nations through Legislation and Slow-Moving Poison,' in *Colonial Genocide in Indigenous North America*, eds. Andrew Woolford, Alexander Laban Hinton and Jeff Benvenuto (Durham: Duke University Press, 2014). This is not to suggest that settler colonial atrocities in Canada do not continue to be ignored or minimized, but rather that recognition has increased in the wake of this mapping and exhumation efforts.
7. See Alyssa Couchie, '(Re)Braiding Frayed Sweetgrass for Niijaansinaanik (Our Children): Understanding the 'Sixties Scoop' Through the Lens of Slow Atrocity Violence,' *Michigan Journal of International Law*, Volume 44, Issue 3 (2023), pp. 405-443.
8. See Paul J. Kim, 'Social Determinants of Health Inequities in Indigenous Canadians Through a Life Course Approach to Colonialism and the Residential School System,' *Health Equity* 3/1 (2019); Davinder Singh, Sarah Prowse, and Marcia Anderson, 'Overincarceration of Indigenous People: A Health Crisis,' *Canadian Medical Association Journal* 191/18 (2019).

above as part of a broader strategy aimed at diversifying and expanding the scope of prevention and justice-seeking efforts.[9] Unlike international crimes, public health catastrophes tend to be viewed as complex, causally multifaceted phenomena, and the lens of public health explicitly focuses on collective wellbeing: health at the population rather than the individual level.[10] The field of public health arguably offers tools of prevention and treatment that may be more useful in addressing health issues—including mental health issues—contributing to and flowing from atrocity violence.[11] Such emphasis on multi-causality and populations as collectives are among the main reasons why situations framed primarily as public health catastrophes tend not to also be viewed through a criminal law lens, focused, as the criminal law is, on individuated assessments of causation and culpability.[12] The notion that individual criminal culpability may exist within a broader public health catastrophe, such as the global COVID-19 pandemic is, even when contemplated, treated as novel and unusual.[13] Yet it is precisely

---

9. I propose such a reconceptualization elsewhere. See Randle C. DeFalco, '(Re) Conceptualizing Atrocity Crimes as Public Health Catastrophes,' in *Public Health, Mental Health and Mass Atrocity Prevention*, ed. Jocelyn Getgen Kestenbaum, Caitlin O. Mahoney and Amy E. Meade (New York: Routledge, 2021).

10. For example, in the realm of atrocity prevention, James Waller describes a public health based approach as a 'population-based health model where the aim is the prevention of the disease of mass atrocities.' James Waller, 'Foreword,' in *Public Health, Mental Health, and Mass Atrocity Prevention*, ed. Jocelyn Getgen Kestenbaum et al. (London: Routledge, 2021), xvi.

11. Jocelyn Getgen Kestenbaum et al., 'Introduction,' in *Public Health, Mental Health and Mass Atrocity Prevention*, ed. Jocelyn Getgen Kestenbaum et al. (London: Routledge, 2021), 8–9.

12. See Matiangai Sirleaf, 'Ebola Does Not Fall from the Sky: Structural Violence and International Responsibility,' *Vanderbilt Journal of Transnational Law* 51/ 3 (2018). Sirleaf notes that while 'structural violence [such as recent Ebola outbreaks in West Africa] does not ordinarily involve cognizable crimes, criminal law doctrine is nonetheless helpful in better understanding the role of causation in structural violence.'

13. For discussions of the theoretical applicability of international criminal law to failures to respond appropriately to the COVID-19 pandemic, see David J. Scheffer, 'Is It a Crime to Mishandle a Public Health Response?,' *PassBlue*, April 26, 2020, accessed 5 July 2023, https://www.passblue.com/2020/04/26/is-it-a-crime-to-mishandle-a-public-health-response/; 'Trump's Coronavirus Response: Genocide By Default?,' *Opinio Juris*, May 15, 2020, accessed 5 July 2023, http://opiniojuris.org/2020/05/15/trumps-coronavirus-response-genocide-by-default/. Brazilian President Jair Bolsonaro has been accused of committing crimes against humanity by a fellow Brazilian politician predicated on his active mismanagement of the pandemic, but it remains unclear whether any legal proceedings will result. See Jack Nicas, 'Brazilian Leader Accused of Crimes Against Humanity in Pandemic Response,' *The New York Times*, October

because a purposeful reframing of atrocities through a public health lens challenges dominant notions of harm, causation, and culpability, as well as what responses thereto are appropriate, that such a reframing of international criminal law may be useful.[14]

To think through the specifically aesthetic possibilities of this proposed normative shift in atrocity conceptualization, this chapter assesses whether the imagery and language of public health might be helpful to tactics of resisting the increasing hegemony of international criminal law in global justice discourses as proposed by Christine Schwöbel-Patel in her book, *Marketing Global Justice*.[15] These tactics, framed by Schwöbel-Patel as potential means of 'occupying' global justice, are: 'unplugging,' 'de-spectacularizing,' 'unmasking,' and 'resisting' current dominant global justice discourses.[16] This chapter considers whether reframing atrocities as public health catastrophes might prove useful to such efforts. To do so, it considers a variety of situations wherein atrocity violence has been ignored altogether, with its gravity artificially downgraded through partial or total denial, and its root causes and/or continuing ramifications for affected populations obscured. For each, it considers whether a public health-based approach might assist efforts to disrupt or 'occupy' prevailing global justice and international criminal law narratives through one or more of the four tactics referenced above. I suggest that there may be some merit in looking to public health as an alternative framework of conceptualizing atrocity violence and that doing so might be helpful to tactics of occupying global justice. Ultimately, however, this chapter concludes that such a shift is at best but one minor component of a much-needed broader reimagining of international criminal law and its relationship to global justice.

The Current Dominant Atrocity Aesthetic: International Crimes as Horrific Spectacles

International criminal law tends to invisibilize a certain kind of violence, specifically violence that is slow, attritive, and decidedly unspectacular in nature.[17] A notable example that I have invoked in my previous

---

19, 2021, accessed 5 July 2023, https://www.nytimes.com/2021/10/19/world/americas/bolsonaro-covid-19-brazil.html.
14. DeFalco, '(Re)Conceptualizing Atrocity Crimes as Public Health Catastrophes,' 25.
15. Schwöbel-Patel, *Marketing Global Justice*, 242–86.
16. Schwöbel-Patel, *Marketing Global Justice*, 243.
17. DeFalco, *Invisible Atrocities*.

work is the creation, enforcement, or perpetuation of famine conditions, including in Khmer Rouge-era Cambodia.[18] I found that in Cambodia and elsewhere, international criminal justice actors and institutions appear to treat famine and other similarly slow and attritive forms of mass harm causation as necessarily situated outside the purview of international criminal justice. While mentioned in passing in judgments and other legal documents, issues such as food availability, starvation, and generalized living conditions tended to be treated as related yet collateral to 'real' atrocity violence, which invariably involves the commission of brutal and spectacular acts of interpersonal violence.[19] Whether a person has access to sufficient food to survive, or other basic necessities meanwhile, seems to repeatedly be framed as related to, but not 'part of' atrocity commission processes. Harmful everyday conditions of life are instead conceptually situated as either (non-justiciable) 'root causes'[20] or collateral consequences of genocide, crimes against humanity, and war crimes rather than part and parcel of them.[21]

Evident in judgments, reports, and other core legal materials, this tendency to view slower forms of violence as outside the scope of

---

18. Randle C. DeFalco, 'Accounting for Famine at the Extraordinary Chambers in the Courts of Cambodia: The Crimes against Humanity of Extermination, Inhumane Acts and Persecution,' *International Journal of Transitional Justice* 5/1 (2011); DeFalco, *Invisible Atrocities*, 152–84.

19. Randle C. DeFalco, 'Justice and Starvation in Cambodia: International Criminal Law and the Khmer Rouge Famine' (LLM thesis: University of Toronto, 2013).

20. On this dynamic in the realm of human rights, including a tendency to identify, and subsequently 'set aside' root causes of human rights violations, see Susan Marks, 'Human Rights and Root Causes: Human Rights and Root Causes,' *The Modern Law Review* 74/1 (2011), 73.

21. For example, in the context of Rwanda, the exclusive focus on atrocities committed during the one hundred day genocide of 1994 has arguably helped obscure various mass harms occurring in the region both before and after the 1995 genocide. Marijke Verpoorten, 'Detecting Hidden Violence: The Spatial Distribution of Excess Mortality in Rwanda,' *Political Geography* 31/1 (2012). Identifying various forms of 'hidden violence' occurring before, after, and alongside the 1994 genocide involving high levels of excess death. Of course, the jurisdiction of the International Criminal Tribunal for Rwanda (ICTR) was temporally limited to 1994 (Statute of the International Tribunal for Rwanda, 8 November 1994, Art. 1). The Tribunal did discuss Rwanda's history and relevant events leading up to the 1994 genocide, but again, such information was not directly relevant to the Tribunal's core work of adjudicating the criminal responsibility of individuals alleged to have participated in international crimes committed solely in 1994. Larissa van den Herik describes the resulting legacy of the ICTR as one of 'spotlighting' certain harms, while relegating other, unaddressed ones to 'black holes' of social and legal invisibility. Larissa van den Herik, 'International Criminal Law as a Spotlight and Black Holes as Constituents of Legacy,' *AJIL Unbound* 110 (2016): 209–13.

international criminal law[22] led me to consider the role of an aesthetics of horrific spectacle in structuring dominant notions of what international crimes are. There seems to be a widely held belief that because international crimes are large in scale and massive in terms of the severity of suffering inflicted, that their commission will necessarily involve the production of horrific spectacles of wrongdoing and harm causation. It is this constructed notion of international crimes as horrific spectacles that I describe as a reigning dominant aesthetic model of atrocity commission.[23] I view this tendency toward horrific spectacles as part of a troubling broader tendency toward oversimplification, decontextualization, and dehistoricization within international criminal law.[24]

Focusing on the most dramatic, spectacular forms of atrocity violence plays a role in tendencies to present those who commit international crimes as devilishly evil and those victimized as feminized and passive individuals, wholly defined by their victimhood.[25] More broadly, these aesthetic proclivities are arguably key components in international criminal law's own colonization and domination of global justice discourses,[26] narrowly focusing such discussions

---

22. For examples of this tendency, see generally DeFalco, *Invisible Atrocities*, 24–62. Evelyne Schmid identifies a similar recognition gap when it comes to the possibility of international crimes being committed through violations of economic, social, and cultural human rights. See generally Evelyne Schmid, *Taking Economic, Social and Cultural Rights Seriously in International Criminal Law* (New York: Cambridge University Press, 2015).
23. DeFalco, *Invisible Atrocities*.
24. These problems are key themes in much of the scholarship critical of international criminal law. See Tor Krever, 'International Criminal Law: An Ideology Critique,' *Leiden Journal of International Law* 26/3 (2013); Karen Engle, "Anti-Impunity and the Turn to Criminal Law in Human Rights,' *Cornell Law Review* 100/5 (2015). For a more recent analysis of the uncritical acceptance of 'requiring penal action for human rights abuses without interrogating what is involved in the relationship between [human rights and criminal legal regimes]' see Mattia Pinto, 'Historical Trends of Human Rights Gone Criminal,' *Human Rights Quarterly* 42 (2020).
25. Stolk, 'A Sophisticated Beast?'; Schwöbel-Patel, 'Spectacle in International Criminal Law." See also Mark Osiel, 'Who Are Atrocity's 'Real' Perpetrators, Who Its 'True' Victims and Beneficiaries?,' *Ethics & International Affairs* 28/3 (2014). Osiel suggests that a set of 'implicit sociological premises—almost ontological assumptions—about what mass atrocity *is*, about who the parties to it really were' create conflicting impulses within atrocity law,.
26. On this colonization process and its implications, see Zinaida Miller, 'Effects of Invisibility: In Search of the 'Economic' in Transitional Justice,' *International Journal of Transitional Justice* 2/3 (2008); Sarah M. H. Nouwen and Wouter G. Werner, 'Monopolizing Global Justice: International Criminal Law as Challenge to Human

on decontextualized, dehistoricized eruptions of mass violence and individual bad actors at the expense of more pressing global justice issues relating to questions such as those of power and inequality.[27] Famine represents one concrete example of a process of mass harm causation often involving a mix of structural causes and culpable acts by individual domestic and/or international actors. Despite persistent myths to the contrary, contemporary famines are overwhelmingly predictable products of human agency rather than unforeseeable 'natural' disasters or products of overpopulation.[28] Nonetheless, outside the context of sieges or the strategic use of starvation of a civilian population as a warfare tactic, famine continues to be viewed as a subject international criminal law has little, if anything, to do with.[29] The relative invisibility of harms such as those associated with famine within international criminal law thus exemplify how the reigning atrocity aesthetic of horrific spectacle may obscure the culpabilities associated with certain exercises of domestic and international power, while highlighting others.

Recasting Atrocities as Public Health Catastrophes: An Overview

In thinking through potential models of atrocity commission, ones with the potential to better capture the complexity and heterogeneity of mass harm causation processes, public health-based approaches to crime and violence developed primarily at the domestic level may prove instructive. In a highly generalized sense, such approaches treat violence and crime as problems to be dealt with by drawing from the fields of public health and epidemiology, rather than primarily criminal justice.[30]

Diversity,' *Journal of International Criminal Justice* 13/1 (2015); Engle, 'Anti-Impunity and the Turn to Criminal Law in Human Rights'; Pinto, 'Historical Trends of Human Rights Gone Criminal."

27. Along these lines, see Frédéric Mégret, 'What Sort of Global Justice Is 'International Criminal Justice'?,' *Journal of International Criminal Justice* 13/1 (2015).

28. See generally Amartya Sen, 'Ingredients of Famine Analysis: Availability and Entitlements,' *The Quarterly Journal of Economics* 96/3 (1981), 433; Cormac Ó Gráda, *Famine: A Short History* (Princeton: Princeton University Press, 2009); Olivier Rubin, *Contemporary Famine Analysis* (New York: Springer, 2016); Alex de Waal, *Mass Starvation: The History and Future of Famine* (Cambridge: Polity Press, 2018).

29. See generally Tom Dannenbaum, 'Siege Starvation: A War Crime of Societal Torture,' *Chicago Journal of International Law* 22/2 (2022), 75; Bridget Conley et al., 'Introduction,' in *Accountability for Mass Starvation: Testing the Limits of the Law*, ed. Bridget Conley et al. (New York: Oxford University Press, 2022).

30. See Roberto Hugh Potter and Jeffrey W. Rosky, 'The Iron Fist in the Latex

Public health-based approaches can be used as a potential alternative framework for understanding and responding to atrocity violence for at least four main reasons.

First, as a discipline focused first and foremost on health outcomes at the population rather than individual level, public health-based approaches tend to recommend a combination of short and long-term interventions aimed at reducing harms associated with crime commission.[31] This dual emphasis, on both present harms and their more diffuse, longer-term root causes, would be a welcome addition to current discourses of international crime, which tend to decentre structural root causes, even when recognizing their salience in a limited way.[32] Such an approach might also help to challenge the false notion that atrocities are events with clearly identifiable beginning and ending points.[33] For example, the spectacular escalation of longstanding anti-Rohingya violence in Myanmar since around 2008 has firmly placed this situation within the canon of contemporary atrocity crimes.[34] Arguably 'slow burning' anti-Rohingya atrocity crimes have a far longer duration, dating

---

Glove: The Intersection of Public Health and Criminal Justice,' *American Journal of Criminal Justice* 38/2 (2013): 276–88.

31. Potter and Rosky, 'The Iron Fist,' 282. This theme, of pushing for greater recognition of root causes of violence and negative public health outcomes and an associated de-emphasis on policing and criminal prosecutions is prevalent in contemporary prison abolition literature, which focuses primarily on domestic criminal justice systems, especially that of the United States.

32. Marks, 'Human Rights and Root Causes'; Rachel López, 'Black Guilt, White Guilt at the International Criminal Court,' ed. Matiangai Sirleaf (Oxford: Oxford University Press, forthcoming).

33. Many scholars of genocide and atrocity, especially non-legal scholars, have resisted the notion that genocides and mass atrocities are discrete 'events' with such clear beginnings and ends, instead viewing them as complex social processes that can wax and wane in terms of intensity and duration. See Sheri P. Rosenberg, 'Genocide Is a Process, Not an Event,' *Genocide Studies and Prevention* 7/1 (2012); Peter B. Owens, Yang Su and David A. Snow, 'Social Scientific Inquiry Into Genocide and Mass Killing: From Unitary Outcome to Complex Processes,' *Annual Review of Sociology* 39/1 (2013); Kerry Whigham, *Resonant Violence: Affect, Memory, and Activism in Post-Genocide Societies* (New Brunswick: Rutgers University Press, 2022); Melanie O'Brien, *From Discrimination to Death: Genocide Process Through a Human Rights* (London: Routledge, 2023).

34. Indeed, legal action characterizing anti-Rohingya violence as involving the commission of international crimes has been undertaken at the International Court of Justice, International Criminal Court, and in Argentinian domestic courts. For an overview of these efforts and this recent framing of anti-Rohingya violence as involving international crimes, see DeFalco, 'Time and the Visibility of Slow Atrocity Violence,' 922–23.

back many decades and having roots in regional imperialism and British colonialism.[35] By looking at how the health and livelihoods of Rohingya populations has been intentionally compromised over many decades, a public health lens might render these older, slower atrocities more visible.

Second, public health-based approaches to crime and violence also minimize the role that criminal prosecutions should play in reducing crime.[36] This acknowledgment—that even if crimes are legally defined, they need not be dealt with solely through criminal, or even legal responses more broadly—tends to get lost when it comes to atrocity commission and the overwhelming emphasis on criminal prosecutions as the preferred, even sole, suitable response.[37] A public health-based understanding of atrocity violence may help illuminate the need for a multifaceted set of health-promoting responses, rather than mere 'accountability' in the form of criminal prosecutions.

Third, public health-based approaches to violence and crime tend to adopt a more expansive understanding of violence itself. For example, in its influential 2002 'World Report on Violence and Health,' the World Health Organization defines violence as the 'intentional use of physical force or power, threatened or actual, against oneself, another person, or against a group or community, that either results in or has a high likelihood of resulting in injury, death, psychological harm, maldevelopment or deprivation.'[38] By including both actual or 'threatened' uses of either 'physical force *or* power,' and encompassing a wide array of harms to individuals or 'communities,' such a definition could help centre the critical role organisational power plays in virtually all processes of mass domination, oppression, and killing.[39]

---

35. See Maung Zarni and Alice Cowley, 'The Slow-Burning Genocide of Myanmar's Rohingya,' *Pacific Rim Law and Policy Journal* 23/3 (2014), 72; Azeem Ibrahim, *The Rohingyas: Inside Myanmar's Hidden Genocide* (London: Hurst, 2016).no. 3 (2014
36. Liana B. Winett, 'Constructing Violence as a Public Health Problem,' *Public Health Reports* 113/6 (1998). See also Achim Wolf, Ron Gray and Seena Fazel, 'Violence as a Public Health Problem: An Ecological Study of 169 Countries,' *Social Science & Medicine* 104 (2014): 220–27. The authors find income inequality to be related to rates of violent crime in low and middle-income countries and recommending 'global action to moderate income inequality to reduce the global health burden of violence.'
37. Along these lines, see Karen Engle, Zinaida Miller and D.M. Davis, eds., Anti-Impunity and the Human Rights Agenda (Cambridge: Cambridge University Press, 2016); Sirleaf, 'Ebola Does Not Fall from the Sky.'
38. World Health Organization, 'World Report on Violence and Health" (Geneva: World Health Organization, 2002), https://apps.who.int/iris/bitstream/handle/10665/42495/9241545615_eng.pdf, 5.
39. See Laurel E. Fletcher and Harvey M. Weinstein, 'Violence and Social Repair:

Fourth and finally, a normative coupling of atrocity and public health could also be useful insofar as the 'spotlight' effect of international criminal law might help emphasize the individual culpabilities routinely involved in the production of large-scale negative public health outcomes.[40] Thus, international criminal law, and its oft-problematic myopic focus on individual culpability for mass harms, might provide a useful method of highlighting the overlooked fact that many public health catastrophes can be at least partially blamed on an identifiable set of individual actors, as well as institutional and structural forces.[41]

In sum, I view a public health paradigm of atrocity commission as valuable primarily in terms of its implications for the visibility of a wider array of harms and associated culpabilities within international criminal law. I posit that if we view atrocities as 'situations wherein powerful actors intentionally bring about catastrophic public health outcomes amongst victim groups,' that this framing may help visibilize not only spectacles of violence, but other slower, more insidious means of harming large numbers of victims, as international crimes.[42]

A Public Health Paradigm as an Effective Counter-Aesthetic Model?

If the primary utility of recasting atrocities as public health catastrophes is the recognition of a broader array of forms of atrocity violence,

---

Rethinking the Contribution of Justice to Reconciliation,' *Human Rights Quarterly* 24 (2002). The authors observe that 'a careful review of the process of social breakdown reveals that the rapidly escalating process of group or collective violence may have its origin in strategy and planning by a select group of individuals but ultimately relies on the force of group power to achieve its ends.'

40. On the 'spotlight' effect of international criminal law, see Larissa van den Herik, 'International Criminal Law as a Spotlight and Black Holes as Constituents of Legacy,' *AJIL Unbound* 110 (2016), 209–13.

41. This approach, of using criminal law general concepts, especially in relation to culpability, does not necessarily require a criminal prosecution-based response to public health crises, even when we can identify individuals bearing some degree of direct culpability. Along these lines, Sirleaf deploys criminal law principles 'to reveal how certain international actors enabled structural violence with Ebola through omission. ... However, [Sirleaf notes that] this does not suggest that the appropriate response to structural violence once attribution of responsibility has occurred is to resort to criminal law ... as a form of securing redress for structural violence internationally.' Sirleaf, Sirleaf, 'Ebola Does Not Fall from the Sky,"12.

42. DeFalco, '(Re)Conceptualizing Atrocity Crimes as Public Health Catastrophes,' 31. There is, of course, a tension in this model between utilization of international criminal law as a means of emphasizing culpable agency, and the emphasis on structural root causes and the reduced role of criminal prosecutions.

the question remains whether such an approach might provide pathways for resisting the broader aestheticized marketing practices that Schwöbel-Patel convincingly demonstrates pervade international criminal law and global justice discourses.[43] As Schwöbel-Patel argues, there is clearly market value to be derived from the current spectacle-based dominant atrocity aesthetic in the attention economy.[44] The spectacle is alluring in its drama and simplicity, and has the ability to compete in a marketplace flooded with information.

The remainder of this chapter considers how such a reconceptualization of atrocity crimes as public health catastrophes may or may not provide pathways for resisting the broader aestheticized marketing practices that Schwöbel-Patel proposes.[45] More specifically, it considers whether adoption of a public health-based understanding of atrocity violence may or may not be helpful in efforts to adopt the four tactics aimed at 'creat[ing] ruptures in the dominant norms, institutions, representations, and ways of thinking and being; and to consider alternatives, not of argument, but of *being* shaped by common themes of struggle and resistance.'[46] These are:

> first, unplugged global justice, which concerns the abandonment of marketized visual and linguistic habits; second, de-spectacularised global justice, which emphasizes the slow and quiet, therefore finding the time and means to focus on context; third, unmasked global justice, which reveals and unsettles stereotypes by means of irony and satire and has a theatrical element to it; and fourth, resistance global justice, which foregrounds agency and insists on an internationalism of solidarity.[47]

Unplugged Global Justice: Looking Away from the Spectacle and Toward Communal Health?

The reigning aesthetic model of atrocities as horrific spectacles is part of a broader, highly successful branding process grounded in the attention economy.[48] The horrific spectacles of atrocity commission processes themselves are the centre-points of a broader drama, replete with stock characters: evil perpetrators, devastated 'grotesque' victims, and

---

43. Schwöbel-Patel, *Marketing Global Justice*.
44. Schwöbel-Patel, *Marketing Global Justice*, 45–50.
45. Schwöbel-Patel, *Marketing Global Justice*.
46. Schwöbel-Patel, *Marketing Global Justice*, 244. Emphasis in original.
47. Schwöbel-Patel, *Marketing Global Justice*, 243.
48. Schwöbel-Patel, *Marketing Global Justice*, 250.

'cool-headed' lawyers and judges, who deliver justice.[49] Courts present the stage where these legal dramas play out.[50] Drawing on Tim Wu's work, Schwöbel-Patel suggests that intentionally looking away, or refusing to consume, spectacles of atrocity can offer a means of 'active resistance' to the 'normalization of spectacle' within international criminal law.[51] One example of such unplugging as resistance provided by Schwöbel-Patel is the objecting to and refusing to consume or share 'images of sad African children that are used to grab the attention of a Western donor community.'[52] The ultimate goal of this tactic is not simply the reduction of the circulation of these stereotypical images of atrocity victims, but rather challenging the marketization of global justice itself, by pushing us (the target consumers of such images) to reconsider how we discuss and think about atrocity and the current (marketized) global justice framework, especially international criminal law.

In terms of unplugging global justice, the question is whether a reframing of atrocities as public health issues may provide us with an alternative language that may be useful in efforts to resist the current marketized rhetoric and imagery that pervades international criminal justice. While we must remain aware of the fact that what we see and recognize is not neutral, but reflects a wide array of choices and underlying assumptions, the language of public health may provide some useful concepts that can be used to challenge the prevailing reliance on spectacle in representing atrocity violence. Along these lines, the process of 'unplugging' is not only looking away from spectacular, stereotypical images of atrocities and their victims/perpetrators, but also resisting the spectacularized language used to describe such events. Rather than (decontextualized and dehistoricized) horrific spectacles of violence, we may describe atrocities as largely predictable public health catastrophes that are the products of both historical factors and 'specific choices made by powerful actors that shape the health outcomes of specific populations' to disastrous effect.[53] Instead of emphasizing the visceral horror of such events, we can unplug by looking away whilst highlighting historical and structural factors that combine to bring about such

---

49. Schwöbel-Patel, *Marketing Global Justice*, 250.
50. Schwöbel-Patel, *Marketing Global Justice*, 250.
51. Schwöbel-Patel, *Marketing Global Justice*, 251.
52. Schwöbel-Patel, *Marketing Global Justice*, 252.
53. DeFalco, '(Re)Conceptualizing Atrocity Crimes as Public Health Catastrophes,' 31. Along these lines, see also generally Sirleaf, 'Ebola Does Not Fall from the Sky."i

violence, along with focusing on a broader array of actions negatively affecting the material conditions of life of relevant populations.

For example, in the context of ongoing discussions of the alleged commission of genocide and other atrocity crimes against Rohingya populations in Myanmar, refusing to look at or recirculate predictable images of burned villages and desperate, malnourished refugees may be a form of 'unplugging.' Instead of recirculating these horrific images, it may be more productive to highlight the roles that colonialism, global anti-Muslim prejudice, and other key factors played in rendering the Rohingya population vulnerable and encouraging their oppression. We may also expand the temporal dimensions of the debate concerning the commission of international crimes against Rohingya victims by unplugging from the stale debate concerning whether the Rohingya have, in a legal sense, been victims of genocide over the past decade or so.[54] The orientation of public health can aid in this process by offering a way to broaden our temporal view in terms of atrocities committed against Rohingya victims. For instance, focusing attention on how overall health within this group has been quite intentionally impaired and mortality rates increased via a longstanding, multifaceted project of persecution through economic, social, and political ostracization carried out by powerful government actors in Myanmar for decades.[55]

Leveraging the language of public health as part of a tactic of unplugging from spectacularized and marketized global justice might also be useful in other contexts by providing an alternative language through which we can demand the lens of justice be expanded, temporally and in terms of the forms of violence involved. To give another example, the disaggregation of violence committed through processes of settler colonialism into a series of largely unrelated discrete events obscures settler colonialism as a broader, multifaceted, long-term atrocity project through which the health of Indigenous populations

---

54. This is not to suggest that the legal question of whether the Rohingya have been victims of genocide is irrelevant or inconsequential, but rather that the tendency to focus on this questions obscures the broader history of violence and oppression experienced by the Rohingya spanning multiple generations. For an excellent overview of issues related to whether the Rohingya have experienced genocide, see Michael Scharf and Paul Williams, 'Talking Foreign Policy - October 1, 2019 Broadcast: 'The Rohingya Genocide," *Case Western Reserve Journal of International Law* 52 (2020), 546–50.
55. See Zarni and Cowley, 'The Slow-Burning Genocide of Myanmar's Rohingya'; Ibrahim, *The Rohingyas: Inside Myanmar's Hidden Genocide*; DeFalco, 'Time and the Visibility of Slow Atrocity Violence.'

have been devastated.⁵⁶ The myth of the 'peaceful frontier' becomes an (even more) absurd proposition than it currently is if we have the tools to conceptually link intermittent spectacular acts of violence committed against Indigenous populations with the various forms of everyday oppression over time that continue to be deeply entangled with such spectacular violence.⁵⁷

Indeed, recent events in Canada exemplify the obsession with horrific spectacle in the recognition of atrocity violence. Evidence that the commission of extremely large-scale atrocities—including genocide—were central facets of settler colonial processes of land acquisition and political domination of Indigenous populations has been abundant and compelling for some time.⁵⁸ Nonetheless, even as the Canadian government and (portions of) its settler population have been forced to begrudgingly admit wrongdoing in the treatment of Indigenous populations, this recognition has remained limited and focused on spectacular atrocity acts. Forced by impending litigation to acknowledge the criminality of its residential school system and the failure to meaningfully investigate violent crimes committed against Indigenous women and girls, the government created a truth commission and a commission of inquiry. Yet, partially through an emphasis on these spectacles of state violence and indifference, settler Canadian society was able to replace the myth of the peaceful frontier with the myth that only a (non-legal, non-criminal) 'cultural' genocide was committed in Canada against Indigenous populations.⁵⁹

---

56. DeFalco, '(Re)Conceptualizing Atrocity Crimes as Public Health Catastrophes,' 21.
57. For examples of discussions of slower forms of atrocity violence in settler colonial contexts, see Jennifer Huseman and Damien Short, "'A Slow Industrial Genocide': Tar Sands and the Indigenous Peoples of Northern Alberta,' *The International Journal of Human Rights* 16/1 (2012): 216–7; Ladner, 'Political Genocide: Killing Nations through Legislation and Slow-Moving Poison'; Wakeham, 'The Slow Violence of Settler Colonialism'; Whigham, *Resonant Violence*."
58. See 'A Legal Analysis of Genocide: Supplementary Report,' National Inquiry into Missing and Murdered Indigenous Women and Girls, June 2019, accessed 5 July 2023, https://www.mmiwg-ffada.ca/wp-content/uploads/2019/06/Supplementary-Report_Genocide.pdf; Patrick Wolfe, 'Settler Colonialism and the Elimination of the Native,' *Journal of Genocide Research* 8/4 (2006); Andrew Woolford and Jeff Benvenuto, 'Canada and Colonial Genocide,' *Journal of Genocide Research* 17/4 (2015); Kona Keast-O'Donovan, 'Convicting the Clergy: Seeking Justice for Residential School Victims through Crimes Against Humanity Prosecutions,' *Manitoba Law Journal* 45/4 (2022).
59. John Barber, 'Canada's Indigenous Schools Policy Was 'Cultural Genocide,' Says Report,' *The Guardian*, 2 June 2015, accessed 5 July 2023, http://www.theguardian.

'Unplugging' from this narrative and associated representations of violence against Indigenous Canadian populations that are limited to the residential school system and indifference of authorities investigating crimes and disappearances, while using the language of public health, can help insist on a more complicated, and more complete picture when it comes to the central role atrocity commission has played in settler colonial processes in Canada and elsewhere. For example, by emphasizing the close relationships between the logic of residential schools ('kill the Indian in the child') and the broader calamitous demographic impact on Indigenous populations in Canada (and the United States,[60] as well as elsewhere), we may begin a much-needed reframing of settler colonialism as a systematized form of atrocity commission. In this new framing, settler colonialism is inextricably intertwined with atrocity commission.[61] Moreover, if we are able to centre everyday forms of past violence and oppression, connections with ongoing anti-Indigenous violence and oppression in Canada and elsewhere may be more readily made.[62] Again, there is a possibility that the language of public health may be of assistance here, by allowing us to talk in terms of demographic impacts and disparate health outcomes, rather than fretting over the now-unknowable subjective motivations of those responsible and whether they possessed genocidal intent.

The need to push back against reductionist apologias for the ongoing atrocities committed against Indigenous populations is especially pressing in Canada, which is in the midst of yet another (extremely limited) reckoning with its violent past in the wake of the unearthing of numerous mass graves at former residential school sites.[63] The discovery

---

com/world/2015/jun/02/canada-indigenous-schools-cultural-genocide-report.
60. Roxanne Dunbar-Ortiz, *An Indigenous Peoples' History of the United States* (Boston: Beacon Press, 2014).
61. On the logic of 'kill the Indian in the child' see Truth and Reconciliation Commission of Canada, 'Honouring the Truth, Reconciling for the Future: Summary of the Final Report of the Truth and Reconciliation Commission of Canada,' 2015, 130, 369, 375–76, http://www.trc.ca/assets/pdf/Honouring_the_Truth_Reconciling_for_the_Future_July_23_2015.pdf.
62. For example, despite being deeply intertwined with the residential school system, the mass removal of indigenous children from their homes and their placement in non-indigenous households remains largely overlooked as a potential process of atrocity crime commission in Canada. Couchie, '(Re)Braiding Frayed Sweetgrass for Niijaansinaanik (Our Children): Understanding the 'Sixties Scoop' Through the Lens of Slow Atrocity Violence."
63. See Ian Austen, 'How Thousands of Indigenous Children Vanished in Canada,' *The New York Times*, 7 June 2021 accessed 5 July 2023, https://www.nytimes.

of mass graves, themselves aesthetically paradigmatic 'evidence' of atrocity violence, is a prime example of the persistence of spectacle in orienting social attention.[64] Evidence that members of Indigenous populations were killed en masse through a variety of means throughout the construction of Canada as a nation-state has been abundant for decades. Yet, the spectacle of unmarked mass graves containing the remains of Indigenous children has become national and international news. Such a horrific spectacle is highly competitive in the attention economy. As Schwöbel-Patel reminds us however, we must be cautious to resist the easy route of trying to harness the marketized attention economy in an attempt to bend it to our will, to turn injustices we view as in urgent need of redress into spectacles in an attempt to gain attention.[65]

The potentialities of public health approaches as a tactic of resisting the spectacle and unplugging global justice are limited however and not without risk, as Schwöbel-Patel herself recognizes.[66] On one hand, unplugging risks perpetuating complacency in the wake of atrocity violence. Most, if not all, of the world's currently wealthiest and most powerful nations became wealthy through the commission of extractive atrocity violence. Countries such as Britain, the United States, Canada, various other Western European Nations, Russia, China, Japan, and many others accumulated vast amounts of wealth through plundering the resources of other nations and peoples. This plunder was carried out through various combinations of conduct that now would run the gamut of international crimes: aggression, war crimes, crimes against humanity, and genocide. Ignoring the past is in the interest of those who continue to benefit from the unrecompensed plunder and so unplugging always risks aiding in efforts to not see.

To return to the context of Canada, narrating, documenting, visualizing, and memorializing the real injustices that have taken place requires the kind of sustained effort and attention that the visual economy of spectacle helps us to avoid. To some extent this work has been

---

com/2021/06/07/world/canada/mass-graves-residential-schools.html.
64. Alyssa Couchie and Randle DeFalco, 'Rebraiding Frayed Sweetgrass: The Spectacle of Residential School Exhumations and Invisible Anti-Indigenous Atrocity Violence in Canada,' *Justice in Conflict*, 29 August 2022, accessed 5 July 2023, https://justiceinconflict.org/2022/08/29/rebraiding-frayed-sweetgrass-the-spectacle-of-residential-school-exhumations-and-invisible-anti-indigenous-atrocity-violence-in-canada/.
65. Schwöbel-Patel, *Marketing Global Justice*, xx.
66. Schwöbel-Patel, *Marketing Global Justice*, 256–58.

carried out by Canada's Truth and Reconciliation Commission, whose ninety-four 'calls to action' amount to demands for deep structural reforms to Canada's relationship with Indigenous sovereign nations, including sustained efforts to improve public health equity.[67] In 2015, Prime Minister Justin Trudeau pledged to 'fully implement' all of the calls to action.[68] Yet, a 2021 analysis by the First Nation-led Yellowhead Institute research center concluded that the Canadian government had only moved toward the meaningful implementation of a handful of 'symbolic' calls to action, while failing to take any action toward implementing the calls to action requiring broad structural reforms to Canada's relationship with Indigenous peoples.[69] Notably, this report came out well after the identification and exhumation of mass graves at former residential school sites made national headlines. Thus, even the spectacle of children's bodies being removed from mass graves appears to have failed to move the Canadian government toward anything more than symbolic gestures in implementing the broad reforms called for by the Truth and Reconciliation Commission.

    The spectacle also still seems to grip public imagination. We, the Canadian settler public and its government, may collectively grimace at the ongoing exhumation spectacle and pledge to take action, but such action remains shallow and generally unresponsive to the deep structural reforms necessary to address the continuing harms flowing from the sustained genocidal settler attitudes toward Indigenous populations that enabled the children to be killed and buried in mass graves in the first place. If we insist on replacing the imagery and rhetoric of horror and spectacle surrounding the mass graves, with one couched in the language of public health, might this help combat erasure of experience and harm? If we refer to how the mass graves are but one data point in a broader, longer, deeper public health catastrophe foisted on Indigenous populations by settlers pursuing land and resources, this may conceptually connect the graves and victims to the structural causes contributing to their killings and the structural reforms needed

---

67. Truth and Reconciliation Commission of Canada, 'Honouring the Truth,' 322–23.
68. 'Statement by Prime Minister on Release of the Final Report of the Truth and Reconciliation Commission,' Prime Minister of Canada, 15 December 2015, accessed 5 July 2023, https://pm.gc.ca/en/news/statements/2015/12/15/statement-prime-minister-release-final-report-truth-and-reconciliation.
69. Eva Jewell and Ian Mosby, 'Calls to Action Accountability: A 2021 Status Update on Reconciliation,' Yellowhead Institute, December 2021, accessed 5 July 2023, https://yellowheadinstitute.org/trc/.

to improve the lives and health of Indigenous populations in Canada today.[70]

On the other hand, even if those committed to structural reforms and deeper justice try to 'unplug' from the standard narrative regarding the schools and graves, such efforts could be derailed and routed back toward spectacle by focusing on the most dramatic and horrific examples of health catastrophes foisted on Indigenous populations, such as for example, documented cases of appalling human experimentation on children at residential schools.[71] That is, even if one group of activists and advocates committed to de-spectacularizing Canada's colonial history by couching it in an aesthetics of public health focused on community wellbeing and community harm, such efforts may be recast within the familiar frame of spectacle and in the process, (re)stripped of nuance and context.[72]

De-spectacularized Justice: Public Health and Banal Atrocities

The potential void created by unplugging from dominant global justice narratives grounded in spectacle, and the harms that may flow from such withdrawal from engagement, could potentially be mitigated by combining this tactic with that of 'de-spectacularized global justice.'[73] In contrast to unplugging, which involves a looking away, de-spectacularizing global justice provides an alternative way of engaging with questions of global justice, one grounded in an 'active quietness' which insists on complexity and contextualization.[74] In contrast

---

70. For example, Pauline Wakeham refers to the 'long emergency' of settler colonial violence committed against Indigenous nations in Canada. Wakeham, 'The Slow Violence of Settler Colonialism.'
71. Ian Mosby, 'Administering Colonial Science: Nutrition Research and Human Biomedical Experimentation in Aboriginal Communities and Residential Schools, 1942–1952,' Social History 46/91 (2013).
72. Arguably, we have seen this very dynamic play out within the realm of Canada's ongoing problem of lack of Indigenous representation within juries. Following the acquittal of white farmer Gerald Stanley for the killing of Indigenous victim Colten Boushie by an all-white jury, the Canadian government responded by banning the use of peremptory challenges, rather than pursuing the broader array of structural reforms arguably critical to actually improving Indigenous participation in juries within Canada. Kona Keast-O'Donovan, 'A Band-Aid on a Broken System: Moving Beyond Peremptory Challenges to Increase Indigenous Juror Representation in Canada,' UCLA Criminal Justice Law Review 6/1 (2022).
73. Schwöbel-Patel, Marketing Global Justice, 254–58.
74. Schwöbel-Patel, Marketing Global Justice, 254.

to unplugging, the tactic of 'de-spectacularizing' provides an alternative aesthetic lens, one that may mitigate some of the risks of unplugging in contexts where many actors would prefer a return to invisibilization of relevant harms, victims, and beneficiaries. Returning to the example of longstanding, multifaceted anti-Indigenous atrocity violence in Canada, this section considers what 'active quietness' as a tactic might consist of in this context, and whether such an approach could mitigate risks of a retrenchment of the 'peaceful frontier' myth in Canada attendant to deployment of the tactic of unplugging. To do so, this section considers whether public health gives us a framework through which connections can be made between spectacular and unspectacular harms suffered by Indigenous populations through the settler colonial process.

A good starting point for settlers who view themselves as committed to justice for Indigenous populations may be a quiet process of self-questioning. Have we used the relative invisibility of certain slow, unspectacular forms of mass violence committed against Indigenous populations as an excuse (consciously or not) to not recognize this violence? Is this process of *not seeing* partially due to the discomfort *seeing* causes us? After all, as settlers we are beneficiaries of the land, wealth, and socio-economic capital accumulated through such violence.

This potential grounding of invisibility in the avoidance of discomfort connects Schwöbel-Patel's discussion of 'occupying' global justice with her previous work on the 'comfort' of international criminal law.[75] While her article focuses primarily on the shift away from human rights and toward international criminal law as the primary benchmark for 'Good and Bad acts' globally, the notion that this shift has been at least partially driven by an 'increasing trend towards comfort (ICL) at the expense of discomfort (human rights)' may help us to think through why even settlers ostensibly committed to redressing harms done to Indigenous populations struggle to see certain harms.[76] As Schwöbel-Patel points out, we often find comfort in certainty and simplicity, while finding contention and complexity discomforting.[77] In the Canadian context, the settlers most likely to be discomforted by the recognition of how deeply their comfortable lives have been made possible by settler colonial atrocity violence are those who care about Indigenous rights. Such individuals, myself included, can reduce their discomfort

---

75. Christine Schwöbel, 'The Comfort of International Criminal Law,' *Law and Critique* 24/2 (2013).
76. Schwöbel, 'The Comfort of International Criminal Law,' 188.
77. Schwöbel, 'The Comfort of International Criminal Law,' 188.

by subtly minimizing the harms suffered by Indigenous populations and the connections between such harms and their own privileges.

Returning to where an aesthetics of public health may serve a small purpose in efforts to de-spectacularize Indigenous justice issues in Canada, and understandings of atrocity violence more generally, such a framing might serve as a pathway toward what Schwöbel-Patel refers to as finding 'comfort in discomfort.'[78] The public health frame can perhaps allow those of us with an interest in decolonizing our understandings of our shared histories by shifting our focus away from typical genocide spectacles towards more nuanced understandings of mass harm causation as longstanding multifaceted 'processes' that evolve over time, rather than static 'events' that are perpetrated by one-dimensional evildoers.[79] We may also begin to identify how to begin to become comfortable with the discomforting reality that we are beneficiaries of these ongoing genocidal processes if we see them as ongoing public health challenges, as such a framing orients us toward structural reform as the necessary solution, and away from the kinds of largely empty symbolic gestures Canada has thus far peddled almost exclusively in.

In my understanding, one of the valuable aspects of thinking about unplugging and de-spectacularizing as tactics in unison is that it offers a process to follow in the oft-difficult and counter-intuitive practice of resisting dominant social narratives and frames of understanding. If step one is to look away, step two may be to spend time in quiet contemplation regarding what to look *toward*. For me, as a settler, questions of responsible advocacy and solidarity when it comes to Indigenous peoples are fraught with risks of cooption, and the perpetuation of epistemic violence. On a fundamental level, it is not my place to say what we should look toward in terms of framing and representing Indigenous experiences of settler colonial violence. Rather, I view my role as one of solidarity with Indigenous activists and communities. However, the notion of 'active quietness' has been helpful to me in terms of creating time and space to contemplate questions raised by the spectacle of the ongoing mass grave exhumations.

If we set aside our moral outrage, shock, disgust, and other negative visceral emotions we may feel upon being confronted with stories

---

78. Schwöbel, 'The Comfort of International Criminal Law,' 188.
79. This framing is inspired by the late Sheri Rosenberg's framing of genocide as a dynamic 'process' rather than a static 'event.' Rosenberg, 'Genocide Is a Process, Not an Event.'

and images of children's bodies being exhumed from mass graves, and try to ruminate on how such victims are connected to longer, slower, quieter, less spectacular forms of violence and suffering, this may result in a more nuanced understanding of Canadian history and settler positionality in relation thereto. Rather than immediately seizing on these human remains as 'evidence' of the horrific nature of settler colonial violence, de-spectacularizing encourages thinking of alternative frames of understanding. Are these graves 'new' 'evidence'? That is, do they really provide information that we did not already have? Moreover, if we care about the lives and experiences of these children now that we have located and documented their physical remains, can we think more broadly about their experiences, in terms of their physical and mental health, beyond focusing myopically on how they ended up in these mass graves? Can we pause and reflect and listen to survivors, and realize that we should have been listening to them all along? Or, will we predictably view those who died as 'ideal victims,' since they were killed and are now truly silent? And, how might a public health lens aid or restrict our ability to conceive of a less spectacular, more nuanced and capacious understanding of settler colonialism as a complex, still-unfolding atrocity process? Finally, there is a question of audience and advocacy. Namely, whether a personal process of reconfiguring one's *self*-narration, documentation, visualization, and perhaps even memorialization of mass injustices such as those experienced by Indigenous populations through quiet contemplation is 'successful' in terms of reorienting one's own conceptualization, while the real challenge is one of shifting *public* perception.

This section considers these challenges by considering what forms of slow, unspectacular anti-Indigenous violence, are excluded from the current focus on the spectacular violence committed at residential schools, and whether a public health orientation might help us engage in a witnessing of these hidden harms.[80] In the context of Canadian settler colonial violence, these hidden harms are unfortunately myriad in nature. The remainder of his section focuses on the removal of Indigenous children from their communities through supposed child welfare laws as one example of a slower, less visible form of settler colonial violence that may be rendered visible through a public-health informed process of de-spectacularisation.

---

80. Rob Nixon refers to this as 'a different kind of witnessing: of sights unseen.' Rob Nixon, *Slow Violence and the Environmentalism of the Poor* (Cambridge MA: Harvard University Press, 2011), 15.

Returning to the questions raised above, if we are to value the lives of victims of residential school violence by taking their full experiences seriously, one thing we must do is attend to processes of removing Indigenous children from their communities.[81] In her work, Alyssa Couchie demonstrates the intertwined nature of fast/spectacular and slow/unspectacular violence both within the context of victim experiences at residential schools and in connections between the schools and other forms of anti-Indigenous atrocity violence. Most notably, Couchie frames processes of large-scale removals of Indigenous children from their homes, families, and communities commonly referred to as the Sixties and Millennial 'Scoops' as perpetuations of anti-Indigenous atrocity processes. In contrast to the increasing documentation of more paradigmatic forms of spectacular atrocity violence perpetrated at residential schools, such as widespread sexual and other forms of direct interpersonal violence (beatings, withholding of adequate food and medical care, and even medical experimentation), the removal of Indigenous children has remained at the periphery of discussions of justice for settler colonial harms, despite being interwoven with other forms of violence and the massive scale of such removals.[82]

Quiet contemplation of such experiences through a public health lens offers a connection between slow and fast anti-Indigenous violence in Canada and thereby aids in moving toward a more accurate and capacious understanding of such violence, including its ongoing nature. The focus on population-level outcomes of public health helps to situate child removals as a component of a larger process of political and material domination of Indigenous populations by settler populations that is ongoing and often hidden in slower forms of violence masked as 'neutral' laws or other policies. In this way, public health orientations serve as a kind of roadmap for avoiding the trap of the spectacle once we move from unplugging to de-spectacularizing global justice. If we adopt a process-based, public health-informed conceptualization of atrocity violence, this might provide a pathway toward narrating, documenting, visualizing, and memorializing the real injustices that have taken place, rather than myopically focusing on a subset of spectacular harms.

A normative shift to a public health-based conceptualization of mass harm is by no means a panacea. The siren call of the spectacle, with its alluring combination of emotional resonance, seeming simplicity,

---

81. Couchie, '(Re)Braiding."
82. For an overview of statistics relevant to the Sixties and Millennial Scoops, see Couchie, '(Re)Braiding,' 26–32.

and easy marketability, remains ever-present. This temptation may itself be obscured. For example, activists and Indigenous rights advocates may be tempted to replace shocking images and descriptions of horrific acts of interpersonal violence with potentially shocking public health statistics to demonstrate the scale and severity of harms such as those of mass child removals. Indeed, in writing this section I have struggled to avoid recitations of such shocking statistics, as a means of evidencing the scale and scope of such harms. Thus, public health may be of limited utility when it comes to resisting the spectacle, by merely offering a means of *expanding* the spectacle in order to capture new harms. There may be value in such an expansion, yet there seems to always be the risk of replacing one spectacle with another, and in doing so continuing to invisibilize that which defies easy spectacularization. To return to the context of Canada, focusing on disparate health outcomes and demographic impacts risks transforming health disparities into spectacles and in so doing, loses space for more careful contemplation and redress.

Indeed, scholars of public health have themselves expressed frustration with the decontextualization of public health issues, to the exclusion of social factors and forms of structural violence.[83] Excavating complicated experiences of oppression and suffering in a more fulsome, nuanced way takes sustained effort. At best, borrowing the orientation of public health can get us only partway there. At worst, such an orientation may simply replicate that which it is intended to displace.

Again, adopting a public health lens in attempting the necessarily uncomfortable self-reflective work that goes into quietly interrogating our own internalized biases regarding individual and collective relationships with spectacle and atrocity violence is not a guarantee of success. In short: The spectacle is easy, while nuance is hard. The spectacle is central to our socialization, especially when it comes to how we understand genocide and atrocity. It takes sustained effort to resist spectacle, even if we may be slightly aided in our thinking by a public health-based strategy of reframing atrocity violence.

Unmasking Global Justice: Recognizing Linkages Between Atrocity and Public Health

As demonstrated in the previous two sections, a public health-based understanding of harm may aid tactics of unplugging from and

---

83. See Paul E Farmer et al., 'Structural Violence and Clinical Medicine,' *PLoS Medicine* 3/10 (2006); Sirleaf, 'Ebola Does Not Fall from the Sky."

de-spectacularizing global justice. This section turns to the tactic of 'unmasking' global justice. Again focusing on the lack of recognition of anti-Indigenous atrocity violence in Canada, it looks at whether public health information can aid in ironic unmaskings of global justice priorities in Canada and elsewhere. Ironically juxtaposing Canada's clear indifference to the present health and welfare crises afflicting Indigenous populations in Canada (for example, over-incarceration, lack of access to safe water, high suicide rates, generally worse health, and various other co-morbidities reducing quality and length of life) with the sudden (post-mortem) caring about the lives of the children in the mass graves may be a way of 'unmasking' the justice priorities of the Canadian government in the face of its own role in longstanding anti-Indigenous atrocity processes.[84]

The tactic of unmasking global justice through irony and satire is one that is particularly fraught with the risk of being viewed as minimizing the suffering of victims. Yet, the tactic is one that can be quite effective at laying bare our collective biases and blind spots if wielded carefully. An example of comedy and irony used to great effect in unmasking social and governmental failures in Canada to acknowledge and redress large-scale atrocities is the satirical website *Walking Eagle News*, created by Indigenous humorist and activist Tim Fontaine.[85] The site and its posts on various social media platforms such as Twitter and Instagram powerfully demonstrates the hypocrisy of the Canadian government and public in the treatment of Indigenous peoples through searing satire in the same vein as the well-known US comedic news site, *The Onion*.

While the scathing satirical articles published in *Walking Eagle News* touch on a wide range of social justice issues, many of them operate to highlight the centrality of health and land issues to Indigenous peoples in Canada. Some of these articles cleverly connect Canada's failure to address its legacy of settler colonial atrocity violence

---

84. For overviews of some of these health disparities and their connections to settler-colonial violence, see Kim, 'Social Determinants of Health Inequities'; Department of Justice Government of Canada, 'Causes of Overrepresentation - Research and Statistics Division - Overrepresentation of Indigenous People in the Canadian Criminal Justice System: Causes and Responses,' 12 February 2020, accessed 5 July 2023, https://www.justice.gc.ca/eng/rp-pr/jr/oip-cjs/p4.html; United Nations, 'Discrimination of Aboriginals on Native Lands in Canada,' United Nations (United Nations), accessed 8 June 2023, https://www.un.org/en/chronicle/article/discrimination-aboriginals-native-lands-canada; Singh, Prowse and Anderson, Overincarceration of Indigenous People."
85. 'Walking Eagle News,' accessed 13 April 2022, https://walkingeaglenews.com/.

with continuing major public health challenges facing Indigenous communities. For example, a March 2022 article titled 'BC to host world's first Reconciliation Games in 2030,' describes 'the 100-kilometer intergenerational trauma carry for Indigenous participants, and the 30-second land acknowledgement for non-Indigenous competitors' as 'events' in these 'games.'[86] These references highlight one major facet of the serious health challenges facing Indigenous populations in Canada (intergenerational trauma), while juxtaposing this massive challenge with the easy symbolic act of land acknowledgements that have become popularized in Canada and elsewhere. The article further notes that the planned 'Reconciliation Games … are not without controversy' as the land needed to host the games 'would be expropriated from several host First Nations.'[87] This tying-in of land expropriation issues also reminds the audience that land claims continue to be primary justice issues for many Indigenous communities in Canada, subtly challenging the continuing preference for symbolic acts of contrition by settlers and their government, at the expense of material acts of returning stolen land.

A variety of other articles satirize the apathy of the Canadian government and public in the face of extreme health disparities between settler and Indigenous populations. The closing line in an article titled 'Rescued Manitoba pups to receive equitable funding, have all-season road, water treatment plant constructed' states that 'First Nations children on nearby reserves are considering dressing themselves like pups in the hopes of also receiving attention from Canada.'[88] This article draws attention to the Canadian government's longstanding failure to provide funding and infrastructure critical to improving the health and welfare of Indigenous communities. Another article, titled 'In bold move, Liberals give First Nations little bit of money generated from their own lands, resources,' draws attention to the chronic underfunding of Indigenous healthcare in Canada.[89] Again, it reminds the audience

---

86. 'BC to Host World's First Reconciliation Games in 2030,' *Walking Eagle News*, 29 March 2022, accessed 5 July 2023, https://walkingeaglenews.com/2022/03/29/bc-to-host-worlds-first-reconciliation-games-in-2030/.
87. 'BC to Host World's First Reconciliation Games in 2030."
88. 'Rescued Manitoba Pups to Receive Equitable Funding, Have All-Season Road, Water Treatment Plant Constructed,' *Walking Eagle News*, 7 August 2018, accessed 5 July 2023, https://walkingeaglenews.com/2018/08/07/rescued-manitoba-pups-to-receive-equitable-funding-have-all-season-road-constructed/.
89. 'In Bold Move, Liberals Give First Nations Little Bit of Money Generated from Their Own Lands, Resources,' *Walking Eagle News*, 12 September 2018, accessed 5 July 2023, https://walkingeaglenews.com/2018/09/12/in-bold-move-liberals-give-first-nations-little-bit-of-money-generated-from-their-own-lands-resources/.

of the centrality of land issues to the health of Indigenous individuals and communities.

More recently, in the wake of the exhumation of mass graves adjacent to former residential schools and the ongoing COVID-19 pandemic, *Walking Eagle News* has continued to centre Indigenous public health issues and inequitable treatment. Articles such as 'Guy acting like wearing mask in coffee shop is oppression thinks Indigenous people need to "just get over it",' 'Touching your face during Covid-19 outbreak linked to blockades somehow,' and 'Businesses struggle to racially profile Indigenous shoppers amid Covid-19 pandemic,' all work on multiple levels to highlight how Canadian society continues to neglect and fear Indigenous peoples.[90] Another article, 'Trudeau town hall includes 37-min hug with First Nations man,' mocks the Trudeau government's tendency toward largely empty symbolic gestures, stating that 'witnesses said the 37-minute hug was triggered by a question … about housing and water issues in Ontario First Nations communities.'[91]

Walking Eagle News is one example of how satire may be used to point out failures to meaningfully address atrocity violence, as well as to highlight the root causes and ongoing legacies of such violence. While the powerful critiques made by *Walking Eagle News* are not in any way limited to public health issues, by couching certain satirical critiques in the language of public health, ongoing population-level harms that are so often ignored within international criminal justice discourses are repeatedly placed front and centre. As such, *Walking Eagle News* demonstrates how skillful satirists may 'unmask' our collective focus on spectacles of violence, and in so doing shift our gaze toward broader, more nuanced understandings of mass violence, its root causes, and legacies.

---

90. 'Guy Acting like Wearing Mask in Coffee Shop Is Oppression Thinks Indigenous People Need to 'Just Get Over It," *Walking Eagle News*, 5 October 2021, https://walkingeaglenews.com/2021/10/05/guy-acting-like-wearing-mask-in-coffee-shop-is-oppression-thinks-indigenous-people-need-to-just-get-over-it/; 'Touching Your Face during Covid-19 Outbreak Linked to Blockades Somehow,' *Walking Eagle News*, 5 March 2020, accessed 5 July 2023, https://walkingeaglenews.com/2020/03/05/touching-your-face-during-covid-19-outbreak-linked-to-blockades-somehow/; 'Businesses Struggle to Racially Profile Indigenous Shoppers amid Covid-19 Pandemic,' *Walking Eagle News*, 10 April 2020, accessed 5 July 2023, https://walkingeaglenews.com/2020/04/10/businesses-struggle-to-racially-profile-indigenous-shoppers-amid-covid-19-pandemic/.
91. 'Trudeau Town Hall Includes 37-Min Hug with First Nations Man,' *Walking Eagle News*, 12 January 2018, accessed 5 July 2023, https://walkingeaglenews.com/2018/01/12/trudeau-town-hall-includes-37-min-hug-with-first-nations-man/.

As with other tactics, the language and aesthetics of public health is unlikely to be a wholesale panacea capable of singlehandedly rupturing the prevailing atrocity aesthetic grounded in spectacle when combined with the tactic of unmasking global justice. After all, the example discussed in this section, *Walking Eagle News*, appropriately mocks and unmasks various forms of problematic Canadian relationships with and attitudes toward Indigenous communities only loosely tethered to public health. This example, however, does illustrate how such 'unmasking' tactics may push audiences to consider a broader array of forms of violence victims of atrocity may experience and how this necessitates a much broader and more holistic approach to justice if we are to take redress and reparation duties at all seriously.

Resistance and International Solidarity

The final tactic Schwöbel-Patel highlights as a means of occupying global justice is that of 'resistance global justice,' which foregrounds agency and solidarity between those who experience oppression.[92] In considering how a public health based approach to the aesthetics of atrocity might factor into the crucially important process of forging solidarity networks, Noura Erakat's excellent and deeply moving essay discussing questions of Black-Palestinian transnational solidarity in the wake of the murder of her cousin by an Israeli soldier is illuminating.[93] In the essay, Erakat notes how many activists implored her to leverage her cousin's killing, her position as an academic and activist, and the ongoing racial justice uprising in the United States to bring greater attention to bear on Palestinian rights issues.[94] Yet, while deeply

---

92. Schwöbel-Patel, *Marketing Global Justice*, 262–63.
93. Noura Erakat, 'Extrajudicial Executions from the U.S to Palestine,' Just Security, 7 August 2020, accessed 5 July 2023, https://www.justsecurity.org/71901/extrajudicial-executions-from-the-united-states-to-palestine/. For more details on the killing, see 'Joint Urgent Appeal to the United Nations Special Procedures on the Extrajudicial Execution and Wilful Killing of Ahmad Erekat by the Israeli Occupying Forces on 23 June 2020,' Al-Haq, 13 July 2020, accessed 5 July 2023, http://www.alhaq.org/cached_uploads/download/2020/07/14/joint-urgent-appeal-to-un-special-procedures-on-the-killing-of-ahmad-erekat-final-1594706298.pdf.
94. Erakat, 'Extrajudicial Executions from the U.S to Palestine,. Erakat writes that she 'received dozens of calls and messages encouraging me to draw parallels between Ahmad's callous killing and the systematic killing of Black people with impunity in the United States.' Such as: 'they left him out to bleed with his parent watching like they did to Mike Brown'; 'they blamed him for his death like they did with Freddie Gray'; 'there's no accountability for his killing like there hasn't been for Breonna Taylor [or Tony McDade or Sandra Bland or Philando Castile or...]'; 'tell them Pales-

committed to Black-Palestinian transnational solidarity, Erakat ultimately chose not to go down this path, explaining that:

> In part, I refrained because being in ethical solidarity means not inadvertently decentering the much-needed and overdue conversations about anti-Black racism in the United States. I also did not want to flatten the unique contexts that shaped Black and Palestinian lives into mere spectacles of violence. The differences between these two contexts are generative and precisely what have, historically and currently, animated transnational solidarity.[1]

Erakat instead employs Black-Palestinian solidarity as an 'analytic and activist praxis' to insist on a set of similarities and connections between the oppression of Black Americans and Palestinians that cannot be reduced so neatly to both being subject to repeated acts of spectacular violence.[2] Erakat focuses the reader on the 'co-constitutive nature of racism and colonialism' and provides examples of 'specific U.S. and Israeli policy choices that depend on wholesale dehumanization along racialized lines.'[3] Ultimately, how Erakat does connect the experiences of Black Americans and Palestinians is in their experience living under conditions of a colonial military occupation, by framing the former as an 'internal colony' in the Black Internationalist tradition.[4]

Throughout Erakat's essay, experiences of Black Americans are referenced as akin to those of Palestinians living under occupation, driving home the saliency of the 'internal colony' framing of the Black American experience. In connecting these experiences to those of Palestinians, Erakat convincingly demonstrates how the tendency of Israeli police and military to treat all Palestinians as an 'always-already-guilty' security threat is similar to the tendency of militarized law enforcement agencies in the United States to treat Black people as security threats and Black protest 'like an insurgency.'[5] Ultimately, Erakat sees transnational solidarity and calls to defund police and the military in the United States as 'seeds for a decolonial future.'[6]

The remainder of this section considers whether a counter-aesthetic reframing of atrocities as public health issues might help nourish these

---

tinian lives matter.'
1. Erakat, 'Extrajudicial Executions from the U.S to Palestine.'
2. Erakat, 'Extrajudicial Executions from the U.S to Palestine.'
3. Erakat, 'Extrajudicial Executions from the U.S to Palestine.'
4. Erakat, 'Extrajudicial Executions from the U.S to Palestine.'
5. Erakat, 'Extrajudicial Executions from the U.S to Palestine.'
6. Erakat, 'Extrajudicial Executions from the U.S to Palestine.'

decolonial seeds. As with other strategies of pushing back against spectacle and the marketization of global justice, there is no clear answer to this question. However, again, there is a possibility that the language of public health and its emphasis on populations and social determinants of health may be of use. Erakat is clearly well aware of the risks of reducing complex systems of oppression into mere accumulations of violent spectacles. Her move to reframe connections between Black and Palestinian experiences as one of mutual racialized colonial subjugation helps to do so by tying in broader issues of control, wealth extraction, and securitization. Yet, as Erakat herself implies throughout her essay, both colonies (Black/Palestinian) are controlled through military force and militarized policing tactics. If one interprets her essay through the lens of international law (a not too far-fetched interpretation, given that Erakat is an international law scholar as well as activist), this places the reader in the familiar international criminal law spaces of military violence and armed conflict. There is so much more to past and ongoing oppression of Black and Palestinian lives than these experiences of military-style violence. Conditions of life under occupation are compromised in many ways, both spectacular and unspectacular in nature.[7] Again, Erakat gestures toward this in discussing conditions faced by Black Americans in the 'internal colony':

> whose conditions, and futures, mirrored other colonized peoples. These conditions, aimed at limiting Black life in the United States, include ghettoization, exclusion from gainful employment, medical experimentation, forced sterilization, exclusion from quality housing, lack of access to quality health care, education, and credit, and the systematic taking of life with impunity. The criminal justice system – featuring over-policing, racial profiling, selective enforcement, mass incarceration, disproportionate sentencing, lack of adequate representation, and hyper-surveillance – works both to make Black people vulnerable to exploitative deprivation as well as to protect those takings for the enrichment of a White racial class in the United States.[8]

The language of occupation, colony, and what Aslı Bâli describes as the American 'military-industrial-policing complex,'[9] are all useful

---

[7]. I discuss this dichotomy between 'fast' spectacles of violence and 'slower' less spectacular forms of harm causation in more depth elsewhere. See DeFalco, 'Time and the Visibility of Slow Atrocity Violence.'
[8]. Erakat, 'Extrajudicial Executions from the U.S to Palestine.'
[9]. Aslı Bâli, 'Defund America's Endless Wars,' *Just Security*, 29 July 2020, accessed 5 July 2023, https://www.justsecurity.org/71723/defund-americas-endless-wars/.

in helping to make connections and forge international solidarity, as they connect imperialism abroad with American imperialist attitudes toward people of color within its own borders.

The limitation of these framings is the ever-present risk that what makes them valuable—their invocation of armed conflict and military occupation—may have the additional effect of reviving the spectacle, even as authors such as Erakat seek to avoid 'flatten[ing] the unique contexts that shaped Black and Palestinian lives into mere spectacles of violence.'[10] Life under occupation involves the ever-present risk of being subject to spectacular violence. But occupations also produce slower, more insidious public health harms that tend to be much larger in terms of harming affected populations. Chronic lack of access to safe shelter, food, water, and other necessities gradually erode the health of populations living under conditions of occupation. In some cases, such conditions themselves may amount to international crimes, despite typically being overlooked or unrecognized as such.[11] One role an aesthetics of atrocities as public health catastrophes can play is that of forging additional links in chains of inter- and transnational solidarity. That is, if colonialism and imperialism are framed as vectors of mass harm, ones with disastrous implications for the health of the populations exposed to them, perhaps this may help make additional connections between the experiences of groups such as Black Americans and Palestinians.

Returning to the Canadian context reframed in this way, solidarity between groups such as Black Americans living in the 'internal colony' within the United States with groups such as Indigenous peoples who have similarly suffered massive negative health consequences at the population level following exposure to the 'disease' of imperialism may be fostered. This could also be helpful in forging solidarity between Indigenous groups within and beyond Canada with one another and with other anticolonial movements, including those of Black Americans and Palestinians. While the violence carried out in the name of imperialism takes many forms, spectacular and not, the common thread is that imperialism invariably brings with it disastrous consequences for the public health of the colonized and subjugated. In the Canadian context, this may mean making affirmative connections between the conditions foisted on non-Canadian victims of imperialism, such as

---

10. Erakat, 'Extrajudicial Executions from the U.S to Palestine.'
11. See generally Schmid, *Taking Economic, Social and Cultural Rights Seriously*; DeFalco, *Invisible Atrocities*.

Black Americans and Palestinians, and those foisted on Indigenous populations within Canada. While the forms of violence may differ significantly in terms of when and how they have been (and continue to be) committed, the root causes (desires for land, wealth, and power) and continuing effects (marginalization and ongoing severe public health problems) may be more similar. Demands for material, rather than symbolic actions, may also be similar in their orientation toward recompense and improving the health of affected communities and populations.

Of course, this is asking an aesthetic and rhetorical strategy to do a major amount of conceptual work. The gravity and allure of the spectacle tend to pull and bend efforts to resist it back on themselves, with the danger of refolding them into a 're-formed' spectacle that may be conveniently marketed and sold. Thus, the real lesson may be that regardless of which tactic one adopts in trying to escape the gravity well of spectacle, one must remain diligent in resisting the siren calls of spectacle and simplicity. At best, a strategy of reframing atrocity violence through the lens of public health offers a vocabulary of resistance in this regard. A language that may allow one to consistently point to large scale population-level harms and which focuses on the production of such harms as multifaceted and tied up in structural relations of power and subordination.

Conclusion: Opportunities and Shortcomings

If intentionally leveraged to do so, public health approaches to crime and violence provide certain tools that can help in resist marketized global justice and the obsession with spectacle that accompanies it. This utility is limited however, as 'success' in efforts to in Schwöbel-Patel's words 'occupy global justice' may be measured less by identifying the best tools—linguistic, descriptive, otherwise—and more in what sustains a commitment to an evolving anti-colonial, anti-racist, anti-neoliberal mindset emphasizing context and demanding solidarity. The all-encompassing nature of market capitalism, and the branding practices and emphasis on spectacle that come with it, also inevitably permeate and influence public health discourses and practices. Efforts to marketize the pandemic, by weighing the 'cost' of predictable excess deaths against those of market inefficiencies stemming from adopting public health best practices, were common, especially in the United States, where infections and death rates soared amidst constant handwringing about protecting markets from the ravages of the pandemic.

The allure of the spectacle, with its seductive combination of sensory excitement and seeming moral simplicity has proven difficult to shake. However, aesthetically reframing global justice issues and priorities as a question of global public health priorities represents a useful method in the ongoing struggle to demand a reorientation of the gaze of global justice to look past the spectacle and focus on what is producing the oppression and violence Indigenous, Black, Palestinian, and other marginalized peoples continue to experience. Only through such dogged insistence can we reorient the gaze to global justice to focus on improving the lives of the world's most vulnerable populations.

11

Violence

Jo Frank

When I say violence, I mean my violence, I mean his violence[1],[2].

---

1. Keep coming back to this: Can't write violence abstract. Write violence concrete. Write fist against temple, write foot on wrist, write knuckle against eye socket, write knee on neck. Writing violence concrete requires thinking violence abstract. Write fist, think: his – write temple, think: my. Write foot, think: his – write wrist, think: my. Write ankle, think: his – write eye socket, think: my. He and I, his and my, distinguishable by body, by body parts, bodies assignable by affiliation, he and I, his and my, separated by body, by body parts, separated by properties, by property: his fist, my temple. Property, I think, and language asserting property. His foot, my wrist. Body, body parts as property, properties of violence. My violence, his violence. Start again: Think: him, think: me, think: we in his violence, think: 'our,' hand wants to write that down, picks up pen, but hand is blocked and pen only scratches, tears the paper, and behind scullstone thought wound, thought blood, thought scab, thought tissue fluid, thought scar - Stop. And back: our. 'Our' - no, no, no, violence not our violence. If our violence then whose property? When I say violence, I mean my violence, I mean his. Doesn't mean, his violence is my violence. My violence is not his violence: When I say my violence, I think of myself without contribution to his violence. Or think contribution trembling, contribution tears, contribution speechless pleas, without contribution no possession, no property. My violence property; property without contribution. His, my, my, his, pronouns not related to relationality, not related to property.[1]

    [1] Before violence, in violence, after violence: we are property. Before violence, violence claims proclaims property. His violence proclaims through words, through escalation, through lips drawn over his teeth. Asserts and claims, proclaims entitlement: I am violence, this is my right.
    You are mine.

2. Experiences of violence are not interpersonal in the sense of representation. Re-presentation. When I say violence, I mean my violence, I mean his violence. I don't mean those who experience violence outside of mine and his. Don't mean you, you, or you. I mean my violence, I mean his violence.

His violence announces itself.³

---

3. His violence pulls his lips over his teeth, places a curved index finger between his lips. His violence pulls his lips over his teeth, language ends. This language. Language shifts, speaking to you now: Violence. Organs of articulation hands,² elbows, feet, body weight.

² Close my eyes and see his hands. Olive green skin, protruding veins, tendons dancing under the skin. Wrists inflammation red, hair black, creeping up to knuckle ridges. Long, thin fingers. Thumb bent from pressure on violin neck. Close my eyes and see them. Dream variations uncounted, untold.
Example: Walk across Lambeth Bridge, Berlin grey over London view, House of Lords to the left, Big Ben just visible, walk slowly, stop, look right towards the Tate, look, then light shock. Light shock, then eyes fixed on the road – cars gone. Look towards the footpath, no one to be seen. Light shock. Something moving. Inhale once, twice, three times to understand: middle lettering mercury, converges, merges, curves its path, arches out of the asphalt, branches burst from the middle stream, turn pale blue, begin to pulsate; potholes turn birthmark brown, asphalt shimmers grey, then olive green, then sprouting from the tarmac: hair. Hair that claws up my body: heels, thighs, abdomen, stomach, chest, neck, lips, eyes – hair cornfield, hair forest. Stare. See buildings collapsing into debris dust, rebuilding, reshaping into olive green palm. Olive green thumb. Olive green fingers. Olive green fingers seizing into fist. Turn around, Lambeth gone, now upper arm and shoulder, see neck, see chin, see lips. upper arm and shoulder, see neck, see chin, see lips drawn over teeth. Bridge forearm, his, he in Gulliver size, lying over the city. Balance breaks. He pulls up forearm up like drawbridge. Me, bite-size, legs break into run – run, run, run, as fast as I can – run, run, run, but hair like gauntlets, cut heels, cut thighs, cut abdomen, cut stomach, cut chest, cut neck, cut lips: run, run, run, cut, cut, cut, legs not strong, reach for hair before fall on stomach, hold tight, but hands wet with blood cuts, hands wet with cut sweat, no grip, wake up. Last sequence before eyes open: Second hand, thumb, forefinger, plucking me like insect from hair, holding me between thumb and forefinger, thumb and forefinger press together.
When I say *see his hands*, I don't mean see his hands, I mean feel his hands.

His violence has kinship signified in language.⁴

4. Designated by systematization, classification, attribution. Designations in ambiguities, obscurities, in overlaps and questions of perspective.³ Even the simplest distinctions: Structural - Personal | Physical – Psychological fail because of internal affinity.⁴ Failure due to mixing of categories. Violence includes, among other things, deliberate injury to people, deprivation of liberty, sexual abuse, rape, damage to property, theft, vandalism. Failure in thinking, failure in Language: connotation spectrums. *We need a new lexicon of violence*,³ my growl while writing.

³ Take his violence:
A) His violence is not domestic. Domestic. /dəˈmɛs.tɪk/. Domestic is feather duster and doily, is vinegar cleaner and armchair, is television table and coat rack, is pine wood. Horkheimer's 'lousy petit bourgeois' ring around the 'domestic.'
Step back: Domestic. 'Belonging to the house' – Possession and property. His violence does not belong to a house. Does not live in a house. Is not tied to a house. Radiates beyond the house, *maybe it's everywhere*. His violence is not domestic. Is his violence, is mine.
Take his violence:
B) His violence is not abuse. Abuse. /əˈbjuːs/. Abuse as: Use of something for a purpose for which it was it was not originally intended to be used. Alcohol abuse, abuse of authority, abuse of medicines, abuse of asylum, abuse of data, abuse of drugs, abuse of discretion, abuse of trade, abuse of power, abuse of drugs, abuse of justice, welfare abuse, tablet abuse, abuse of process, abuse of trust.
Translate: Use of a child for a purpose for which it was not originally intended to be used.
Then, please, explain purpose, explain originally, explain intended, explain use.
We need a new lexicon of violence.
His violence is not abuse. Is his violence, is mine.

⁴ Try again and again, cram books behind scullstone. Ideas, convictions, explanations. Nothing helps. Nothing helps: Sit at my desk, Benjamin shuffles through the room. Shuffles, shuffles, adjusts his glasses, talks about *violence and the temporality of law-making power*; I shake my head. Arendt takes a seat, hands me a cigarette, says *violence as an extreme manifestation of power*. Žižek intervenes, plucks his nose, runs his snotty hand through his hair, rumbles *radical change in social systems*; nodding in embarrassment, Žižek sniffles off. Tariq Ali, verbose intoxication, wisps words like *freedom* and *resistance* – but his violence, mine as resistance? Against whom? Me? Him? Both? Rubbish. Fanon behind the curtain, steps out, proposes *colonisation of the mind* – rolled out into a metaphor? No, no, no. Foucault puts elbows on knees, hums silkily, *expression of biopolitical power*; no, no, no. Pinker rushes over, says *violence to avoid greater violence* and *best time to be human*; does that get us anywhere? No. Galtung, sitting cross-legged, throws a triangle on the floor, direct, structural, cultural; helpful, ok, but equiangularity? α=β=γ=60°? No. Galtung sulks, no more triangles today.

His violence exposes language.⁵

Byung-Chul Han floats in: *Virtual Violence!*; fuck off. Butler: *oscillating frames of reference*; yes,yes,yes, but, that's not his violence, my violence. Structure, structure, structure: everybody writes violence as political agent, speaks violence as structure, worse: substance – the horrific chasm must remain.

5. What language can do: a lot. What language can't do: the most important thing. Can't take anyone with her into violence. Can take you by the hand, take you to the children's room, to the living room, to the kitchen, to the bathroom, can show you colours yellow and light shocks, can let you hear: sound cracking body, sound fracturing bone, can paint blood onto your tongue: full-bodied first impressions, robust richness, unbalanced depth, metal, musty notes and salty smears, earthy hints, acidic overtones and a toasty edge, lingering coarse aftertaste of melted butter, salt, baking spices, prunes, black pepper, fear. Can attach words to movements: boxing, burning, flailing, pressing, thrashing, punching, shaking, pushing, kicking, throwing, choking. She can tell of trembling, of shivering, of lightning, of throbbing, of pulsating, of ringing, of buzzing, of stabbing, of pulling, of hissing. Can tell you rigidity, can tell you horrific numbness, can tell you signalless nerve endings on cheek, on thigh, on stomach, on back, on buttocks, can tell you the words spoken inward after impact: don't move. Turn yourself off. Feeling dangerous. Don't save anything. I can say the darkness. I can say the darkness drop, the darkness surface, the darkness like bubble, the darkness like cloak. The darkness as it moves from liquid to fibre to scar. I can speak of humiliation, of praying and begging, of shame. Of shame, of guilt. Of shame, of guilt, of disappearance. Screaming anger, whispering sadness, howling hurt, shrieking disappointment, roaring mortification, crying humiliation, moaning degradation, whimpering pain, sobbing belittlement, screeching indignity.
Language can do all that. I can do all that with language.
But as much as language allows itself to be led, to be led over its own pitfalls, she can't take you with me into violence. Can't make you feel impact, can't cause wounds, let you see light shock, taste blood.⁵
Translate, it thinks behind scullstone, translate. And there comes Benjamin with Pannwitz in tow to the scullstone screen: 'Our translations, even the best, are based on a false principle.' They want to translate Violence to English, instead of translating English to Violence. Translation approximation. Everything asymptote. Approximation, approximation, approximation. But that would be my wish: to take you with me into his violence.

⁵ This is what I mean. You see: light shock. You see: nostrils. You see: nose hairs. You see: cheekbones. You see: lip retraction. You see: eyelids, eyelashes. You see: black pupils, around them oceanic current in blue-grey, around them red-drawn river arms across greyish dry wasteland. You see: brows and lightning-shaped crevasse. You see: forehead furrows, furrows, furrows. You see: right hand – after

Translated excerpt from Jo Frank, *Gewalt* (Wien: Edition Atelier, 2023).

Translation by author.

---

impact. You see colour cones in front of brain grey, distinguish flat and fist by colour. You see his body in turmoil, increasing rotation speed, spinning into a new lunge: Shoulders drawn back, torso forcing itself to turn against gravity. You only ever see that out of the corner of your eye, your left eye, your skull smashed to the right. You ask me: was there a crack? We listen, hear nothing, relief. We listen, hear a crack, horror. What was that? Nose? Cheekbone? Jaw? Tooth? Vertebra? A hand shakes it's way to check, we stop it mid-way, don't touch, we say to ourselves, dangerous, wait, otherwise hand in the way on second impact, impact on hand and fingers can be forced into the eye, not good with dirty-edged child's nails. We feel: second impact shift from fist to flat, know his hand hurts, have seen it many times, the shaking out and the rage. His blows hurt his knuckles. We hear: His shouting, second impact, wordless, lips still retracted, still drawn over teeth. We hear coughing, lips won't release breath, force it back, force it back, until pressure presses breath through his nose, from his nostrils projectiles snot. Runs over his lips, hand wipes it away, then lashes out again. Head whipped into unknown angles. We anticipate next impact, initiate avoidance movements, fail: arms not too high or fist will catch fingers. Fist catches fingers, but we need fingers, use our forearm, press fingers towards our chest. Forearm is strong, forearm can take it. Can take it better than face, now numb on one side, skin under shock, no more signals, body absorbs numbness inwards, moves everything inwards, switches everything to mute. If blows move downwards, different avoidance movements. Avoidance movements, until we curl up, curl up towards darkness. Don't forget to breathe. We must breathe. Don't tremble. All muscles effort, shift the trembling inwards. Don't make a noise. Noise annoys him. Noise only inwards, speak only inwards, shout only inwards, there's a place there that absorbs every sound. We can tell it everything, whisper everything into it, shout anything at it, but do not make a noise. Move everything inwards, body tries to move itself inwards. Fails. Disappearance into the floor, disappear into the carpet, that his feet can pass through your back without resistance. Without resistance. Resistance useless, resistance means pain. We can only do pain for a moment, we know that. Become transparent until no resistance, become transparent until invisible. Doesn't help. Still there. Still there with the cries and whimpers. Still there, the numbness, still there, the trembling. Still there, the tears forced inwards. Still there, the despair. Still there, the sadness. Everything there, everything in the body, there's still room, somewhere. There is still room. There must be more room. After the violence, don't move. Just lie there. Do not move. Do not move until we hear his last contempt for now. Do not move until light shock recedes from the corner of our eyes. Do not move until we hear footsteps retreating from the room. Until we hear his voice in another room. Until we hear his voice in the bathroom, humming, washing his hands. Only then: We can move. Careful now, check whether movement possible. Try to uncurl. Just try. Of course, there's pain, but we have to press on. Press on like dog, like beetle, like child. You are with me in his violence.

12
Why Eichmann Couldn't Laugh: Fifteen One-Minute Parables
Gerry Simpson

#1: The Transparent Man

Henri Bergson spoke about the comedy of correction.[6] This is perhaps the harsh laughter of a God who knows us in our entirety and before whom we are ridiculous and transparent. Søren Kierkegaard, in *Fear and Trembling*, says: 'a man in a glass cage is not so constrained as is each human in his transparency before God.'[7] I can't help thinking of Eichmann in *his* glass cage and in *his* opaqueness, a transparency that failed to reveal much at all except a lack of depth, further descending layers of transparency. And, to over-pursue this motif of transparency and glass partitioning, let me say that it is a bit risky to be talking about laughter in any self-conscious way. It would be especially foolish to try to be funny. Albert Camus once defined the absurd as 'seeing a man talking on the phone behind a glass partition.'[8] Yesterday, anyone walking past my apartment in the East Village and looking through the window would have recognised the absurdity of a man in a grim-faced struggle with his computer trying to finish a paper on laughter.

---

6. Henri Bergson, *Laughter: An Essay on the Meaning of the Comic* (Connecticut: Martino Fine Books, 2014).
7. Søren Kierkegaard quoted in: James Wood, *The Irresponsible Self: On Laughter and the Novel* (London: Pimlico, 2005), 5.
8. Albert Camus, *The Myth of Sisyphus*, trans. Justin O'Brien (Middlesex: Penguin Books, 1979), 21.

#2: The Unfunniness of Jokes

Joking is a grim subject: Sigmund Freud's treatise on wit is one of the least amusing books I have ever read. Indeed, none of the illustrative jokes seem very funny at all. Some are downright baffling. John Carey, the English literary critic, in an introduction to Freud's *The Joke and Its Relation to the Unconscious*, describes an old German joke as 'one of the few jokes collected by Freud that still seems funny to today's reader.'[9] But that joke isn't funny either. The implication that readers of the past were in convulsions about any of the other jokes strikes me as unlikely.[10] This problem, of course, has been well documented over the years. Collections of jokes are strictly for the comically challenged. As one writer put it, reviewing a (Canadian) anthology of humour: 'give me an 800-page extravaganza by a Guatemalan magical realist, give me a book on German accountancy.'[11] Meanwhile Henri Bergson's rapidly multiplying taxonomies of comedy made me feel as if I would never laugh again.

#3: Göring Considers it Unsportsmanlike to Kill Children

Hermann Göring, who considered it 'unsportsmanlike'[12] to kill children, said in an interview just before his suicide that one or two of his fellow defendants were 'not normal men.'[13] This implies that the rest of them were, and, of course, here we are immediately confronted with the stories of Hideki Tojo tending his garden, or footage of Adolf Hitler playing with his nieces. George Steiner wonders about 'the man who can read Geothe or Rilke in the evening, that he can play Bach and Schubert, and go to his day's work at Auschwitz in the morning.'[14] This is our modern mystery. For Giorgio Agamben, the full horror

---

9. John Carey, 'Introduction,' in Sigmund Freud, *The Joke and Its Relation to the Unconscious*, trans. Joyce Crick (London: Penguin, 2002), 3.
10. Though I had the same reaction to Karl Kraus's *The Last Days of Mankind*, which people claim as a great comic masterpiece of the Viennese early twentieth century. Karl Kraus, *The Last Days of Mankind: The Complete Text* (London: Yale University Press, 2015).
11. Martin Amis, *The War Against Cliché: Essays and Reviews 1971-2000* (London: Vintage Publishing, 2002), 366.
12. Leon Goldensohne, *The Nuremberg Interviews: Conversations with the Defendants and Witnesses* (London: Pimlico, 2007), 132.
13. Goldensohne, *The Nuremberg Interviews*, 109.
14. George Steiner, *Language and Silence: Essays and Notes 1958–1966* (New York: Macmillan, 1967).

of the mass killings is expressed in the football game, played in one of the camps, between the Sonderkommando and the SS each Sunday.[15] For Agamben we are always in the midst of this soccer match: averting our eyes from some horror as we play. This is the seduction and 'normality' of evil. How could the players laugh and celebrate in the mode of the great comic festivals of play?

#4: Hess Looks Unwell

One of Göring's fellow defendants and surely one of the abnormal individuals he refers to is Rudolf Hess. In photos of the trial, Hess has the faraway look of a man who has either seen too much or understood too little. He gazes blankly, perhaps pitilessly: a rough beast indeed. The question of his sanity was a funny question to ask in the midst of a trial involving men who were said to be responsible for murdering Europe's Jewish population. There is a joke. Hess flew to Scotland in order to sue for a peace with the United Kingdom. He is captured by a Scottish Laird who asks him if he is the mad man. 'No, I'm his Deputy,' replied Hess. Later, mapping Hess's apparent madness onto a bureaucratic, penitentiary logic, he becomes the only prisoner in Spandau, guarded by the four great powers on a rotating basis: MAD (Mutually Assured Detention). When the Americans and Soviets exchange keys, they each send out their tallest soldier in a mini-arms race. The soldiers get taller and taller. Eventually, the game ends when the Soviets appear with their smallest soldier. This is perhaps the end of the Cold War.

#5: Eichmann's Humour

Adolf Eichmann became known, via Hannah Arendt, for his thoughtlessness.[16] He just couldn't place himself in another person's shoes. Arendt, too, has been accused of a failure of imagination. She, perhaps, also could not or was not willing to place herself in the shoes of the Jewish Leadership. But she understood something about Eichmann. His banality was extraordinary. Another interrogator—this time a psychiatrist—was asked whether Eichmann was 'normal.' 'More normal than I am having interviewed him. This is amusing but wrong. Eichmann himself would not have understood the joke. 'I was especially struck

---

15. See Giorgio Agamben, *Remnants of Auschwitz: The Witness and the Archive* (New York: Zone Books, 2002).
16. Hannah Arendt, 'Eichamnn in Jerusalem II,' *New Yorker*, 16 February 1963.

by his complete lack of humour.'[17] Eichmann hardly represents what it means to be human but he shared something with humanity. Humanity, with a capital 'H' also lacks a sense of humour.

#6: Mankind Receives an Unwelcome Shock

Raymond Poincaré, the French President, announced, also at Versailles: 'Humanity can place confidence in you, because you are not among those who have outraged the rights of humanity.'[18] But humanity here included the Belgians, French and British each of whom were, by this time, responsible for three centuries of sometimes violent, certainly racially-inflected, Empire. Though the Imperial War Cabinet meeting on 20 November began at noon, there was a lot to get through. The main line of business was the disposition of the Kaiser. What were the representatives of humanity going to do about this outlaw? But first, there were some minor matters to take care of. Lloyd George: 'there are two or three questions we are not clear about ... Palestine, East Africa ... questions of that kind.'[19] 'We have not quite settled in our minds *what sort of government we will set up* in Mesopotamia.'[20] It was ever thus. Here are the representatives of civilization, just prior to elaborating the idea that aggressive war would be a crime against humanity, reordering their imperial outposts, themselves, as Justice Pal remarked at Tokyo, the result of three centuries of aggressive war.

I went back recently to the National Archive documentation from this meeting. How did the Imperial War Cabinet get from its own imperial consolidations and restructurings to the enemy's crimes against humanity? After all they each seemed to be grounded on precisely the same combination of non-consensual territorial acquisition and mass violations of human rights. Was there a hint of self-consciousness? What was the hinge?

---

17. Avner W. Less, 'Introduction,' in *Eichmann Interrogated: Transcripts from the Archives of the Israeli Police*, eds. Jochen von Land and Claus Sibyll, trans. Ralph Manheim (Toronto: Lester & Orpen Dennys, 1983), vii.
18. Department of State, United States, 'Papers Relating to the Foreign Relations of the United States' (US Government Printing Office 1919), 159.
19. Imperial War Cabinet, Shorthand Notes of the 37th Meeting, 20 November 1918, 2.
20. Gerry Simpson, *The Sentimental Life of International Law: Literature, Language, and Longing in World Politics* (Oxford: Oxford University Press, 2001), ch 4.

Well, between the surprisingly cursory discussion of Palestine, Syria, and Iraq and the lengthier debate about the Kaiser there is one short announcement. A telegram is read out from the *Association of Universal Loyal Negroes of Panama*. It reads: 'Negroes throughout Panama send congratulations on your victory and in return for services rendered by the negroes throughout the world in fighting … beg that their heritage wrested from Germany in Africa may become the negro national home with self-government.'[21] This is passed over in silence and the discussion moves on to the Kaiser's terrible crime of making war on Europe and the shock this delivered to the conscience of mankind.

#7: …And Then Another One

> The Tribunal shall not be bound by technical rules of evidence. It shall adopt and apply to the greatest possible extent expeditious and non-technical procedure, and shall admit any evidence which it deems to be of probative value.[22]

For Arendt, a show trial is a 'spectacle with prearranged results' or the obliteration through compulsive staging of 'the irreducible risk' of acquittal.[23] The point of the trial is the trial itself: its ramifications, its warnings, its effluxions of terror. George Orwell understood this. When I was sixteen, we were told at my High School that we had to write a major essay on a literary figure. I chose Orwell because it was 1980 and everyone was very excited about the prospects for 1984. The *New Musical Express* had predicted that, by that time, the levels of surveillance would be much more widespread than in the novel of the same name. I went to the English master and told him I wanted to write on irony in the novels of George Orwell. 'Which novels?' he asked, archly. 'The minor novels,' I replied building irony upon irony. So, I began wading through *Keep the Aspidistra Flying* and *Coming Up For Air*. There is a reason, it turned out, why these books are largely unread.

Mrs Parsons lives with her two little daemonic children at Victory Mansions. Her drains are blocked, as they often are, and she calls Winston Smith down to help her unblock the sink. The two children torment Winston, calling him a Eurasian spy, threatening to vaporise

---

21. Imperial War Cabinet, Shorthand Notes of the 37th Meeting, 20 November 1918, 6.
22. Charter of the International Military Tribunal ("London Agreement" signed 8 August 1945, recorded 15 March 1951) 251 UNTS 280 art 19.
23. Arendt, 'Eichmann in Jerusalem II,' 120.

him and shouting 'Goldstein' as he leaves the flat. Mrs Parsons is apologetic; the children are furious, she explains, because she failed to take them to the hanging:

> Some Eurasian prisoners, guilty of war crimes, were to be hanged that evening ... this happened once a month and was a popular spectacle.[24]

War Crimes Trials: not depoliticized programmes of management but wild-eyed theatres of revenge. Human rights with a vengeance. As one of the observers of the Moscow Show Trials eerily put it: these were 'dramas of subjective innocence and objective guilt.'[25] This objective guilt was repeatedly enunciated in the months preceding the major trials at Nuremberg and Tokyo where the Nazis were repeatedly described as the world's worst criminals and where the defendants were chosen with great care on the basis of political impact. The show trials, themselves, continued into the 1950s, most famously in Prague where the purpose was not to determine guilt or innocence. Nor, even, to remove political opponents, but rather to create them.

The proceedings there were initially conceived as trials of fairly low-level *apparatchiks*. Under pressure from Moscow, President Gottwald (perhaps still wearing his disappeared Comrade Klement's hat from *The Book of Laughter and Forgetting*) found a higher level defendant, Otto Sling, a district party secretary. Under torture, Sling implicated Rudolf Slansky, the General Secretary of the Czech Communist Party, in a fantastic and implausible conspiracy. Finally, the Soviet advisers had a defendant of sufficient seniority. The Czechs were initially shocked and bemused. What about the evidence? One Soviet legal adviser, soon to be himself purged, said: 'we have been sent here to stage trials not to check whether the charges are true.'[26]

As for the existence of legal norms. Again this didn't matter. The instincts of the proletariat would stand in for what Kyrlenko, one of the Moscow prosecutors, called 'bourgeois sophistry.'[27] And this recalls, too, a Nazi Law of 28 June 1935 referring to the need to punish criminals and deviants according to 'the sound perceptions of the people.'[28]

---

24. George Orwell, *Nineteen Eighty-Four* (London: Penguin, 1974), 22.
25. Maurice Merleau-Ponty, *Humanism and Terror* (Boston: Beacon Press, 1969), 202.
26. Meir Cotic, *The Prague Trial: The First Anti-Zionist Show Trial in the Communist Bloc* (New York: Herzl Press, 1987), 69.
27. Simpson, *The Sentimental Life of International Law*, 103.
28. Richard Minear, *Victors' Justice: The Tokyo War Crimes Trial* (Princeton, MA: Princeton University Press, 1971), 17.

Ten years later, though, President Roosevelt was worrying about acquittals on technicalities and Robert Jackson—pressed on the existence of crimes against humanity or aggression—replied by saying 'we can avoid these pitfalls of definition if our test of what is a crime gives recognition to those things which fundamentally outrage the conscience of the American people.'[29] This became at trial the idea of 'shocking the conscience of mankind.'[30]

#8: Adolf Eichmann Receives a Shocking Book

Mankind is, of course, shocked by many different things at different times. This was something the US advisors, Robert Lansing and James Brown Scott, argued at Versailles when they resisted the whole idea of crimes against humanity, claiming that there was no such thing as humanity only nations with different moral outlooks. In Jerusalem, Adolf Eichmann seemed unshockable. His thoughtlessness, indeed, was his most remarkable quality. Arendt, again: 'the longer one listened to him the more obvious it became that his inability to speak was closely connected to his inability to think ... he was genuinely incapable of uttering a single sentence that was not a cliché.'[31] He seemed curiously affectless, in other words. At one point, he is handed some novels to read. One of them is *Lolita*. After two days Eichmann returned the novel, visibly indignant: 'that is quite an unwholesome book,' he tells the guard.

#9: Hayden White Emplots the Shoah

A famous World Court judge once told me that humour and genocide were an impossible—probably blasphemous—combination. Richard Evans, arguing against postmodernism, wanted us to accept that there are limits to the ways in which one could emplot the Holocaust.[32] In Saul Freidlander's *Probing the Limits of Representation*, he states: 'Auschwitz was indeed inherently a tragedy and cannot be seen either as comedy or farce.'[33] *Life is Beautiful* is a comedy set in a concentration camp. Hayden

---

29. United States Department of State Bulletin, 'Justice Jackson's Report to the President on Atrocities and War Crimes; June 7 1945' (Government Printing Office 1945).
30. See Nina Jorgensen, *The Responsibility of States for International Crimes* (Oxford: Oxford University Press, 2000), ch 9.
31. Arendt, 'Eichmann in Jerusalem II,' 328–329.
32. Richard Evans, *In Defence of History* (London: Granta Books, 2001), 124.
33. Saul Friedlander, *Probing the Limits of Representation: Nazism and the "Final Solution"* (Cambridge, MA: Harvard University Press, 1992), 124

White said: 'every field is constituted by what it forbids its practitioners to do.'[34] White, roundly criticized for claiming that history could be emploted in multiple ways, would have appreciated the animating spirit behind this book. The question: to take our field more or less seriously. In *White Noise,* Don de Lillo's airborne toxic event novel, the protagonist Professor Gladney has established a Centre for Hitler Studies. A Junior Visiting Faculty member is deeply impressed at this initiative. He makes a lengthy sycophantic speech about how Gladney has more or less invented Hitler Studies. He goes on to say at a meeting: 'Professor Gladney, no one can so much as mention Hitler without a metaphorical glance in your direction. It's what I want to do with Elvis.'[35]

#10: Tojo Loses His Head

Shumei Okawa, the Japanese propagandist, was eventually declared insane, and unfit to stand trial by William Webb, the Presiding Judge at the Tokyo War Crimes Tribunal. Okawa had slapped Tojo over the head in a piece of slap-stick comedy. But how comic is this? How long did Tojo swing in the air before dying? Maybe like Joachim von Ribbentrop, for several minutes. But Okawa is a key figure in the history of ironic disjunctions.

Prior to his removal, Okawa argued that the trial is not the realisation of justice but the continuation of war. This brilliantly Clausewitzian but ultimately unacceptable formula anticipates later critiques of the Trial and of international criminal justice itself. Okawa asserted that Japan's imperial war was not an aggressive war at all but an act of pre-emptive self-defence. This argument was rejected by the Tribunal, of course. The Soviets, in particular (later to pre-emptively attack Czechoslovakia) declared the doctrine to be disreputable. Meanwhile, half a century later, Okawa's insanity was to become a key marker of President Bush's foreign policy. Okawa is the Shakespearean Fool: a madman speaking obscure sense.

#11: Eichmann Loses His

In 1998, just around the time of the execution by lethal injection of Karla Faye Tucker in Texas (her appeal for clemency having been turned

---

34. Hayden White, *Tropics of Discourse: Essays in Cultural Criticism* (London: The Johns Hopkins University Press, 1978), 126.
35. Don DeLillo, *White Noise* (New York: Penguin Books, 1985).

down by a Governor Bush), Martin Amis, Saul Bellow and several others were having dinner and discussing the case. Almost everyone was in agreement that the death penalty was an outrage not just in this case but in every case. There was a classic liberal consensus at the dinner table punctuated only by the silence of Bellow. Amis turns to Bellow astonished: 'I can't believe it, Saul, you don't agree with us do you?'[36] How could the author of *Herzog* or *The Dean's December* believe in capital punishment? Bellow's response consisted of two words: 'Adolf Eichmann.'

#12: How many Americans Does it Take to Commit Genocide?

As Eichmann was being tried in 1960, Stanley Milgram was curious about whether there would have been a sufficient number of people in the United States prepared to guard the concentration camps. He set up a famous experiment in which average citizens were given fairly non-coercive instructions to torture fake subjects. His conclusion: that there were sufficient numbers of willing torturers and guards in New Haven alone.

#13: Raskolnikov Finds it Amusing

In *Crime and Punishment* when Raskolnikov confesses his double murder he asks Sonia: 'you think its funny?'[37] Before answering his own question; 'well, yes, the funny part about it, Sonia, is that that's exactly how it was.'[38]

Sonia did not think it at all funny.[39]

#14: Erdogan Finds it Libellous

Two satirists speak on this question. In *The Resistible Rise of Arturo Ui*, Brecht said 'the greatest political criminals must be exposed and exposed especially to laughter.'[40] Peter Cook opening his new club 'The Establishment' in Soho said he had consciously imitated 'those

---

36. Martin Amis, *Experience* (New York: Hyperion, 2000), 260.
37. Fyodor Dostoevsky, *Crime and Punishment*, trans. David McDuff (London: Penguin Classics, 2003).
38. Dostoevsky, *Crime and Punishment*, 429.
39. Dostoevsky, *Crime and Punishment*, 429.
40. Bertolt Brecht, *The Resistible Rise of Arturo Ui* (London: Bloomsbury, 2016).

wonderful Berlin cabarets which had done so much to stop the rise of Hitler and prevent the outbreak of the Second World War.'[41] But maybe we should keep Cook in mind while trying to side with Brecht. Laughter can, surely, be dangerous. One might laugh too hard at a joke of Stalin's. Not hard enough at a quip of Mugabe's.

> When he laughed, respectable senators burst with laughter,
> And when he cried the little children died in the streets.[42]

What is humanity's law? A satirist under arrest for laughing at another country's head of state? This is the law of laughter. Humanity's extra-jurisdictional law of laughter.

#15: Sonia Finds it Blasphemous

Ironic laughter arises, as it were, organically from the gap between our hopes and the abridgement of these hopes, or in the abyss between illusion and experience. It is already there then as part of the discipline or field, built into its very structure. To think in terms of what comic law might be, then: at worst, simply counter-hubristic or frivolous; at best, it might mark a tentative step towards a better or more supple language with which law can gesture at murderous violence. 'Our vocabulary for moral blame soon runs out when we want to condemn the murder of six million persons or the torture of children. To say that these acts are wrong sounds like a kind of irony.'[43] Not all laughter is ironic though. Another form of laughter might be understood as less intellectual or reflective: it is the rebellious, instinctive laughter of a world in which some lives and deaths are more sacred than others, a laughter through tears, anxiety, hysteria. This is the laughter we all experience perhaps when we have narrowly avoided danger.

Ironic laughter arises, as it were, organically from the gap between our hopes and the abridgement of these hopes, or in the abyss between illusion and experience. It is already there then as part of the discipline or field, built into its very structure. To think in terms of what comic law might be, then, at the worst, simply counter-hubristic or frivolous, at best it might mark a tentative step towards a better, or more supple,

---

41. Jonathan Coe, 'Sinking Giggling into the Sea,' *London Review of Books*, 18 July 2013, 31.
42. W H Auden, 'Epitaph for a Tyrant (1940),' in W H Auden, *Collected Poems* (London: Vintage, 1991), 183.
43. Carlos Santiago Nino, *Radical Evil on Trial* (New Haven, CT: Tale University Press, 1996), 141.

language with which law might gesture at murderous violence. 'Our vocabulary for moral blame soon runs out when we want to condemn the murder of six million persons or the torture of children. To say that these acts are wrong sounds like a kind of irony.'[44] Not all laughter is ironic though. Another form of laughter might be understood as less intellectual or reflective: it is the rebellious, instinctive laughter of a world in which some lives and deaths are more sacred than others, a laughter through tears, anxiety, hysteria. This is the laughter we all experience perhaps when we have narrowly avoided danger.

In *Crime and Punishment*, Raskolnikov talks about being tempted by the devil by his own double murder and by the comedy of it.

'Funny, isn't it?' he asks.

'Don't laugh, blasphemer!' exclaims Sonia.[45]

Are there representational limits to laughter? When Titus first sees his daughter (horribly mutilated) and the heads of his sons, he utters the line: 'Ha Ha Ha.'[46]

---

44. Nino, *Radical Evil*, 141.
45. Dostoevsky, *Crime and Punishment*, 429.
46. See Jonathan Bate, *Shakespeare and Ovid* (Oxford: Clarendon, 1993), 116.

13

'Poetic Justice Products'

INTERNATIONAL JUSTICE, VICTIM COUNTER-AESTHETICS, AND THE SPECTRE OF THE SHOW TRIAL

Alex Batesmith

> This ECCC [is] a political farce, an irreversible sham of extraordinary perversion in denying justice to victims, exploiting their suffering, soiling the memories of their loved ones and embedding cynicism in an already fragile population living in paranoia, mistrust and distrust.[1]

International criminal justice is used to receiving more brickbats than plaudits. Whether charged with over-promising or under-performing, or that the discipline is based on questionable structural foundations, critique has been trenchant as well as sustained. Such criticism typically emanates from the academy, or from the international defence Bar, but it takes on a particular significance when it emanates from the class of people upon whom the entire edifice is essentially premised: the victims themselves.[2] The uncompromising denunciation quoted above was delivered by Theary Seng, a victim-survivor of the Khmer Rouge regime in Cambodia, as part of her very public renunciation of civil

---

1. 'Theary Seng Withdraws Her Civil Party Status, Denounces ECCC as "Irredeemable Political Farce",' *Ki-Media*, 15 November 2011, accessed 17 January 2023, http://ki-media.blogspot.com/2011/11/theary-seng-withdraws-her-civil-party.html.
2. Frédéric Mégret, 'The Anxieties of International Criminal Justice,' *Leiden Journal of International Law* 29/1 (2016); Christine Schwöbel, ed., *Critical Approaches to International Criminal Law* (Abingdon and New York: Routledge, 2014); David Luban, 'After the Honeymoon: Reflections on the Current State of International Criminal Justice,' *Journal of International Criminal Justice* 11/3 (2013); Mikael Rask Madsen et al., 'Backlash Against International Courts: Explaining the Forms and Patterns of Resistance to International Courts,' *International Journal of Law in Context* 14/2 (2018); Joseph Powderly, 'International Criminal Justice in an Age of Perpetual Crisis,' *Leiden Journal of International Law* 32/1 (2019).

party status at the Extraordinary Chambers in the Courts of Cambodia (the ECCC). The ECCC, from which Seng withdrew her participation, is the hybrid domestic-international criminal tribunal that was established to prosecute those accused of international crimes committed in Democratic Kampuchea between 1975 and 1979.[3] Seng's words were written in 2011 after a protracted three-year battle with the ECCC during which she sought, and was denied, more extensive participation in the trials of the Khmer Rouge than the Trial Chamber was prepared to countenance. Her words and her actions are atypical of victims who, according to the canon of international criminal law, variously seek 'justice,' 'catharsis,' and 'empowerment' through engagement with formal justice mechanisms.[4]

Contemporary international criminal tribunals, including the International Criminal Court and the Special Tribunal for Lebanon as well as the ECCC, present themselves as victim-centric institutions. Not only are victims seen as integral to the normative framework of international criminal justice, their support is a prerequisite for the success and legitimacy of this entire system of law.[5] However, notwithstanding their centrality to its processes and institutions, international criminal justice has certain expectations of and places particular preconditions on victims. This chapter thus begins by revisiting the concept of the 'ideal' victim as essentialized by and for international criminal law and its principal institutions, and how characteristics of vulnerability, dependency, compliance, and blamelessness are often represented aesthetically by traumatized or physically mutilated women and children.[6] Situating this discussion within the context of victim participation in the criminal trials of the Khmer Rouge leaders

---

3. The Law on the Establishment of the Extraordinary Chambers in the Courts of Cambodia, 27 October 2004 ('ECCC Law').
4. For an overview of the vast literature on victims in international criminal law, see Luke Moffett, *Justice for Victims Before the International Criminal Court* (London: Routledge, 2014); Maria Elander, *Figuring Victims in International Criminal Justice: the Case of the Khmer Rouge Tribunal* (London: Routledge, 2018) and Rachel Killean, *Victims, Atrocity and International Criminal Justice: Lessons from Cambodia* (London: Routledge, 2018).
5. Killean, *Victims*, 2.
6. Nils Christie, 'The Ideal Victim,' in *From Crime Policy to Victim Policy*, ed. Ezzat A. Fattah (London: Palgrave Macmillan, 1986); Joris Van Wijk, 'Who is the "Little Old Lady" of International Crimes? Nils Christie's Concept of the Ideal Victim Reinterpreted,' *International Review of Victimology* 19/2 (2013); Christine Schwöbel-Patel, 'The "Ideal" Victim of International Criminal Law,' *European Journal of International Law* 29/3 (2018).

at the ECCC in Cambodia, I then examine the case study of Theary Seng's involvement in and disengagement from the judicial processes, as an example of what happens when victims do not conform to the expected aesthetic. In particular, I analyse how Seng represents a counter-aesthetic to the archetypal victim, challenging expectations of what was expected of her both within and outside formal legal mechanisms. I explore how she addressed the Court, her engagement with the media, and her writing and images posted on her own personal website. On her website, Seng developed what she styled 'Poetic Justice Products' as a vehicle for venting anger and for playfully and provocatively engaging public debate outside the courtroom.[7] The chapter then goes on to explore a counter-aesthetic of victimhood in international criminal justice. Drawing upon and developing the concept of 'rupture' within the criminal process, I reflect on how such a counter-aesthetic, especially when created by the victims themselves, challenges the legitimacy and credibility of international criminal law's institutions, raising the spectre of the show trial as the ultimate expression of the failure of procedural justice.

The Aesthetic of the Ideal Victim in International Criminal Justice

The legitimacy sought by international criminal justice is increasingly dependent on victims. At the International Military Tribunal at Nuremberg, victims and their interests did not play a prominent role either in the courtroom or in the broader justification of prosecutions.[8] Similarly, victims did not figure to any meaningful extent in the 'second coming' of the discipline at the *ad hoc* tribunals for the Former Yugoslavia or Rwanda. The Rome Statute of the International Criminal Court ('ICC') in 1998 further formalized victims as the *raison d'être* of international criminal justice, both 'deserving recipients of legal justice and morally entitled to accountability.'[9] In the generation

---

7. Theary Seng's personal website can be found at https://thearyseng.com/, with specific pages relating to her former status as an ECCC civil party listed here: https://thearyseng.com/eccc-civil-party accessed 17 January 2023.
8. See Killean, *Victims*, 22–25. However, Lawrence Douglas notes how the film *Nazi Concentration Camps* showing footage of victims immediately after the liberation of the camps was nevertheless used by the Prosecution to convey the horrific scope of the crimes in such a way as the images 'spoke for themselves': Lawrence Douglas, 'Film as Witness: Screening Nazi Concentration Camps Before the Nuremberg Tribunal,' *The Yale Law Journal* 105/2 (1995).
9. Laurel Fletcher, 'Refracted Justice: The Imagined Victim and the International

that has passed, a vast literature on victims and victim studies has developed to explore the place of victims relative to the development of the discipline, both within and outside the courtroom.[10] 'Justice for victims' is at once international criminal justice's rallying cry, reflexive justification and response to its critics. However, in their seminal article on victims appearing before and as invoked by the International Criminal Court ('ICC'), Sara Kendall and Sarah Nouwen identify the disparity between the very limited participation of victims in proceedings and the extensive reliance on victims as an abstract rhetorical concept.[11] As they express it, 'the figure of "The Victim" is deployed as a kind of new sovereign of ICL, yet its looming presence in the discourse surrounding the work of the ICC overstates the role of actual victims within the legal proceedings.'[12] As the reality of victim participation has inevitably failed to keep up with the rhetoric, scholarship critical of how international criminal justice and its principal institutions and actors reflexively instrumentalize the victim and their interests is now common.[13]

Although the gap between the 'abstract' and the 'juridified' victim may be considerable, the 'figure'—or aesthetic—of both is unitary. Several scholars writing on international criminal justice take criminologist Nils Christie's view of 'the ideal victim' from domestic justice discourse as the starting point of this discussion. For Christie, an ideal victim is 'a person or category of individuals who—when hit by crime—most readily is given the complete and legitimate status of being a victim.'[14] The status of 'ideal victim' is bestowed upon deserving individuals by the system, typically where five characteristics are present: firstly, the victim is weak; secondly, the victim is engaging in a 'respectable' project; thirdly, the victim is blameless; fourthly, that the offender is 'big and bad' who is, fifthly, unknown to the victim.[15] Adapting Christie's

---

Criminal Court,' in *Contested Justice: The Politics and Practice of International Criminal Court Interventions*, eds. Christian de Vos, Sara Kendall and Carsten Stahn (Cambridge: Cambridge University Press, 2015), 306.
10. For summaries, see Killean, *Victims, Atrocity and International Criminal Justice*; Moffett, *Justice for Victims*, and Elander, *Figuring Victims*.
11. Sara Kendall and Sarah Nouwen, 'Representational Practices at the International Criminal Court: The Gap Between Juridified and Abstract Victimhood,' *Law and Contemporary Problems* 76 (2013), 235.
12. Kendall and Nouwen, 'Representational Practices,' 241.
13. Fletcher, 'Refracted Justice.'
14. Christie, 'The Ideal Victim,' 18.
15. Christie, 'The Ideal Victim,' 19.

typography, Christine Schwöbel-Patel suggests that there are three necessary components for the ideal victim in international criminal justice: victims must be weak and vulnerable—'feminized, racialized, infantilized'; victims must be dependent—they must be spoken for by professional, emotionless representatives; and victims must be 'grotesque,' the 'abnormal and therefore unpleasant, but ... also weird and empathy inducing.'[16] Schwöbel-Patel argues that all three characteristics are a prerequisite for 'spectacularized attention grabbing'[17] for the marketing of international criminal justice to its consumers, being nation states and others with the money to fund the institutions of global justice.[18] This 'ideal-type' aesthetic of vulnerability, dependency and grotesqueness can be seen both within and outside the courtroom.

Maria Elander identifies three modes through which victims participate within the courtroom: as the visitor/spectator; as a party to the proceedings, in this case the 'civil party' as we will see at the ECCC; and as a witness providing testimony within the proceedings.[19] For each of these three modes there appears to be an expected behaviour: a spectator who will calmly witness the justice being enacted in their name; a civil party conforming to strict procedural rules once selected as a representative for a larger collective; and a witness providing affective yet controllable evidence. As Elander puts it, an international tribunal's invitation to the victim is to 'demonstrate our humanity by giving voice to his or her injury and victimization,' but this same invitation 'comes with restrictions that are difficult to meet: to give voice to suffering, without becoming "emotional" and demonstrating humanity.'[20] Outside the courtroom, victimhood is visually represented in similar ways. The ICC's 'Justice Matters' photographic exhibition toured venues around Europe before returning to the Court's seat in The Hague. Among other images, the photographs and videos display maimed and mutilated black women, juxtaposed with robed judges

---

16. Schwöbel-Patel, 'The "Ideal" Victim,' 710–718.
17. Schwöbel-Patel, 'The "Ideal" Victim,' 722.
18. See, generally, Christine Schwöbel-Patel *Marketing Global Justice: The Political Economy of International Criminal Law* (Cambridge: Cambridge Studies in International and Comparative Law, 2021); Van Wijk, 'Who is the "Little Old Lady" of International Crimes?,' 167.
19. Elander, *Figuring Victims*.
20. Maria Elander, 'The Victim's Address: Expressivism and the Victim at the Extraordinary Chambers in the Courts of Cambodia,' *International Journal of Transitional Justice* 7/1 (2013), 111.

and on-location crime scene teams.²¹ The dominant aesthetic is also popularized through films and documentaries that explain the ICC's work, in which footage of anonymous, suffering victims that have endured 'unimaginable atrocities' are seen as 'desperately seeking [the] intervention' of the international criminal justice community.²² Yoav Mehozay develops the idea that the 'victim aesthetic' is instrumentalized (and grossly simplified) for political capital.²³ Writing about the domestic US criminal justice system, he argues that the aesthetic of the victim is a social construct with deep symbolic power that 'puts a premium on superficial manifestations while ignoring deep structural pathologies.'²⁴ The victim's role, as he later puts it, is to 'validate emotions, not to vindicate rights.'²⁵ The emotional urge to punish is arguably even greater within international criminal justice. Here, the distance between victims at the rhetorical pinnacle of the discipline and their concrete enjoyment of rights and recompense is at its most stark. The ECCC, recently having published its final judgment after sixteen years of operation, provides a very useful case study to explore such theories of victim aesthetics.²⁶

The ECCC and Khmer Rouge Victim Aesthetics

The criminal conduct of the ruling Communist Party of Kampuchea, known colloquially as the Khmer Rouge, is estimated to have caused the deaths of between 1.8 and 3 million out of the then population of 8 million Cambodians, either through execution, maltreatment,

---

21. For a discussion of the exhibition, see Immi Tallgren, 'Come and See? The Power of Images and International Criminal Justice,' *International Criminal Law Review* 17/2 (2017), 259–280 and Schwöbel-Patel, 'The "Ideal" Victim,' 715.
22. Wouter Werner, '"We Cannot Allow Ourselves to Imagine What it All Means": Documentary Practices and the International Criminal Court,' *Law and Contemporary Problems* 76 (2013), 330; Wouter Werner, 'Justice on Screen – A Study of Four Documentary Films on the International Criminal Court,' *Leiden Journal of International Law* 29 (2016).
23. Yoav Mehozay, 'From Offender Rehabilitation to the Aesthetics of the Victim,' *Social and Legal Studies* 27/1 (2018).
24. Mehozay, 'From Offender Rehabilitation to the Aesthetics of the Victim,' 98.
25. Mehozay, 'From Offender Rehabilitation to the Aesthetics of the Victim,' 102.
26. 'Cambodia: UN-backed tribunal ends with conviction upheld for last living Khmer Rouge leader,' *UN News*, 22 September 2022, accessed 14 January 2023, https://news.un.org/en/story/2022/09/1127521; James Hendry, 'The End of the Judicial Mandate of the Extraordinary Chambers in the Courts of Cambodia is Near' *PKI Global Justice Journal* 6 (2022), 2.

imprisonment, enforced labour, and other policies leading to mass starvation and disease.[27] The significance of such numbers is frequently cited as being that every household in Cambodia has been touched by tragedy, either through the loss of multiple family members or through the pain and suffering caused by witnessing or directly experiencing the violence and extreme hardship.[28] The ubiquity of victimhood in Cambodia is a clear distinguishing feature of its post-1979 society. During the ECCC's first trial, Case 001 against Kaing Guek Eav, known as 'Duch,' psychologists testified that the entire country suffered post-traumatic stress from living through the regime.[29] The trials have provided a focal point for extensive and more recent scholarship on psychological trauma, the 'hidden scars' of which are still being carried by Cambodia's contemporary population.[30]

As is typically the case after conflict, the narrative of the Khmer Rouge era is a contested political issue, which has implications for how the notion of victimhood is perceived within Cambodian society. Elander notes that a self-identity has been consciously fostered, from Cambodia's lifetime Prime Minister Hun Sen downwards, to enable all Cambodians to consider themselves as victims, a message she says is reinforced by the ECCC.[31] Alexander Laban Hinton describes how the tribunal's own outreach materials convey how the experiences of an ordinary Cambodian citizen are relevant to the ECCC's proceedings.[32] Hinton draws the contrast between such official, idealized narratives (and, we could add, aesthetics) of victimhood in the narrow judicialized

---

27. Ben Kiernan, *The Pol Pot Regime: Race, Power, and Genocide in Cambodia Under the Khmer Rouge, 1975–79* (New Haven and London: Yale University Press, 2002); Craig Etcheson, *After the Killing Fields: Lessons from the Cambodian Genocide* (Westport: Praeger Publishers, 2005), 117–119.
28. Elander *Figuring Victims*, 115, citing Cambodian Prime Minister Hun Sen's words in the *Introduction to the Khmer Rouge Trials* (Public Affairs Section, ECCC, 4th Edition): 'not a single one of our people has been spared from the ravages brought upon our country during...the regime known as Democratic Kampuchea.'
29. For example, the evidence of Mr Ka Sunbaunat, given during the trial of Kaing Guek Eav at the ECCC on 31 August and 1 September 2009, available at https://www.eccc.gov.kh/en/witness-expert-civil-party/mr-ka-sunbaunat, accessed 17 January 2023.
30. Beth Van Schaack et al., *Cambodia's Hidden Scars: Trauma Psychology in the Wake of the Khmer Rouge, An Edited Volume on Cambodia's Mental Health* (Phnom Penh: DC-Cam, 2011).
31. Elander *Figuring Victims*, 115.
32. Alexander Laban Hinton, *The Justice Façade: Trials of Transition in Cambodia* (Oxford: Oxford University Press, 2018).

sense, and Cambodian Buddhist concepts of suffering and death beyond the transitional justice 'imaginary.'[33] Resisting the temptation to descend into an obvious local/global split on the question of a victim imaginary, Hinton nevertheless reminds us that Cambodians 'have selectively and creatively engaged with human rights and transitional justice, blending, adapting, and sometimes more or less ignoring them.'[34] Such an anthropologist's perspective on victimhood adds a very useful dimension to the debate when analysing international criminal justice's victim aesthetic as instantiated at the ECCC, for which the pre-existing context of Khmer Rouge victimhood is relevant.

When the Khmer Rouge were driven from power in January 1979, the occupying Vietnamese forces set about making an example of the vanquished. A five-day trial in absentia for two of the former regime's senior leaders was staged in August 1979 by the Vietnamese authorities at the People's Revolutionary Tribunal in Phnom Penh, at which witnesses testified against the '"Pol Pot / Ieng Sary 'genocidal clique"' in a process that was widely derided as a show trial.[35] What was labelled 'the genocide'[36] was also memorialized by the Vietnamese in 1980 at notorious crime sites, principally to discredit the ousted Khmer Rouge, who were still fighting a civil war from their strongholds in the northwest of the country until the late 1990s.[37] The two most important of these sites of memorialization were the Tuol Sleng

---

33. Hinton, *The Justice Façade*, 21; Caroline Bennett, 'The Justice Facade: Trials of Transition in Cambodia' review of *The Justice Facade: Trials of Transition in Cambodia*, by Alexander Laban Hinton, *Anthropological Quarterly* 93/1 (2020).
34. Bennett 'The Justice Façade,' 1669 citing Hinton, *The Justice Façade*, 87.
35. The People's Revolutionary Tribunal of Kampuchea, in which Pol Pot and fellow Khmer Rouge senior leader Ieng Sary were tried in absentia: Frank Selbmann, 'The 1979 Trial of the People's Revolutionary Tribunal and Implications for ECCC' in *The Extraordinary Chambers in the Courts of Cambodia*, eds. Simon Meisenberg and Ignaz Stegmiller (The Hague: TMC Asser Press, 2016).
36. Rebecca Gidley, 'The Political Construction of Narrative and Collective Memory in Cambodia,' *Situations* 10/1 (2017).
37. Caitlin Brown and Chris Millington, 'The Memory of the Cambodian Genocide: The Tuol Sleng Genocide Museum,' History Compass 13/2 (2015); David Chandler, 'The S-21 Project,' Sciences Po: Violence de masse et Résistance – Réseau de Recherche, 3 February 2008, accessed 18 January 2023, https://www.sciencespo.fr/mass-violence-war-massacre-resistance/fr/document/s-21-project.html; Judy Ledgerwood, 'The Cambodian Tuol Sleng Museum of Genocidal Crimes: National Narrative' in Genocide, Collective Violence and Popular Memory: The Politics of Remembrance in the Twentieth Century, eds. David Lorey and William Beezley (Wilmington: Rowman and Littlefield Publishers, 2001), 116.

Genocide Museum, situated in the grounds of Khmer Rouge Security Office S-21, the regime's apex torture and execution centre in the city, and Choueng Ek, the 'killing fields' just outside the city where S-21's victims were, in the contemporary revolutionary vernacular, taken to be 'smashed.'[38] Both museums have significantly contributed to the way in which the Khmer Rouge era is represented—and consequently how the victims are 'figured'—both for the political narrative and for the purpose of 'dark tourism.'[39] At Tuol Sleng in the former communal detention cells of S-21, hundreds of black and white photographs are exhibited within giant two-sided glass display cases and on the walls. These anonymous images are the faces of S-21 detainees, each photographed upon entry before their incarceration, torture, and execution.[40] Similarly, the centrepiece memorial stupa at the Choeung Ek museum houses the bleached skulls and bones stacked and visible through the glass sides of the monument, the remains of a fraction of the estimated 14,000-17,000 victims executed in the surrounding shallow mass graves.[41]

Originally with minimal accompanying explanatory material,[42] both Tuol Sleng and Choeung Ek act as visual representations of genocide that invite an emotional response rather than an understanding of the complex causes of the violence.[43] This ties in with the official Cambodian government position on the Khmer Rouge era: that it was a regime driven by a handful of fanatical apex *génocidaires*, or what Michael Vickery describes as the 'Standard Total View.'[44] There were no state-backed judicial investigations into Khmer Rouge-era crimes,

---

38. Rachel Hughes, 'Memory and Sovereignty in Post-1979 Cambodia: Choeung Ek and Local Genocide Memorials' in *Genocide in Cambodia and Rwanda: New Perspectives* ed. Susan E. Cook (London, Routledge, 2017).
39. Elander *Figuring Victims*; Christine Schwöbel-Patel 'Maria Elander: Figuring Victims in International Criminal Justice: The Case of the Khmer Rouge Tribunal,' review of *Figuring Victims in International Criminal Justice: The Case of the Khmer Rouge Tribunal*, by Maria Elander, *European Journal of International Law* 31/4 (2020).
40. Cheryl Lawther et al., 'Making (In?) Visible: Selectivity, Visibility and Authenticity in Cambodia's Sites of Atrocity,' *Journal of Genocide Research* 24/1 (2022).
41. Julie Fleischman, 'Working with the remains in Cambodia: Skeletal Analysis and Human Rights After Atrocity,' *Genocide Studies and Prevention: An International Journal* 10/2 (2016), 122.
42. Audio guides are now provided to visitors of both museums: see Lawther, 'Making (In)Visible.'
43. Brown and Millington, 'The Memory of the Cambodian Genocide,' 33.
44. Michael Vickery, *Cambodia 1975–1979* (Seattle: University of Washington Press, 2000).

and the history of Democratic Kampuchea was not taught at schools.[45] The result was, as Zucker explains, that the Cambodian population took their Khmer Rouge stories from 'popular … survivor memoirs and autobiographies and the stories told by guides and taxi drivers along the tourism trail,' which largely conformed to Vickery's Standard Total View.[46] The victim aesthetic portrayed through Tuol Sleng and Choeung Ek is powerful yet simplified: as Elander notes, the message is '"we" all suffered,' and therefore 'we' all demand justice.[47] However, the presentation of evidence and artefacts is never a neutral process. The visual display of images at Tuol Sleng does not make clear that a majority of documented S-21 victims were in fact Khmer Rouge cadre themselves, and photographs of female victims are occasionally duplicated throughout the museum, giving a misleading impression that women made up a greater proportion of Khmer Rouge victims than was in fact the case.[48] Returning to Mehozay's argument that victims are only important for their aesthetic significance rather than in and of themselves, we are entitled to ask whether the presentation of the victim at these dark tourism sites is qualitatively any different to that at the ECCC.[49]

Standing in parallel to the museums of Tuol Sleng and Choeung Ek is the Documentation Center of Cambodia (DC-Cam), a non-governmental organization created to research and document the era of Democratic Kampuchea and its aftermath.[50] In its twenty-five year history, DC-Cam has expanded its research across the whole country in a vast number of projects taking in documentation, trauma, memory, accountability, education, family tracing, drama, and mapping and is the largest repository of Khmer Rouge era documents in the world.[51] As DC-Cam developed its projects in the twelve years before the ECCC became operational, there was a turn towards identifying documents

---

45. Khamboly Dy, 'Challenges of Teaching Genocide in Cambodian Secondary Schools,'
Policy and Practice: Pedagogy about the Holocaust and Genocide Papers, Paper 4 (2013), 6.
46. Eve Zucker, 'Contested Narratives of Victimhood: The Tales of Two Former Khmer Rouge Soldiers' in *Societies Emerging From Conflict: The Aftermath of Atrocity*, ed. Dennis E. Klein (Newcastle: Cambridge Scholars Publishing, 2017), 36.
47. Elander, *Figuring Victims*, 115.
48. Lawther, 'Making (In)Visible.'
49. Mehozay, 'From Offender Rehabilitation to the Aesthetics of the Victim.'
50. The website of the Documentation Centre can be found at https://dccam.org/homepage, accessed 17 January 2023.
51. Hinton, *The Justice Façade*, 221–240.

and potential witnesses. However, in addition to accountability at the heart of DC-Cam's ethos is the reflexive desire to 'search for the truth,' suggestive of the aims of truth and reconciliation commissions established elsewhere as transitional justice mechanisms.[52] In Cambodia, this truth is not only complex—when so many victims were also perpetrators—but it is deeply personal and is woven into individual ideas of what is meant by justice.[53]

Adequately responding to the enormity of victim suffering is something that international criminal justice finds difficult to manage, but the foregrounding of 'justice for victims' has been a deliberate strategy for the ECCC from the very beginning. The now extensive literature on victims and the ECCC spans a number of separate but linked themes, including expressivism,[54] procedural and substantive justice,[55] effectiveness and agency,[56] spectacle and theatricality,[57] and institutional legitimation.[58] The siting of the ECCC in Cambodia, despite misgivings from many quarters,[59] was ultimately justified as having greater immediacy, relevance, and meaning to the affected population, and as enabling easier participation of victims and witnesses, not to mention the supposedly exemplar effect it would have on the Cambodian municipal criminal justice system.[60]

---

52. Hinton, *The Justice Façade*, 223–226.
53. Meng-try Ea and Sorya Sim, *Victims and Perpetrators?* (Phnom Penh: Documentation Centre of Cambodia, 2001); Julie Bernath, '"Complex Political victims" in the Aftermath of Mass Atrocity: Reflections on the Khmer Rouge Tribunal in Cambodia,' *International Journal of Transitional Justice* 10/1 (2016).
54. Barrie Sander, 'The Expressive Limits of International Criminal Justice: Victim Trauma and Local Culture in the Iron Cage of the Law,' *International Criminal Law Review* 19/6 (2019).
55. Luke Moffett, 'Reparative Complementarity: Ensuring an Effective Remedy for Victims in the Reparation Regime of the International Criminal Court,' *The International Journal of Human Rights* 17/3 (2013).
56. Kieran McEvoy and Kirsten McConnachie, 'Victims and Transitional Justice: Voice, Agency and Blame,' *Social and Legal Studies* 22/4 (2013).
57. Christine Schwöbel-Patel, 'Spectacle in International Criminal Law: the Fundraising Image of Victimhood,' *London Review of International Law* 4/2 (2016); Nigel Eltringham, 'Spectators to the Spectacle of Law: The Formation of a "validating Public" at the International Criminal Tribunal for Rwanda,' *Ethnos* 77/3 (2012).
58. Bernath, '"Complex Political Victims".'
59. Duncan McCargo, 'Cambodia: Getting Away with Authoritarianism?' *Journal of Democracy* 16/4 (2005); Kheang Un, 'The Khmer Rouge Tribunal: A Politically Compromised Search for Justice,' *The Journal of Asian Studies* 72/4 (2013). For an overview of the negotiations that led to the creation of the ECCC, see Sebastian Strangio, *Cambodia: From Pol Pot to Hun Sen and Beyond* (Newhaven: Yale University Press, 2020).
60. Helen Horsington, 'The Cambodian Khmer Rouge Tribunal: The Promise of a

However, in practical terms, the ECCC's 'victim-centrism' has been inconstant and uneven. As a hybrid Cambodian-international criminal tribunal, the ECCC was founded through an agreement between the United Nations and the Cambodian Government, implemented through a domestic establishing law and informed by both Cambodian and international criminal law.[61] Procedurally, the ECCC was shaped by the plenary of judges, who determined the Internal Rules that set out the way in which parties and other actors participate.[62] Although the original Agreement and Law contained only cursory references to victims' involvement in the proceedings,[63] the Internal Rules were drafted to include what Rachel Killean describes as 'some of the most extensive procedural and substantive rights ever granted to victims in an international or hybrid criminal court.'[64] Victims were granted the right to file complaints, become witnesses or to apply to become civil parties.[65] Civil party status, as it is suggested, affords victims their best opportunity for 'empowerment' through direct involvement in the proceedings.[66] The first iteration of the ECCC's Internal Rules afforded civil parties and their legal representatives extensive rights of participation in the court proceedings, including giving testimony, cross examination of witnesses (through their lawyers), and addressing the Court.[67] To the dismay of many who had been civil parties in Case 001, such ostensible procedural and participatory justice for victims was not matched by concrete or substantive justice measures: the Internal Rules only empowered the Trial Chamber to award 'collective and moral reparations' in the event of a conviction.[68] Moreover, the extensive civil party participation in Case 001 was abandoned in advance of the much longer

---

Hybrid Tribunal,' *Melbourne Journal of International Law* 5/2 (2004).
61. ECCC Law 2004
62. Killean, *Victims, Atrocity and International Criminal Justice*, 76, fn 57.
63. Killean, *Victims, Atrocity and International Criminal Justice*, 64; Article 23 ECCC Agreement ('protection of victims'); Articles 23 and 36 of ECCC Law 2004 (Co-Prosecutors can question victims; victims can appeal decisions of the Trial Chamber).
64. Killean, *Victims, Atrocity and International Criminal Justice*, 69.
65. Rules 12(2)(c) and 49(2), Internal Rules of the Extraordinary Chambers in the Courts of Cambodia ('ECCC Internal Rules').
66. For a critique of these views, see Mahdev Mohan, 'The Paradox of Victim-Centrism: Victim Participation at the Khmer Rouge Tribunal,' *International Criminal Law Review* 9/5 (2009), 768, who argues that 'the promise of 'empowerment' through participation is a rhetorical device.'
67. Killean summarizes these in *Victims, Atrocity and International Criminal Justice*, 70.
68. Rules 23 and 23 *quinquies*, ECCC Internal Rules.

and more complex Case 002 on the grounds of trial efficiency and as a reaffirmation of pure retributive justice,[69] including the streamlining of legal representation and curtailment of speaking rights.[70] As Case 002 began, modalities of victim engagement expanded, through the Court's Victims' Support Section and country-wide outreach activities facilitated with the assistance of Cambodian civil society, but the sense remained that proper preparations for participation in proceedings had not been made from the outset.[71]

As discussed above, the ECCC developed a victim aesthetic of calm reflection, engagement, and progress; it would be through participating in ECCC court proceedings victims could be both at peace with the past and help to secure the country's future stability, harmony, and prosperity. Hinton describes this as the 'transitional justice imaginary' that creates a 'façade'[72] of justice in which, as Mehozay expresses it, 'superficial manifestations' take preference to lived realities.[73] Specifically, Hinton refers to the ECCC's claims that ordinary Cambodian citizens can help contribute to 'justice' through their participation in the proceedings, the benefits of which are understood as national reconciliation, stability, peace, and security. Applying to become a civil party, says the fictionalized Cambodian victim-survivor Uncle San in the ECCC's explanatory outreach booklets, provides 'the right to participate in all of the court proceedings, plus a right to request collective and moral reparations.'[74] This ultimately enables Uncle San to sleep without being disturbed

---

69. 93 civil parties participated in Case 001, whereas 3,866 were admitted to participate as civil parties in Case 002. See also Alain Werner and Daniella Rudy, 'Civil Party Representation at the ECCC: Sounding the Retreat in International Criminal Law?' *Northwestern Journal of International Human Rights* 8/3 (2009), 301–309; Silke Studzinsky, 'Participation Rights of Victims as Civil Parties and the Challenges of their Implementation Before the ECCC,' in *Victims of International Crimes: An Interdisciplinary Discourse*, eds. Thorsten Bonacker and Christoph Safferling (The Hague: Asser Press, 2013).
70. Killean, *Victims, Atrocity and International Criminal Justice*, 91.
71. Hinton, The Justice Façade, 109–11; Killean, Victims, Atrocity and International Criminal Justice, 135–143; Christoph Sperfeldt, 'The Role of Cambodian Civil Society in the Victim Participation Scheme of the ECCC' in Bonacker and Safferling, Victims of International Crimes.
72. Hinton, *The Justice Façade*, 21.
73. Mehozay, 'From Offender Rehabilitation to the Aesthetics of the Victim,' 98
74. Alexander Laban Hinton, 'Transitional Justice Time: Uncle San, Aunty Yan, and Outreach at the Khmer Rouge Tribunal,' in *Genocide and Mass Atrocities in Asia: Legacies and Prevention*, eds. Deborah Mayersen and Annie Pohlman (London: Routledge, 2013), 93.

by bad dreams.⁷⁵ Julie Bernath notes how victims are pivotal to the ECCC's 'rhetorics and rituals of self-legitimation,' how they are 'constantly invoked as the ECCC's main symbolic beneficiaries.'⁷⁶ Elander writes that the ECCC 'needs ... victims for its message,' where a 'simplistic narrative of [the victims'] innocence'⁷⁷ shattered by the criminal conduct of the accused can only be resolved through retributive justice that acts as a rite of passage from the prior state of chaos to order.⁷⁸ The reality of the victim aesthetic at the ECCC was however somewhat different.

Within the courtroom, victims and their participation were constrained both in fact and by degree. In fact, the condensing and consolidating of victims' voices into the voice of a single lawyer,⁷⁹ the removal of a victim's previously granted right to speak (as I shall shortly discuss), and the bypassing of individual victimhood through collectivity of justice, have all reduced the practical ability of victims to present themselves in court as they would wish to.⁸⁰ By degree, when and if victims are permitted to address the court, they were faced with very restrictive parameters. Victims must have suffered 'but not so much that they become unmanageable in the courtroom'⁸¹ and should avoid being 'disruptive' or 'difficult to deal with,' illustrating the clash of expectations on what constitutes ideal victimhood.⁸² ECCC judges have reprimanded victims for demonstrating excessive emotion during proceedings, in particular anger and anguished sadness.⁸³ Outside the courtroom, the victim aesthetic is typically expressed and represented in weight of numbers: the ECCC auditorium housing the largest number of observers (who are all also victims, as all Cambodians are victims);⁸⁴ the villagers (again, all of whom are victims) being bussed in to

---

75. Hinton, *The Justice Façade*, 1–21.
76. Bernath, '"Complex Political Victims",' 52.
77. Elander, 'The Victim's Address,' 101, 105.
78. Elander, *Figuring Victims*, 189
79. Elander, *Figuring Victims*, 125.
80. Mohan, 'The Paradox of Victim-Centrism,' 768.
81. Bernath, '"Complex Political Victims",' 61.
82. Mohan, 'The Paradox of Victim-Centrism'; Elander, 'The Victim's Address.'
83. On 'emotional testimony,' see Beth Van Schaack et al., eds., *Cambodia's Hidden Scars: Trauma Psychology in the Wake of the Khmer Rouge* (Phnom Penh: Documentation Centre of Cambodia, 2011), 131–134.
84. 'Visitor information for public hearings,' ECCC, accessed 17 January 2023, https://www.eccc.gov.kh/en/visitor-information-public-hearings.

the tribunal every day from outlying provinces in their hundreds.[85] The massed victims-as-observers/victims-as-participants appear to be seen as part of the tableau of the tribunal: as they queue to pass through security screening to enter the ECCC compound, or take their breaks in the communal cafeteria, the victims become a legitimising backdrop, a reminder of the tribunal's popular(izing) aesthetic.

Disruption, Subversion, and 'Rupture' of the ECCC Victim Aesthetic

The dominant aesthetic of the victim, both within and outside the ECCC courtroom, as the 'racialized, feminized and infantilized' victim, clearly fits within the established understanding of the 'ideal' victim as envisaged by international criminal justice more broadly.[86] Civil parties are dependent on the court for their status as juridical victim. They are dependent on their lawyers (who in turn are dependent on the Lead Co-Lawyers) to question the accused and witnesses and to make legal submissions, and they are dependent on the President of the Trial Chamber to frame acceptable speech when they are permitted to speak. Constrained in this way, victims do not pose a threat to the order and legitimacy of the court.[87] In contrast, victims that do not conform to the ideal—i.e. who offer a counter-aesthetic—tend to manifest a disruptive presence to the structures and forces at play within international criminal justice. The focus for the rest of this chapter will be on the actions of one such civil party at the ECCC, the unsettling counter-aesthetic of victimhood that they presented, and what atypical engagement and subsequent rupture might say about international criminal justice and the ultimate discreditable label of the show trial.

Theary Seng was the first victim recognized as a civil party at the ECCC. 'In many ways,' as Hinton writes, she was 'an ideal civil party, someone whose suffering and loss corresponded closely to conceptions of victimhood the transitional justice imaginary asserts.'[88] Seng had experienced profound suffering. Both her parents were killed

---

85. Rachel Hughes, 'Showing now: The Bophana Audiovisual Resource Centre and the Extraordinary Chambers in the Courts of Cambodia,' *Civil Society and Transitional Justice in Asia and the Pacific* (2019), 111.
86. Schwöbel-Patel, 'Spectacle in International Criminal Law,' 250.
87. Christine Schwöbel-Patel, 'Nils Christie's "Ideal Victim" Applied: From Lions to Swarms,' *Critical Legal Thinking*, 5 August 2015, accessed 18 January 2023, https://criticallegalthinking.com/2015/08/05/nils-christies-ideal-victim-applied-from-lions-to-swarms/.
88. Hinton, *The Justice Façade*, 89.

by the Khmer Rouge when she was a very young girl. She witnessed awful violence and experienced hunger, anguish, and trauma before escaping to a refugee camp on the Thai-Cambodian border from where she emigrated to the United States, eventually qualifying as a lawyer. When she settled back in Cambodia, she developed a television and media presence, worked as a commercial lawyer and had volunteered extensively on democracy projects before joining a prominent Cambodian NGO, the Center for Social Development ('CSD').[89] On becoming CSD's Executive Director in 2006, she looked to harness the momentum of the newly-created ECCC by focusing the NGO's system of public forums on 'justice and national reconciliation,' a theme that she also pursued thought her application to become the first civil party at the Court.[90]

Despite her putative status as an 'ideal victim'—she was at one stage described as the 'poster child' for the civil parties—Seng had initially been highly sceptical of the ECCC.[91] In her 2005 autobiography she had expressed the view that a domestically-controlled tribunal would *'inevitably lead to a parody of justice that would curdle even the blood of the dead'* given the lack of judicial independence and competence.[92] Such forthright language prefigured her words to come. Persuaded otherwise in the early days of the ECCC's existence, she filed for and was granted the first application for civil party status in 2007, explaining her belief in the importance of the tribunal as a court of law to influence the 'court of public opinion.'[93] In other words, Seng viewed victim interest and involvement in the ECCC as the catalyst for wider democratization across Cambodia.[94] Seizing her opportunity, in February 2008 Seng directly addressed the ECCC's Pre-Trial Chamber during preliminary hearings. Outlining her interests—both individual and collective on behalf of others—she spoke assertively and confidently, more like a lawyer than a victim:

> for victims, this is your court. Participate. Do not fear. May I remind the Court to provide greater protective measures.[95]

---

89. As detailed in her memoirs: see Theary Seng, *Daughter of the Killing Fields: Asrei's Story* (London: Fusion Press, 2005).
90. Hinton, *The Justice Façade*, 98.
91. Hinton, *The Justice Façade*, 89.
92. Seng, *Daughter of the Killing Fields*, 257–8.
93. Hinton, *The Justice Façade*, 98–99.
94. Author's interview with Theary Seng 27 July 2021.
95. Seng's composed, lawyerly demeanour can be seen in footage from the hearing itself: 'Theary Seng's Direct Arguments in Pre-Trial Hearing Against Nuon Chea, Feb

At one point, unchallenged, she directly addressed the accused Nuon Chea, offering him a copy of CSD's publication on post-traumatic stress without complaint from the Judges, Prosecutors, or Defence.[96] Although conforming to the necessary decorum within the confines of a formal courtroom, perhaps there was something in the direct and confident nature of Seng's address. That is, something about the advocacy on display that departed from the usual position of victims speaking through legal representatives, or the unsettling agentic power of a voice in the courtroom calling upon victims *as a victim* that subverted the accepted order. Four months later, when Seng next attempted to address the Court directly, she was prevented from doing so after the Judges upheld an objection from the Defence.[97] This prompted Seng to walk out of the courtroom frustrated, angry, and upset at 'being used' with no substance to her participation.[98] The episode led to a change in the ECCC's Internal Rules stipulating that only civil parties' lawyers could address the court.[99] The ECCC had slammed the door shut on expansive victim participation that had previously been opened so wide.

Theary Seng attempted to regain her voice and agency at the ECCC by creating the Association of Khmer Rouge Victims of Cambodia and by continuing to play a very active role in pursuing accountability for Khmer Rouge crimes as well as highlighting ongoing domestic human rights abuses and corruption in Cambodia. However, she became disillusioned with the ECCC and with the system of victim participation and civil party representation, and publicly renounced her civil party status.[100] Her plainspoken and self-possessed courtroom advocacy already presented a very different image to the typical dependent atrocity victim—by 'talking back' as a survivor,[101] she was criticized both publicly for forcefully 'demanding' too much,[102] and privately

---

2008 (Part 2 of 2),' KI Letters, accessed 6 August 2021, https://youtu.be/_rZ7u-Fgj9g.
96. As discussed in Mohan, 'The Paradox of Victim-Centrism,' 752.
97. Civil party lawyer Mahdev Mohan wrote at the time that the Pre-Trial Chamber's decision to prohibit Theary Seng from addressing the Court was 'misconceived.' Mohan, 'The Paradox of Victim-Centrism' 753.
98. Hinton, *The Justice Façade*, 127.
99. Rule 24(7)(i), ECCC Internal Rules, introduced 6 March 2009; Mohan, 'The Paradox of Victim-Centrism,' 753–758; Hinton, *The Justice Façade*, 129.
100. Theary Seng press release 15 November 2011.
101. Antonius Robben and Carolyn Nordstrom, 'The Politics of Truth and Emotion Among Victims and Perpetrators of Violence,' *Ethnographic Fieldwork: an Anthropological Reader*, 23 (2012), 175.
102. Sarah Thomas, 'Civil Party's Repeated Attempts to Address Bench and Poor

for 'manipulating the process' whilst 'stand[ing] on her soapbox.'[103] But it was Seng's subsequent words and actions that cemented the victim counter-aesthetic that she represents.

Firstly, via a press release and conference in November 2011, she denounced the ECCC as a 'sham' and an 'irredeemable political farce.' Instead of disengaging from the issues and disappearing from the spotlight, Seng announced that as she couldn't seek justice through the ECCC, all that was left to her was to pursue 'poetic justice.'[104] Conceiving of representationally novel ideas of what to do with her unfulfilled victimhood, she devized a series of 'Poetic Justice Products' that included a war criminals darts game, war criminals collectors cards, poetic justice cushion covers, door mats, and even a 'poetic justice' Trivial Pursuit game. Seng took more than a dozen giant dartboards down to Phnom Penh's popular riverside area, and invited members of the public to throw darts at targets superimposed on the faces of ECCC accused as well as Richard Nixon and Henry Kissinger. The authorities soon forcibly removed the dartboards, but not before Seng had given interviews to media outlets on site.[105] At the time, she explained that 'Poetic Justice is to negate the nefarious legacy of the Khmer Rouge tribunal … The UN has failed us miserably; the tribunal has failed victims miserably,' and that the dartboards had twin goals: 'firstly, therapy in the form of a way to release aggression and save the faces of the wives and children in Cambodia. Secondly, this is a humorous way to educate people [about the ECCC's Case 002].'[106] Seng published similar views and opinions on her personal website and on regional blogs, where she also posted an arresting photograph of herself depicting her reclining on a comfortable arm chair, head cocked to one side, eyes holding the gaze of the lens, holding a recently-exhaled large cigar between two upturned 'Victory V' fingers.[107] Reflecting on this a decade later, Seng explained that this photograph expressed 'defiance – it was to say "I'm only a victim in the legal

---

Management of Proceedings Force Worrying Precedent for Victim Participation Before the ECCC,' *ECCC Reparations*, 4 July 2008, accessed 18 January 2023, http://eccreparations.blogspot.com/2008/07/civil-partys-repeated-attempts-to.html.
103. Attributed to a 'senior ECCC official' interviewed in Mohan, 'The Paradox of Victim-Centrism,' 754.
104. Theary Seng press release 15 November 2011.
105. Bridget Di Certo, 'KRT Critic Offers "Poetic Justice",' *Phnom Penh Post*, 16 November 2011.
106. Di Certo, 'KRT Critic.'
107. Theary Seng press release 15 November 2011.

sense, I'm not victimized". This was not the image you'd expect of a Cambodian, of a Cambodian woman, a Cambodian victim.'[108] These were deliberate actions and specifically chosen images not commonly associated with victims in international criminal justice.[109] In relation to her 'Poetic Justice Products,' Seng also explained that she 'wanted to engage victims, to show that justice was more than a legal process.'[110] As she put it, 'I saw that part of my role at times was to be a provocateur on certain issues, I wanted to bring the Cambodian public along.'[111] The counter-aesthetic resulting from these visual expressions of defiance, provocation, playfulness, and agency suggest a strategy of deliberate distancing from the proceedings and of challenging the Court's dominant treatment of victimhood, subverting the ideal of the helpless victim.

In her discussion of survivor speech in the context of sexual abuse offences in the US, Katie Gibson highlights a radical approach taken by one trial judge in Michigan who opened the court to 156 survivors to present their victim statements over seven days in the sentencing hearing. The judge placed no restrictions on what was said, nor on how it was said, and many addressed the accused directly and emotionally. The result, Gibson argues, was that the survivors went beyond the constricting parameters of victim impact statements and 'racists logics of worthy victimhood,' instead mobilising a 'rhetoric of collective anger to disrupt courtroom norms, hegemonic scripts, and generic expectations that contain and diminish testimony of [victims].'[112] Gibson describes what happened in this case as a 'rhetorical rupture' of the boundaries of the law.[113] In contrast to the US judge who enabled such a rupture, the judicial officials at the ECCC sought to shut down victim speech whenever there was anger or other unsuitable or excessive emotion,[114] finding it 'difficult to tolerate a victim who appears roguish, unreceptive to the

---

108. Interview with Theary Seng, 27 July 2021, notes on file with author.
109. Seng explained that she was showing defiance in the photograph: this represented an attempt to wrest a sense of agency from her disempowering experience at the ECCC. Interview with Theary Seng, 27 July 2021.
110. Interview with Theary Seng, 27 July 2021, notes on file with author.
111. Interview with Theary Seng, 27 July 2021, notes on file with author.
112. Katie Gibson, 'A Rupture in the Courtroom: Collective Rhetoric, Survivor Speech, and the Subversive Limits of the Victim Impact Statement,' *Women's Studies in Communication*, 44/4 (2021), 518–541.
113. Gibson, 'A Rupture in the Courtroom.'
114. Bernath, '"Complex Political Victims",' 61.

court's process, or simply convinced that her story is unique and deserves special attention.'[115] For a victim such as Theary Seng to be unbowed—both within and outside the courtroom—speaks to a form of resistance that attempts to 'undermine or negotiate different power relations,' and a refusal to 'connive' with the specific processes of international criminal justice.[116]

Albeit from a very different perspective, this brings to mind aspects of French attorney Jacques Vergès and his 'défense de rupture.' Vergès made a career of iconoclasm, serially defending those accused of the most serious crimes to expose what he saw as the hypocrisy of the law.[117] Filip Hasselind and Mikael Baaz explain that Vergès sought to highlight the structural biases in the system by turning the trial into an attack not only on the judges and the prosecutors but also on the system itself.[118] They argue that within the courtroom, for Vergès the choice is either 'connivance' with or 'rupture' from the dominant power. As they express it, 'connivance shares, or at the very least accepts the interests and values of the established order and the legal system it represents while rupture supports an alternative set of interests, namely the goals of the subaltern.'[119] Fundamentally, a trial's success 'is dependent on the consent of the defendant and their defender… [who] must accept the court and recognise its legitimacy.'[120] Not only because Vergès was seen as a defiant presence in the courtroom—who was regularly photographed smoking Cuban cigars outside it—but there are parallels with the counter-aesthetic of Theary Seng's atypical victim. Seng refused to connive with power at the ECCC, and she refused to consent to the constraints of the ECCC's civil party system. Discussing the rupture tactics of Vergès—who for a time also represented accused Khieu Samphan at the ECCC—Seng acknowledged how Vergès understood the need

---

115. Mohan, 'The Paradox of Victim-Centrism,' 740.
116. Mikael Baaz et al., 'Resistance Studies as an Academic Pursuit,' *Journal of Resistance Studies*, 3/1 (2017), 10–28 at 17.
117. Sylvie Thénault, 'Défendre les Nationalistes Algériens en Lutte Pour l'Indépendance. La «Défense de Rupture» en Question,' *Le Mouvement Social* 3 (2012); Jean Danet, 'Sur la Notion de Défense de Rupture: Willard, Vergès, et Après?,' *Histoire de la Justice*, 27/1 (2017).
118. Filip Hassellind and Mikael Baaz, 'Just Another Battleground: Resisting Courtroom Historiography in the Extraordinary Chambers in the Courts of Cambodia,' *Journal of Political Power*, 13/2 (2020).
119. Hassellind and Baaz, 'Just Another Battleground,' 258.
120. Hassellind and Baaz, 'Just Another Battleground,' 258.

to use 'the court of public opinion.'[121] Both Vergès and Seng shared an awareness of the importance of 'mediatization,' or the mobilization of popular support 'to create political pressure and to intensify the political dimension of a case.'[122]

By challenging the aesthetic of idealized victimhood, both within the courtroom and outside through both professional and social media, Theary Seng's words and actions demonstrate that there is potential for victims to rupture the very processes through which international criminal justice seeks to instrumentalize their identity. Drawing upon Christodoulidis's definition of rupture as 'an act of resistance [that] registers without being absorbed, integrated or co-opted into the system against which it stands,'[123] Rachel Hughes suggests that victim participation in the ECCC does not (or not yet) constitute a wholesale rupture of the legal process, despite what she describes as 'hopeful disruptions.'[124] The fact that 'disruptions' such as Seng's continued beyond the courtroom is nevertheless relevant to understanding how a counter-aesthetic of victimhood impacts the legitimacy of the process as a whole. Seng's accusations that the 'Extraordinary SHAMbers' is a 'vacuous grand pageantry'—more theatre than court of law—raise the spectre of that often-used insult to institutional credibility in international criminal justice: the show trial, which is where this chapter will conclude.[125]

Show Trials and Victim Counter-Aesthetics

The theatricality of justice as 'performed' in a courtroom has long been an object of discussion.[126] One strand of this scholarship concerns the extent to which the performance of justice outweighs its normative function, as in order for any proceedings to be considered legitimate they must be more than simply 'for show': the court must be accepted

---

121. Interview of Theary Seng quoted in Hinton, *The Justice Façade*, 99.
122. Hasslind and Baaz, 'Just Another Battleground,' 259.
123. Emilios Christodoulidis, 'Strategies of Rupture,' *Law and Critique*, 20/1 (2009).
124. Rachel Hughes, Hughes, 'Victims' Rights, Victim Collectives and Utopic Disruption at the Extraordinary Chambers in the Courts of Cambodia,' *Australian Journal of Human Rights*, 22/2 (2016), 148.
125. Hinton, *The Justice Façade*, 155.
126. Antoine Hol, 'The Theatre of Justice: On the Educational Meaning of Criminal Trials' in *Transitional Justice: Imagines and Memories*, ed. Christine Bell (London: Routledge, 2016); Denis Brion, 'The Criminal Trial as Theater: The Semiotic Power of the Image' in *Law, Culture and Visual Studies*, ed. Anne Wagner and Richard Sherwin (Dordrecht: Springer, 2014).

by its audience.¹ The concept of a 'show trial' is perhaps the worst criticism that can be levelled at a court, suggesting unfairness and arbitrariness, and is classically associated with totalitarianism.² The accusation of 'show trial' has frequently been directed at the proceedings of the international(-ized) criminal tribunals.³ International trials are 'seemingly inescapably spectacular,' typically following major conflict, involving crimes that 'shock the conscience of mankind,' and attracting global media attention. Despite this, the 'show trial' allegation has accompanied criticisms of international proceedings as taking an inordinate amount of time, costing a huge sum of money, and prosecuting only a fractionally small number of accused.⁴

Martti Koskenniemi identifies a number of features of the show trial: that only a few political leaders are prosecuted; the context of the crimes is assumed by the court, even if disputed by the accused; the trial automatically vindicates the position of the prosecutor; and the accused is not permitted to speak. He expresses the key paradox for international trials that in seeking to convey 'an unambiguous historical truth, the trial will have to silence the accused,' inevitably leading to a form of show trial.⁵ International trials are freighted with expressivist responsibility both to deliver a 'coherent moral message' and to re-constitute 'broken' communities, both functions that may be undermined by inconvenient or incongruous narratives and images.⁶ Jeremy Petersen suggests that there are two key elements of the show trial: firstly, the deliberate reduction of the risk of acquitting the accused (through denial of due process rights, biased judges or relaxed rules of proof); and secondly, that the trial is staged for the benefit of the audience rather than principally for the determination

---

1. Jeremy Peterson, 'Unpacking Show Trials: Situating the Trial of Saddam Hussein,' *Harvard International Law Journal*, 48/1 (2007), 263.
2. George Hodos, *Show Trials: Stalinist Purges in Eastern Europe, 1948–1954* (New York: Greenwood Press, 1987); Awol Allo, 'The "Show" in the "Show Trial": Contextualizing the Politicization of the Courtroom,' *Barry Law Review*, 15/1 (2010).
3. Jessie Allen, 'Theater of International Justice,' *Creighton International and Comparative Law Journal*, 3 (2013); Martti Koskenniemi, 'Between Impunity and Show Trials,' *Max Planck Yearbook of United Nations Law*, 6/1 (2002); Peterson, 'Unpacking Show Trials'; Christina Prusak, 'The Trial of Alberto Fujimori: Navigating the Show Trial Dilemma In Pursuit of Transitional Justice,' *New York University Law Review*, 85 (2010).
4. Schwöbel-Patel, 'Spectacle in International Criminal Law,' 273; Allen, 'Theater of International Justice.'
5. Koskenniemi, 'Between Impunity and Show Trials.'
6. Prusak, 'The Trial of Alberto Fujimori.'

of the guilt of the accused.[7] Christina Prusak refines this further, arguing that there is inevitably some reduction of conviction risk in international cases because the prosecutors select the strongest cases, and that the requirement for publicity necessitates elements of 'show,' and argues that we should not be overly concerned unless the proceedings obscure the trial's primary adjudicatory purpose.[8] A common thread in these opinions is the reflex for show trials to control or to manage 'the message,' to which I will return shortly.

Given the limited number of prosecuted accused, the jurisdictional constraints and the widespread allegations of political interference in case selection, many commentators and academics have applied the 'show trial' epithet to the ECCC.[9] As examples, journalist Nate Thayer expresses his opinion that the ECCC is 'an insidious, dangerous mockery of the rule of law ... a twenty-first century version of a Stalinist show trial.'[10] Resistance studies scholar Mikael Baaz argues that the ECCC's trials can be criticized on the same grounds as the 1979 People's Revolutionary Tribunal because it is 'nakedly political in nature.'[11] Rachel Hughes however suggests that the ECCC's critics are too quick to denigrate the tribunal as a show trial, because this fails to take account of the Global North's own culpability in the geopolitical situation that led to and followed on from the Khmer Rouge, and reveals an inherently Orientalist prejudice. Hughes's principal objection to the critiques is that they fail to acknowledge the essential performative element of international trials that are, she says, central to the domestic and international legitimacy as part of the imperative of transitional justice.[12] In fact, the physical setting of the ECCC is even more reminiscent of theatre than other tribunals, as proceedings take place on a vast stage behind floor-to-ceiling curtains that open when the court is in public session, in front of an arced auditorium housing 500 seated spectators behind plate glass.[13]

---

7. Peterson, 'Unpacking Show Trials.'
8. Prusak, 'The Trial of Alberto Fujimori,' 882–886.
9. For a summary of such accusations, see Rachel Hughes, 'Ordinary Theatre and Extraordinary Law at the Khmer Rouge Tribunal,' Environment and Planning: Society and Space 33 (2015), 722–724. See also Seth Mydans, '11 years, $300 Million and 3 convictions: Was the Khmer Rouge Tribunal worth it?,' New York Times, 10 April 2017; Mikael Baaz, 'The "Dark Side" of International Criminal Law,' Scandinavian Studies in Law 60 (2015), 181.
10. Cited in Hughes, 'Ordinary Theatre and Extraordinary Law,' 722.
11. Baaz, 'The "Dark Side" of International Criminal Law,' 181.
12. Hughes, 'Ordinary Theatre and Extraordinary Law.'
13. Hinton refers to how the 'performativity of justice is ...related to courtroom

Returning to the idea that a key component of a show trial is one in which the message is controlled, the previously cited scholarship has focused on proceedings that shut down an accused's right to speak and to present a counter-narrative to that advanced by the prosecution. Proceedings are considered illegitimate and an 'abuse of process' if the rights of an accused are sufficiently disrespected. Given that international criminal justice is quintessentially premised on bringing justice to victims, on empowering them and 'healing' their suffering, we should consider the extent to which constraining the victims' rights to speak and so closely circumscribing victim participation in court proceedings (or at least privileging an idealized version of victimhood) also vitiates the legitimacy of the proceedings. When a judge unlawfully curtails the accused's right to speak there is a clear argument for the trial to be considered unfair. But when it is the victim whose voice is silenced—or whose distinctive (counter-aesthetic) shunned—we should reflect on the reasons, and the potential consequences. Of course, there is a qualitative difference between the roles of the accused and of the victim in a criminal trial: only the former risks criminal sanction, loss of liberty, and adjudication of guilt. However, where the victim is so central to the overall 'spectacle' of the international criminal trial, yet has such limited agency and voice and wields so little power, the legitimacy of the instrumentalization of victimhood is called into question.[14]

Christine Schwöbel-Patel's discussion of the 'spectacularization' of the trials of international criminal justice invites us to consider the ideological purpose for which the 'spectacle' is being staged, and how this matches what is happening in reality. As she argues, central to the spectacle is the visual (both real and imagined) for which in international criminal justice the stereotypical 'ideal' victim plays the central aesthetic role in attracting funding. The particular 'fundraising brand' of victimhood at play, as earlier discussed, is the 'racialized, feminized, and infantilized' victim, where a victim's agency is restricted to testifying as a witness.[15] This brand is constructed not only within but also outside the courtroom, in documentaries and photographic exhibitions produced to 'educate' observers and donors alike. For Schwöbel-Patel, the essence of the fundraising image of the victim

---

ritual' at the ECCC. Hinton, The Justice Façade, 145, 159.
14. Fletcher, 'Refracted Justice,' 320.
15. Schwöbel-Patel, 'Spectacle in International Criminal Law,' 250.

is not merely rhetorical,[16] it is ideological: the dominant aesthetic of which is 'constructed for the purpose of maintaining the status quo – for keeping those who have power in power.'[17] This takes us back to Yoav Mehozay, who argues that conceptions of the ideal-type victim are governed by the same principle as ideal-type consumers: namely, it is their image value rather than their *actual* value that has currency.[18] Before institutions of justice, both domestic and international, as well as in consumer society, aesthetics as a superficial manifestation triumphs over messy and complex lived experience.

Concluding Thoughts

Victims such as Theary Seng present a distinctive counter-aesthetic of victimhood that does not sit easily either within the inevitably simplified narratives of a trial or with the underlying ideological purposes of the spectacle. Whether challenging the stereotype within the courtroom as a forcefully-voiced agentic civil party/litigant in person—dismissively described as 'soapboxing' by some—or outside the courtroom through defiant, playful or therapeutic images and stratagem, the 'non-ideal' victim engages in both resistance to and exposure of the underlying premises of international criminal justice. Such actors carve out a space for victims to go beyond the stereotype, expanding and pushing at the 'subversive limits' of victim participation in collective rhetoric and survivor speech.[19]

A decade after her public renunciation of her civil party status and denunciation of the ECCC, Theary Seng is more ambivalent about the court and its contribution to Khmer Rouge victims. She still firmly believes that the 'broken' civil party system was a regrettable 'wasted opportunity,'[20] both in terms of the ultimate 'exploitation and disempowerment' of victims during the proceedings and the 'hollowness and insensitivity' of reparations that were ordered after the trial.[21] However, she adds that 'if there had been

---

16. As Mohan also observed: 'The Paradox of Victim-Centrism,' 769.
17. Schwöbel-Patel, 'Spectacle in International Criminal Law,' 267.
18. Mehozay, 'From Offender Rehabilitation to the Aesthetics of the Victim,' 102–3.
19. Gibson, 'A Rupture in the Courtroom.'
20. Interview with Theary Seng, 27 July 2021, notes on file with author
21. Theary Seng, 'Exploitation and Disempowerment of Victims at the KRT, Issues of Reparations – Commentary,' *K.I. Media*, 7 February 2012, accessed 11 August 2021, http://ki-media.blogspot.com/2012/02/exploitation-and-disempowerment-of.html.

no ECCC, we wouldn't have had funding for public forums, we wouldn't have been on the radio, the attention on victims would not have been there ... We can't let go of the judicial mechanism, but we must be aware that it is very limited.'[22] In Seng's view, the ECCC has had an essential catalysing impact for victims in society more broadly, and she views her 'Poetic Justice Products' as a provocation, an outlet for people to express themselves in a way that international criminal justice would not permit.[23]

Obviously, international criminal courts must be able to control their own procedures; to permit any party—whether civil parties or otherwise—to speak without limit would risk compromising the structure of the proceedings. The experiment of collective rhetoric rupturing the standard trial process permitted by the judge in Michigan would be difficult to replicate in an international criminal tribunal where there may be many thousands of victims. However, where international criminal justice draws its principal legitimacy from narratives of empowerment, healing and giving justice 'for the victims,' it is right to observe how little space and voice such court procedures afford to the multitude of varied and complex victims, and how the international court's view of the victim aesthetic is so reductive. Revisiting the legitimacy of the 'show' claimed to be on behalf of the victims not only requires a more realistic assessment of what international criminal trials can hope to deliver, but also a willingness to admit victims into the proceedings who present a disruptive counter-aesthetic, and ultimately a commitment to looking beyond the superficial.

Author's Note:

This chapter is dedicated to Theary Seng and to the dozens of other political prisoners in modern-day authoritarian Cambodia.[24] On 14 June 2022, Ms Seng was sentenced to six years' imprisonment by the Phnom Penh Municipal Court. She had been charged with conspiracy to commit treason and incitement to social disorder with forty-five others, including the leader of the Cambodian opposition Mr Sam Rainsy. The case against Ms Seng and her co-accused was described

---

22. Interview with Theary Seng, 27 July 2021, notes on file with author.
23. Interview with Theary Seng, 27 July 2021, notes on file with author.
24. 'Political Prisoners in Cambodia,' Human Rights Watch, accessed 19 January 2023, https://www.hrw.org/video-photos/interactive/political-prisoners-cambodia.

as politically motivated by the UN Special Rapporteur Rhona Smith.[25] The American Bar Association's Center for Human Rights Trial Observation Report reported in extensive detail the flagrant violation of due process rights in her trial under both Cambodian law and international human rights instruments, and deemed the conviction untenable and the detention arbitrary.[26]

---

25. United Nations Human Rights Special Procedures, 'Cambodia: UN Expert alarmed by reports of mass trial of activists,' 25 November 2020. Available at https://cambodia.ohchr.org/sites/default/files/25112020%20Cambodia%20SR%20mass%20trial-EN.pdf

26. American Bar Association Center for Human Rights, *Trial Observation Report: Cambodia v Theary Seng*, September 2022, accessed 18 January 2023, https://www.americanbar.org/content/dam/aba/administrative/human_rights/trialwatch/theary-seng-trialwatch-report.pdf.

14

Pinan: Comics and International Justice

Carolina Alonso Bejarano and Peter Quach

THIS IS CALLED PINAN 5.

WHEN I FIRST STARTED TAKING KARATE, I THOUGHT *PINAN* MEANT "PEACE AND TRANQUILITY."

MOST PEOPLE STILL TRANSLATE IT THAT WAY. I WASN'T A VERY DEDICATED STUDENT, EITHER.

THESE PAST FEW YEARS, KARATE HAS BEEN THE ONLY THING THAT HAS MADE SENSE. IT'S HELPED CALM ME.

IN MY STUDIES, I LEARNED THAT THE FOUNDERS OF KARATE ADAPTED THEIR FORMS FROM CHINESE KUNG FU, AND IN CHINESE, THE CHARACTERS FOR *PINAN*, 平安, ACTUALLY MEAN "STAY SAFE."

IT'S WHAT YOU'D SAY TO SOMEONE WHO'S ABOUT TO GO ON A TRIP TO SOMEWHERE DANGEROUS.

IN THE FINAL MOVE OF PINAN 5, YOU CRUSH YOUR OPPONENT'S TESTICLES, AND THEN YOU RIP THEM OUT.

STAY SAFE.

PINAN 平安

by Peter Quach and Carolina Alonso Bejarano

WARNING: THIS COMIC CONTAINS SCENES OF SEXUAL ASSAULT.

Published in the Believer No. 121, page 1.

Christine Schwöbel-Patel (CSP): Thank you so much for allowing us to reprint your comic in this collection! And thank you also for agreeing to speak to us about your work.

My first question relates to victims and agency: One of the things that animated this collection was the representations of victims (of international crime) as lacking agency. While your work does not represent international crime and justice directly, it does engage with agency of victims. What made you decide to portray Juliana, the main character in your comic, as a brown belt in karate?

Peter Quach (PQ): The origin story of this comic could be a meta-commentary on the agency of victims, so let me start at the beginning. It was 2018, when I was talking with one of my then-roommates in Chicago about her dating life using Tinder. At the same time, it was the height of the #MeToo movement in the US and I was grappling with new stories of sexual assault from people in my life and trying to understand it in a more concrete rather than abstract way. The Believer magazine commissioned a comic from me, and I decided to write it about all these things swirling around in my life—Tinder, dating as a woman, and sexual assault.

Carolina Alonso Bejarano (CAB): When Peter told me of his new comic idea, I asked him, as a hetero, cis-gender man who's never been harassed, what he could possibly say about sexual violence from the perspective of a woman. I asked him how he planned to do his research, and I told Peter, 'it's time for men to listen.' He replied, 'it's time for men to speak up,' and then he hung up. I was really skeptical of what he would write, especially when I didn't hear from him for a few days.
PQ: It took me a while to overcome my ego and accept that I didn't know anything about this topic. Men think we know everything! But I eventually swallowed my pride, called Caro back, and asked her to write the comic with me, officially.

CAB: I was excited about the idea of writing this comic with Peter. He and I had collaborated in art for many years and we already ran a serial webcomic together. However, as a person who has experienced sexual violence and had never written about it, I really had to consider whether or not I felt capable of writing the story with Peter. In the end I thought that this would possibly help me heal from my experiences of sexual abuse, and I accepted the invitation.

In most of them we make fun of ourselves, yet we have also covered important topics, including abortion access and workers' rights. Creating a message in one panel has brought its own challenges (different from those we face with longer format collaborations), and I see how cartoons are a very effective way to communicate with the reader, sometimes through humor. I look forward to our future creations and, in particular, I am thinking about issues that are important to me, such as the rights of immigrants, reproductive justice, and, increasingly so, prison abolition.

CSP: Let's talk a little more about the comic as a particular form of art and expression. A comic in an academic collection is fairly uncommon. What do you think the comic offers in terms of form that academic writing on themes of suffering and justice might not offer?

CAB: As an academic myself, I feel very aware of the limits of academic writing. In particular working in a Law School in Britain (where the guiding principle for assessing written work is a Research Excellence Framework, which ranks all research according to an arguably Western, obscure, and arbitrary point-based system). If I want my work to be legible for my institution it often has to ascribe to a narrow understanding of what knowledge is and what knowledge production entails. However, my research interests have been driven by my collaborative work as an activist and artist and that has resulted in scholarship that is not always welcome inside the walls of the metaphorical Ivory Tower. So, for instance, publishing *Pinan* in this book and understanding it as a legitimate source of knowledge about suffering and justice in the context of international criminal justice is a welcome but unexpected invitation.

PQ: I am not an academic, although I have read my fair share of academic books. In my readings of poststructuralist theory, I've come to understand that any medium or message claiming objectivity or superiority is constructed. For a long time (and still in some quarters), the medium of comics as a whole was looked down upon as a lesser art form compared to other media such as painting or sculpture. An explicit part of choosing to dedicate my life to creating comics has been rejecting this paradigm and asserting that comics are not only a valid medium, but also might offer a worldview free of the burdens and assumptions that have accumulated in other media around what counts as a valid object of art and who counts as an artist. I feel comics can play a comparable role in academia by offering a new view on the world and challenging the assumptions of academic writing. And I think other art forms can do this, too. For instance, Caro's first book does something similar in its incorporation of theatre into an academic context.

CAB: Yes. My debut manuscript is called *Decolonizing Ethnography: Undocumented Immigrants and New Directions in Social Science* and was published by Duke University Press in 2019.[8] The book is special because it was co-written by four activist ethnographers—two of whom are members of the community where the research was conducted—and because the last chapter is a play in Spanish and English about undocumented people's rights, which the four of us wrote, produced, and performed together. The play to me is the best part of the book because it represents a more accessible way to communicate a very important message: under US law all people have workers' rights, regardless of their immigration status. That is the message of the book as well, but many folks who won't (or can't) read 150 pages in English may be able to read or watch our play. Additionally, performers in the play are able to approach the issue at hand (the precarious nature of the lives of undocumented workers in the USA) in an embodied way, as they act out the different scenes. In that I see the power of art as a way to communicate and create knowledge, and theatre in particular.

PQ: What theatre, comics, and most art forms can offer with concepts such as suffering and justice that academic writing cannot, in my opinion, is empathy. An artistic depiction of suffering will offer the reader or viewer a different—perhaps more direct—understanding of the phenomenon than a description or study of the same phenomenon in academic writing ever could. Whereas the play in Caro's book asks the reader to experience the plight of undocumented workers through performing the play, comics offer their own, special kind of empathy. What has always drawn me to comics is that they are, by their hybrid nature as a combination of words and sequential images, both a visual and a narrative medium. Through their visuals, comics can directly depict injustices and suffering in a powerful way. Sometimes, in fact, images of suffering or injustices can either overwhelm or undermine

---

8. Carolina Alonso Bejarano et al., Decolonizing Ethnography: Undocumented Immigrants and New Directions in Social Science (Durham, NC: Duke University Press, 2019).

the entire work because the reader can be (re-)traumatized through seeing images of suffering or can be made complicit in the abuse through gazing at the images. In *Pinan* specifically, we walked a fine line in depicting the pain and suffering caused by sexual violence while also seeking to avoid retraumatization or exploitation.

CAB: As Peter was saying, in addition to their visual aspect, comics are also a narrative medium that tells stories with sequential images. Through narrative, comics can also offer a deeper understanding of suffering because in narrative the reader experiences time and change. We are introduced to a character as they experience a traumatic event, and then we follow them as they struggle to grow in the aftermath. Think for example of Marjane Satrapi's 'Persepolis,' Joe Sacco's 'Palestine,' or Art Spiegelman's 'Maus.' In *Pinan*, even though we did not depict the entire arc of Juliana's recovery, she ends the story in a different—ambiguous yet slightly more hopeful—place than where she begins, and in this change the reader can tune into her suffering in a way that academic writing cannot offer. Of course, there can also be narrative in an academic text, but it traditionally has a descriptive or argumentative nature. Comics, on the other hand, don't simply describe a situation but invite the reader to experience it with the characters.

PQ: The dual visual and narrative nature of comics is what drew me to them when I was a little kid in kindergarten, and it continues to fascinate me.

CSP: What is your view on hegemonic visuals and narratives? International criminal justice is replete with stereotypical imagery of white saviourism, Black victims and Black perpetrators. How do you deal with stereotypes in your comics?

PQ: I am a dark skinned Vietnamese-American man and Caro is a light skinned Colombian woman. We are gendered and racialized differently, of course, but as people from the Global South diaspora in a Eurocentric, patriarchal, white supremacist world, we have both encountered negative stereotypes associated with our identity.

CAB: Like, I can't tell you how many people have asked me in my lifetime how to get cocaine or joked to me about cocaine or asked if someone in my family is a drug lord who sells cocaine. Or how many times I have been sent to a little room while going through customs at an airport so some officer can search through my belongings. But we all have been fed these stereotypes and it is hard to see outside of them. For example, when I first started dating Peter I thought he was 'wise,' and he had to remind me that this conception came from my own stereotypes around Asian people.

PQ: But... I am wise!

CAB: A first step in dealing with stereotypes is recognizing that we all have been taught to make them, especially against marginalized peoples.

PQ: Right. Being mindful of how xenophobia, racism, transphobia, anti-Blackness, or misogyny operate through stereotypical associations is an important step for creating believable characters. And let me say that there is something about the widespread use of white saviorism in storytelling that is not just a matter of international criminal justice imagery but is also relevant when discussing art and fiction. Short story: one of my first long format comics, *Freedman* (2011), deals with a formerly enslaved man who is trying to find his enslaved wife after the end of the Civil War.[9] *Freedman* was originally conceived as a multi-volume series, but a year after I published the first issue, Quentin Tarantino released *Django Unchained*, which basically had the same premise. However, in Tarantino's version—unlike in mine—it is a white man who teaches the Black man to shoot and it is that white man who finally kills the slaveowner. That white man is the hero of Tarantino's movie.

CAB: *Django Unchained* (By The White Man).

PQ: Exactly. This made me lose interest in continuing the *Freedman* project, but the experience taught me about the types of stories I want to tell in my comics and the tropes I want to avoid.

CAB: To sum up our answer, I think a further step for dealing with stereotypes in fiction beyond recognizing one's own learned biases against people and avoiding the trope of the white savior can be what we did with *Pinan*, which is basing the characters on actual people we know. The adage in writing is, 'write what you know,' but that doesn't

---

9. Peter Quach, Freedman (Self-published, 2011), accessed 7 June 2023, http://peterquach.com/Comics/Freedman/index.html.

just mean write about your own life. Writers are taught to observe the people in our lives and use those observations as fuel for our writing. In this way we can hopefully avoid stereotypes and approach verisimilitude.

CSP: Biases can also be found in what we categorise as violence and how that is represented. International justice institutions deal with a particular type of violence, like mass conflict or genocide. There are different ways in which violence is represented—as mutilations, as mass graves—but the catalogue of representations is fairly small. Mostly, the representation of the violence is there to shock. In your comic, the violence is represented in a more nuanced way. What was your thinking with the way in which the violent flashbacks are represented?

PQ: How to represent the sexual violence was perhaps the most difficult question we had to deal with in creating *Pinan*. I think that, as you say is the case in an international justice context, oftentimes representations of sexual violence in fiction are also there to shock, or sometimes even titillate. In particular when written by men. The first draft of the script that I wrote had a lot of those elements in the flashbacks—blood, screams, ripped clothes…

CAB: Yes, that first script Peter wrote was quite rough. I mean, it was exactly what we were going for in the first and last pages (which we ended up changing very little through the editing process). But the whole middle, and in particular the flashbacks, we rewrote several times. As we said earlier, we were thinking of other victims of sexual assault that would read the comic. We didn't want it to be retraumatizing for them, yet we needed to refer to Juliana's rape in the story.

PQ: During our initial research on sexual violence we learnt from our friends who work with survivors that oftentimes rapes take place in the context of dating. We also learnt that for many people being sexually assaulted doesn't entail screaming or fighting.

CAB: So, first we decided on a date rape story with five flashbacks. The last thing we dealt with in the comic was how to illustrate them, because it was such delicate territory. We thought that going for a closeup of Juliana's face would convey her suffering and pain without retraumatizing readers who are survivors of sexual violence, so we went with that idea.

PQ: We left much of the assault to the reader's imagination, for a few reasons. First, to avoid exploitation or retraumatization. Second, from a narrative sense, the story is about the recovery, not the assault itself, so we limited our depiction of the assault to five panels because we felt anything more would have overpowered the rest of the story. And third, in comics the reader fills in what happens between the panels with their imagination, and so dedicating only five panels to the assault leaves the reader to imagine the rest, and sometimes whatever the reader may imagine can be more powerful than what any artist could depict. I think these three points could also serve as a lesson for depicting violence in an international criminal justice context because you are telling a story there, as well. Sometimes shock may be desired, but you want to weigh up whether and how depictions of violence serve your narrative needs and, in particular, if the images themselves further exploit and traumatize the victims or serve to perpetuate negative stereotypes.

CSP: This is a good segue to thinking about the relationship between the ends of international criminal justice and the ending of Juliana's story as you depict it. In academic writing on (international) law, we feel pressured to resolve problems, to offer solutions. We are taught to avoid ambiguity and to tie up loose ends. Was the ending of *Pinan* a way of embracing ambiguity and loose ends for you?

CAB: The ending of *Pinan* has been a topic for debate! I am thinking of when we taught the comic to my Latino Studies class at my previous institution in the USA. The students disagreed among themselves about whether this was a happy or a sad ending. Some of them thought that Juliana would never date again, some of them thought she was smiling in the end. They asked us what we meant by the ending. I will say what Peter told our students that day: what we were trying to convey is less important than what the reader understands by it.

PQ: Right. As we mentioned above, we deliberately chose to make the ending of *Pinan* ambiguous, as we felt embracing the ambiguity would honor the perhaps lifelong journey of sexual assault recovery. Art can sometimes fall prey to the same pressures as academic writing to resolve problems and offer resolutions. In art and writing, these are called clichés, but they're clichés for a reason. Readers and viewers want all the loose ends tied up, and in a capitalist system, art that offers pat resolutions will probably sell more than art that doesn't. In *Pinan*, something to note is that Juliana's present is illustrated inside panels we recently published about British colonialism or the second one we ever published about the World Cup. In that sense, for me, cartooning represents a way of processing little or big events in my life while sometimes also offering commentary on the world as I see it.

PQ: I have made cartoons since I was a kid, and only in hindsight have I realized that, intentionally or not, almost all of my cartooning work has in some way dealt with social justice issues. My stories have variously dealt with: the history of racism in the area of the US where I grew up; the life of a formerly enslaved man in the aftermath of the US Civil War; the experience of being a powerless exploited worker in a capitalist system; and the histories of colonialism and linguistics that shaped the pronunciation of my last name. Of course, I've also written about being a Miley Cyrus fan, shopping at IKEA, and having a man-baby as US President, but I did say 'almost all'…

CAB: Peter also uses comics to reflect upon his life, and not just in his longer format comics—for example, *Transit* (2008),[3] *I Am A Racist* (2012),[4] and *Quach* (2023)[5]—but also in his serial webcomic, *But By Laughter* (2017–), which portrays snippets of his everyday life after we separated and he moved to Chicago, then Houston, and finally back to New York City.[6]

PQ: True. The best comics, and art in general, in my opinion are those that reflect the full breadth of the human experience: our pains, our sorrows, our traumas, yes, but also our joys, our silliness, our triumphs, and our absurdities. I try to capture as many of those facets of life as I can, as simultaneously as possible.

CAB: Something to add regarding form and themes is that since 2021, we have been experimenting together with a different format: we are now creating one-panel comics, or cartoons.[7] (and I am happy to say that The New Yorker recently bought one of them for the first time!).

---

3. Peter Quach, Transit (Self-published, 2008), accessed 7 June 2023, http://peterquach.com/Comics/Transit/Transit.html.
4. Peter Quach, I Am A Racist (Self-published, 2012), accessed 7 June 2023, http://peterquach.com/Comics/Racist/index.html.
5. "Peter Quach, Quach (Self-published, 2023), accessed 7 June 2023, http://peterquach.com/Comics/Quach/Quach.html"
6. 'But by laughter,' accessed 7 June 2023, https://butbylaughter.tumblr.com/.
7. https://carolinaalonsobejarano.com/cartoons

PQ: When we were conceiving of the comic together, we knew that we wanted it to be a story about healing. We decided that fifteen pages was too small a canvas to portray recovery from sexual assault, which may take a lifetime. So instead, we aimed to illustrate a snapshot of the process.

CAB: I am a Gender Studies scholar and proposed that we talk to a few of our friends who are experts in sexual violence before brainstorming the storyline. During this research stage, multiple sources said that women who suffer sexual assault often try to reconnect with our bodies during our recovery.

PQ: To circle back to the question, I have been practicing karate for many years, and in our first brainstorming session we decided that having Juliana train in karate would be a good way for her to recover a connection with her body and to reclaim a sense of agency. We could use my own knowledge as a brown belt in karate, and karate could serve as an overarching metaphor for Juliana's healing process and state of mind.

CAB: I understand that karate is about much more than this, but I believe that knowing how to rip someone's testicles off would help me reclaim some of my sense of safety in going through this world as a woman.

CSP: I agree! So, what kinds of themes more generally do you like to broach through the storytelling form of comics? Are there themes that are particularly important to you?

CAB: All of my comic creations are collaborations with Peter, and, except for *Pinan*, they are all autofiction.[1] Our longest running one, *Gumdrops* (2014–), is a one-to-four-panel serial webcomic following our lives, first as a married couple in New York City and later after separating.[2] *Gumdrops* can be funny and cute, like the two we have coming up this summer, about turning forty and getting divorced. But sometimes we address social issues—I'm thinking of the *Gumdrops*

---

1. 'Pinan by Peter Quach & Carolina Alonso Bejarano,' The Believer, accessed 7 June 2023, https://www.thebeliever.net/pinan/.
2. 'Gumdrops,' Carolina Alonso Bejarano, accessed 7 June 2023, https://carolinaalonsobejarano.com/gumdrops.

with borders throughout the comic, and her flashbacks are portrayed in panels unbounded by borders, with art that extends to the edge of the page. If you pay attention, you will notice that on that last page when she deletes Haroun's number and walks away, that last panel is the only panel in the present with unbounded art. Whether that unbounded, free panel implies any resolution or further ambiguity is, also, up to the reader.

CAB: We believe the best art embraces ambiguity and doesn't try to force a simple resolution onto a complex topic. To do so in a story about sexual assault could be offensive and insulting to actual sexual assault survivors, plus life itself is oftentimes ambiguous and open-ended. That is another advantage of artistic media over academic texts. We are not trying to reach any type of 'truth' or 'objectivity' with *Pinan*, rather, we are reflecting on the topic of a woman's attempt at recovery from sexual abuse. No definite conclusion; no happily-ever-after.

CSP: Another disadvantage of (hegemonic forms of) legal storytelling is perhaps that there are commonly just two protagonists or protagonist groups: victims and perpetrators. In your comic, a prominent role is given to the main character's best friend, who helps her process her past and move forwards. Why was this character important to you, and what do you think a character like this can add to storytelling about international justice?

PQ: In narrative forms without inner monologues (so everything except novels really), dramatizing a character's arc has to take place in dialogue with other characters. If you can't hear the character's thoughts, they have to be speaking to someone for the reader to understand their thought processes. Famous examples of these narrative interlocutors include Watson (for Holmes) and Robin (for Batman). So, Juliana's friend Jasmin's role in the story was in a way demanded by the very form of narrative itself.

CAB: One of the topics we wanted to touch upon in *Pinan* is the importance of alternative kinship structures when recovering from sexual trauma, and we explore that through the relationship between Jasmin and Juliana. In this sense, Jasmin is important to our story beyond being the propeller for Juliana's realizations. Indeed, a problem with mainstream depictions of narrative interlocutors, is that they are often people of color, who have no back story and are there to be the sidekick of the main, white, character. We were careful when thinking of Jasmin's character not to make her a caricature and to give her a story of her own. We based the character on one of my best friends, also named Jasmin, and we intentionally tried to depict their care and love for each other as a main part of Juliana's recovery process.

PQ: What this adds to storytelling about international justice is complexity. The legal adversarial system doesn't recognize this, but there are protagonists to every story other than victims and perpetrators. For example, we believe that victims' support networks represent important actors in storytelling about injustice.

CSP: And, finally, if you permit, we'd love to have a 'look behind the scenes.' How does your collaborative creative process work?

PQ: Our artistic collaboration was born almost ten years ago out of our romantic partnership when Caro had the idea to create a short serial webcomic about our life in Brooklyn in the style of Bill Watterson's *Calvin and Hobbes*. We decided on a one-to-four-panel format and a candy-color pallet. As Caro said, *Gumdrops* is usually about random moments in our lives, though we sometimes reflect upon the world at a larger scale. We keep a digital file where we write down interactions between us (like a naked conversation in the shower or a discussion in the back of a taxi) and themes we want to explore (like Black Lives Matter or the US presidential election).Once we choose a story idea, we shape it into a sequence of up to four panels. I make the art and we publish it on our Instagram and Tumblr.

CAB: For longer format comics such as *Pinan*, but also for *Binh and Libertad*, the autofiction graphic novel we are writing about our relationship, we first have a series of storyline brainstorming meetings where we decide the broad strokes of the narrative. So, for instance, with *Pinan* we decided to create a story about a woman, Juliana, who is healing through the practice of karate from being sexually assaulted on a date. We also agreed that she would have a friend, Jasmin, and that the story would revolve around the two of them as Juliana enters the Tinder dating world.

PQ: Once we have spent considerable time creating a storyline, I write a script. Caro edits the script, and we go back and forth until we both agree on the story. And then I do the magic of drawing, inking, coloring, and lettering the comic. I go to Caro for feedback each step of the way, as we discuss set and character design. It's good to collaborate; sometimes I get too into the work and can't see things that are apparent to her. Plus, I trust Caro's sense of fashion and color way more than mine!

CSP: My sense is that international justice actors can not only learn from the comic form, they can also learn from this form of collaboration! Thank you Carolina and Peter for your valuable thoughts and insights. It has been a great pleasure to think with you about comics, counter-aesthetics, and international criminal justice.

15

Alternative Superheroes

Kate Evans

Christine Schwöbel-Patel (CSP): Kate, we approached you for the project on aesthetics and counter-aesthetics of international justice because of your terrific work on Rosa Luxemburg,[1] migration,[2] and climate crisis[3] In your work, you weave personal stories together with structural issues, telling stories of justice and injustice. Can you tell us something about the graphic novel as a medium?

Kate Evans (KE): Using the graphic novel format for historical representations of real-life situations gives you an incredible freedom, because you're essentially creating a docu-drama, a dramatic representation of real events, but you have the ability to historically reference everything you present the public with. So, you have the immediacy and the emotional engagement of a dramatic representation, yet you can take that representation and you can tie it very closely with the actual texts or events. In the case of Rosa Luxemburg, for example, I was able to tie together both her personal life and political work. So, I was able to provide a summary of some of Luxemburg's writings through some of her most engaging and immediate sections of her work and then translate that into a dramatic representation of speech and interaction between characters—representing her and other people in her life. With the graphic novel, you get an incredible freedom to create something that's emotionally engaging yet it's also historically referenced.

---

1. Kate Evans, Red Rosa: A Graphic Biography of Rosa Luxemburg (London: Verso, 2015).
2. Kate Evans, Threads: From the Refugee Crisis (London: Verso, 2017).
3. Kate Evans, Funny Weather: Everything You Didn't Want To Know About Climate Change But Probably Should Find Out (Brighton: Myriad Editions, 2006).

CSP: Does the cartoon offer a way to express complexities that a purely textual form cannot?

KE: I use visual metaphors throughout my work. I am somebody who thinks visually, so I am able to think of visual analogies and use visual metaphors, and the way in which this can really enhance a theoretical text is that you can actually physically illustrate an idea. At one point when I'm demonstrating Luxemburg's work on political economy, I use the dandelion seed to show the precariousness of the worker. And I think that really gives a sense of Luxemburg's original text, which is that the worker floats like a mote of dust in the air and wonders how they'll manage. It's talking about alienation and also about how, without communism of the land and the soil, the basic needs of the workers are ignored, they're irrelevant to society, and so by using this visual image of a dandelion seed you really get the feeling of somebody being unmoored from space. I can layer visual metaphors into my work and then I can break down, not just with diagrams, but with poetic reimagining of concepts of [the] things [that] Luxemburg was saying. I can enhance her text and make her meaning more accessible to people.

Figure 1: Kate Evans, Red Rosa: A Graphic Biography of Rosa Luxemburg (London: Verso, 2015), 97.

CSP: Let's build on the visual metaphors a little. In our project on aesthetics and international justice we're stating that law and understandings of justice are not just about text. So the traditional way of understanding law would be to say, 'you need to read the statutes, read cases law, read the commentary of statutes and case law.' But our proposition is that this leaves out the visual, and more broadly material, aspects of law. If we consider law to be more than its textual life, then this gives us a richer understanding of law. This allows us to highlight some of the problematic aspects of law's aesthetics, like the use of stereotypes. One of the questions we have been asking ourselves is how representations of victimhood, particularly in a visual sense, matter. This connects with another excellent graphic novel of yours, the book *Threads*. You explore the issue of representation of victimhood in that book. Could you tell us something about what you were thinking about representation and victimhood when you were writing and drawing for that graphic novel?

KE: My graphic novels are written out with a narrative structure in mind. They are completely factual; however I intend to engage the reader and take them on an emotional journey. Now, at the centre of *Threads* there is a representation of victimhood, which is of a woman who is incredibly vulnerable. She's pregnant, she has young children, she's stranded at the Dunkirk refugee camp. Her husband has been murdered, she's been separated from her sister, she doesn't know where her sister is—she could be in England, she could be in Spain. So, she's effectively in limbo. (I think one of the things people think about refugees is, 'why are they even there?'). She's powerless. She's trapped in this situation. Now, the riot police come through her camp, destroy their possessions and they physically assault her, they slap her in the face, and I make a representation of that.

The way that I had envisaged this going across a double-page spread was that I would have three representations, because she's been hit three times in the face. So, one slap, and then a second and then a third. Now, this is going to be a double page spread, so you're going to have a spine down the middle page. I couldn't do three images because in the middle one she'd have a line down the middle of her face. It wouldn't work, so I had to make four panels. It's interesting the way that your nonverbal brain takes over when you're planning a page, but it became obvious that she'd have one panel where she was hit, second panel where she was hit, then there'd be a third panel, and then there'd be a fourth panel where she's hit. So, in that third panel, I give her the ability to look back into the eyes of the man who is hitting her with absolute hatred but also with assertiveness, and I felt that was really important because I had given her agency in that situation. I had given her fury, I had given her a look, I had given her the ability to assert her own personhood, just by being able to look back in that page. I think that's what I do in my work, I take representations of people who are 'other' and turn them into *people*.

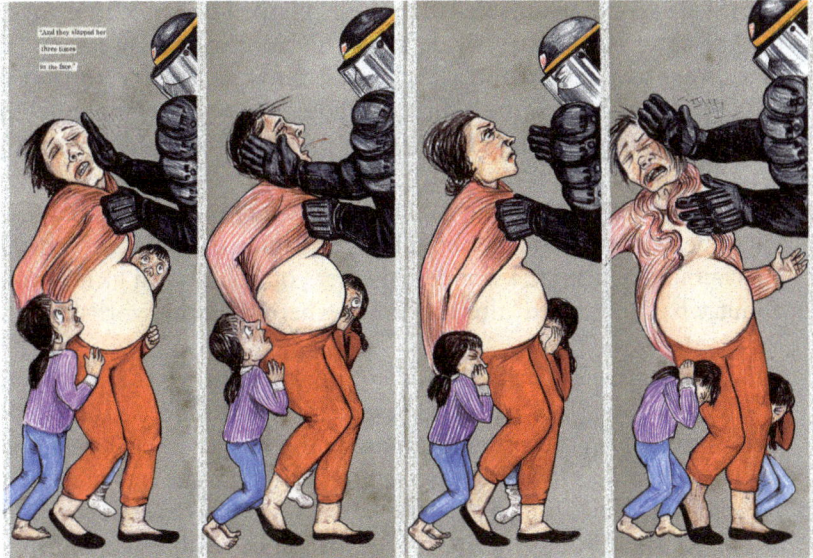

Figure 2: Kate Evans, Threads: From the Refugee Crisis (London: Verso, 2017).

I did this kind of representation early on in the graphic reportage I did for the anti-roads protests in the 1990s, because we were stereotyped by the media and there was massive media hype about 'eco warriors.' So we weren't really thought of as people, we were 'rent a mob,' or we were 'eco warriors,' but we weren't people. But the minute I started making cartoons of us drinking cider, making tea, doing boring and un-brave things, then it made us be people, and I think that my cartoons really reached out to people who thought 'oh, well I can do that,' meaning the more brave things. Well, all of you can, because it's just *people* doing that. And the same thing happened when I went over to Calais. There's a massive moral panic about refugees, and there's incredible dehumanizing that happens in the media and in our representations of migrants all the bloody time. You could take any headline from the current press which says things like 'migrant children selling sex,' 'migrant children drowning at sea,' '200 migrants drown at sea.' Take the word migrant out of that sentence—you've restored those people to full humanity. 200 *people* drowned at sea, that's what happened. The fact they were migrants does not make them not people.

So, I went to Calais and I met people and was able to just show people hanging out and show the crazy little cafes and the funny interactions and all the problematic aspects of the ways people were living.

But it was *people* who were living there. I hope I was able to demystify this idea and simultaneously demystify the idea of the African migrant as a savage invader and the Middle Eastern migrant as a terrorist. I was able to prove the lies of all three of those stereotypes simultaneously, because they are people. They are just people, like you and me.

CSP: In thinking about what a counter-aesthetics of international justice might be, we have thought about this reclaiming of humanness through a reclaiming of agency. I wonder whether you could say a little bit more about what you called 'alternative superheroes' at the workshop?

KE: 'Alternative superheroes' is simply celebrating the heroic-ness of the everyday. So, I have this character—and she's a mother, she's just a mother. Isn't it interesting how under patriarchy motherhood is so undervalued? However, the superpowers that she has are just the superpowers that so many female parents attain in everyday tackling of everyday tasks, but I reframe these as the incredible acts of bravery that they are. I mean, you don't see Spider-Man managing to change nappies and feed twins, do you? Or triplets, come on! Or one! Can't manage one nappy, can he? So much for being able to scale tall buildings - you can scale a supermarket [but] you still need to remember what you needed to buy when you get to the checkout! So everyday superheroes…and in a way that ties back to the eco-warriors stuff that I started with, in that we were dangling off trees and chaining ourselves to bulldozers, but I managed to reframe that from two perspectives. One was to show how incredibly unheroic we were most of the time, and the second was to reframe it as that we had the freedom and the privilege in order to be this heroic. Because there was a Venezuelan guy at one of the protests who saw what we were doing, and he said that in Venezuela they would shoot you and then they would shoot the trees. So I think we always need to look at both finding and celebrating just ordinary acts of kindness and humanity, and also we have to look at the bigger picture about why it is that one person is able to be a hero. Like, what are all the factors around them that enables us to celebrate this heroic-ness? Why is it that we have grown up only with rich white men as our heroes and never poor immigrant people of colour?

Let me talk about comics in that regard. So, I know comics are the perfect way to explore heroism because it is so bound into this trope of the superhero comics. Like, the actual physical images of comic heroes you see are the men who have broad shoulders, and the women who have impossibly anatomical breasts and waists. By making representations of humans that are human shape, it's immediately subversive. I've always created people…women in capes with hairy legs and saggy tits, and that is already subverting the superhero trope into a kind of normality—partly for comic effect, but also because we need to see representations of people that are people-shaped. The comic superhero has tied us into an oppressive way of celebrating exploitation and power, celebrating unattainable body standards, and instead we need to be able to subvert that trope and recognize the beauty and the power in the everyday.

CSP: It's so interesting to hear you talking about subversive comics through representations of the everyday, because there is this really interesting literature in international law about crises and the everyday. In this project, we have been inspired by this literature. So international law usually focuses on wars and on crises or events that are framed as crises for powerful Western states like the refugee crisis, we ask then, well who's crisis is it? Why is it framed as a crisis now? During the workshop, we spoke about how to shift representations to the everyday.

KE: I'd like to state that my work maybe isn't best practice in terms of making comics on this subject, because I'm still making comics *about* refugees—making comics about refugees who I've met. I've placed myself in the middle of their story as a middle-aged mum: I draw links between the children that I meet, the unaccompanied ones, and my unaccompanied and abandoned teenager back at home while I've been in the camps. [Laughs]. But I show the value of motherhood in the way that I do that, because I am meeting 12- and 13-year-old children with no mothers. So, best practice for comics about refugees are made by *PositiveNegatives*. What they do is they interview refugees and migrants and get them to tell their story, and allocate them an artist, and then they get editorial control of the representation that is made of them. So they ultimately give people agency because they give people their own ability to tell their *own* story. Whereas what I'm doing is telling the story of the moments when I met refugees, so again they don't get to be, if you like, the heroes in their own story. What I refuse to do at the point when I go and meet refugees is to get them to tell me their 'refugee story.' I refuse to say, 'so, tell me about all the trauma that brought you to this point.' All I am engaging with is the fact that these are dislocated people from desperate circumstances living in a situation where their humanity is not acknowledged and their basic needs are not being met, and that is bad enough. So, when I'm writing about the refugee crisis, I'm only obliquely referencing the factors that have put these people into this hellish situation. All I'm doing is describing the reality of them being there in a way that helps you to recognize that they are *people*, not that they are a swarm of migrants.

CSP: That is a wonderful way of acknowledging the 'everyday,' with all the contradictions between everyday events and crises that that entails. My final question is about institutions. As international lawyers, we have been attuned to putting a lot of trust into international institutions to deal with crises, whether it's the refugee crisis or wars or climate catastrophe. And what we're doing in this project is also drawing attention to how international institutions have created these problems in the first place. In your role as an activist, have you felt like you've worked against these institutions, or have you felt like you have complemented their work?

KE: Well that's interesting because in *Threads* I document the volunteer efforts to relieve the immediate needs of migrants at the Calais border. Although they don't really relieve the immediate needs of the people at the camp, because actually, the immediate needs of the people at the Calais border are to stick them in the back of your car and drive them across to the UK, which we didn't do. So we're providing a kind of firefighting service whereby we're stepping in and effectively building a refugee camp ourselves. And in a way, that means that we sort of end up being an international institution. We end up being UNHCR [United Nations High Commissioner for Refugees] because the UNHCR isn't there. In fact, France has forbidden them from providing refugee support at this point, which is why what's happening is a volunteer grassroots effort. We were effectively performing the role of an international institution, and that raised ethical questions for us in how much we were compromised by the fact that we were becoming a provider of relief to desperate people. Because there's an inequality there, you're not there relating with another person as a human being. The Western people coming over with all these goods and stuff—we were like Santa handing out food and clothes. But, although the people had nothing, there were still some who asserted their agency through gaming the system. The game for them was to acquire as much from us, the providers, as possible. And I found myself being a border guard, being a policeman, being a bouncer, standing outside a dome in which goods are being distributed and having to prevent someone from entering, and there's a man saying, 'give me one chance, give me one chance,' and I'm going, 'no no no no no no.' And I'm like, how did I put myself in this situation where [such] dehumanizing inequality is being replicated and reinforced? Another person, a volunteer, said to me: 'what we were doing is like a sticking plaster'—it's not addressing the underlying problem. In a way it's cementing it, because if we didn't turn up and clothe and feed children at Dunkirk, yes, they would die, but then maybe somebody would notice that they're there. I mean, on the one hand, it's really important that as people we responded to people and helped them as people, but already our hands were tied by the customs agents preventing us from doing what people really needed to do. I mean if we were people being people, we'd have just dumped the boats at Dunkirk, in a flotilla of people breaking the border restrictions, taking them across. That's what Dunkirk originally was in the English consciousness. Instead, you go over to Dunkirk, and you leave children there in the mud, like, that's not really helping them. It's trying to help them but it's not succeeding.

And I saw amongst the younger generation of activists who were there, [there was] a big separation between the people who are being helped in the camps and the people who are helping. One of the reasons for this is that the people who are doing the helping don't stay there overnight. So they're being accommodated in a trailer park somewhere on the edge of Dunkirk. It's here that I heard two young lads having a conversation, saying, 'what can I do to marketize this work with volunteer relief organizations? Do you reckon I could get a job with *Médecins Sans Frontiers?*.' And I was going, 'hang on, I thought the plan was for us to challenge capitalism and to dismantle international borders? Had you not realised that? Is this all just so you could get a job?.' But of course, you still have to have the material munitions to get a mass movement in place, and that has to happen either through absolute desperation or some kind of citizens income, because at the moment we're not seeing a level of sustained activism because young people don't have the financial security in which to be able to engage with it. All the activism I have ever been involved with has all been volunteer and grassroots led. I have only ever tangentially been supported by any charitable or political institutions.

What fascinates me is this free space where people come together in temporary autonomous zones, and that was something that I very much recognized in the camps at Dunkirk and Calais. People are creating their own spaces. In fact, I did that when I lived as a New Traveller for quite a number of years. We moved with our trucks, and we would create our own temporary autonomous zone under the threat of eviction, but we would try to build something. The best thing is when people come together you get more than the sum of their parts, and when that happens in a free way, that is the sort of flourishing of anarchic principle which in a way gives you a vision of a better world. And then at the same time, you can see the absolute desperation and dysfunction of when that goes badly, and I think I showed that at the Jungle as well, which was a fundamentally unsafe place to be. So, I suppose I've seen an authenticity in people working for themselves, in people being given or being allowed this space to create something for themselves, and I see the best in humanity where that can flourish.

It's always about looking at the bigger picture, and I try and look at the bigger picture with my books on all levels. It's not just the representations that I make of things, it's who I choose to publish them. I go with Verso, who's a radical publisher, so any money it makes goes into more radical ideas, and they're not a huge corporation. My other work is with New Internationalist and they're a co-op. So, I try and look at all aspects of the things that I do, and the compromises, to try and acknowledge that bigger picture.

CSP: Thank you so much, Kate. It has been an absolute pleasure and honour to hear more about your work, and to think through questions of representation with you.

www.ingramcontent.com/pod-product-compliance
Lightning Source LLC
Chambersburg PA
CBHW051530020426
42333CB00016B/1858